THE HISTORY OF GALLAUDET UNIVERSITY

THE HISTORY OF
GALLAUDET UNIVERSITY

150 YEARS OF A DEAF AMERICAN INSTITUTION

DAVID F. ARMSTRONG

MICHAEL J. OLSON,
PHOTOGRAPHY CONSULTANT

GALLAUDET UNIVERSITY PRESS · WASHINGTON, DC

Gallaudet University Press
Washington, DC 20002
http://gupress.gallaudet.edu

© 2014 by Gallaudet University
All rights reserved. Published 2014
Printed in South Korea

Library of Congress Cataloging-in-Publication Data
The history of Gallaudet University : 150 years of a
deaf American institution / David F. Armstrong.
    pages cm.
ISBN 978-1-56368-595-8 (hardcover) —
ISBN 978-1-56368-596-5 (e-book)
1. Gallaudet University—History. 2. Deaf—
Education (Higher)—Washington (D.C.)—History.
3. Deaf—Washington (D.C.)—History.
HV2561.W18G37 2014
378.1'9827209753—dc23   2013042624

∞ The paper used in this publication meets the
minimum requirements of American National
Standard for Information Sciences—Permanence of
Paper for Printed Library Materials,
ANSI Z39.48-1984.

Unless otherwise noted, all photographs are courtesy
of the Gallaudet University Archives.

Jacket and interior design by Bessas & Ackerman

CONTENTS

FRIEND
TEACHER
BENEFACTOR

PREFACE

This book focuses on the history of the unique collegiate program that was established in 1864, which still is the only freestanding institution of higher education in the world designed to meet the specific needs of deaf students. It chronicles Gallaudet's growth from a tiny college of less than two hundred students into a modern comprehensive American university. Along the way, it will discuss the university's achievements as well as its failures, the development of American Sign Language (ASL) as a language of scholarship at Gallaudet during a time when its use in educational institutions was largely discouraged or prohibited, and the struggle by deaf people to gain control of the governance of their university.

Gallaudet University has been known by various names throughout its history. Federal law established Gallaudet as the Columbia Institution for Instruction of the Deaf and Dumb and the Blind in 1857, with the status of a private corporation. It has been governed by an independent board of directors during its entire history. Although it has received a federal appropriation annually since 1858, it is not a government agency, and it has never been controlled directly by the U.S. government. The corporation was relieved of responsibility for educating blind children in 1865 and thereafter was known as the Columbia Institution for Instruction of the Deaf and Dumb. In 1954, federal law changed the name to Gallaudet College, then the Education of the Deaf Act of 1986 renamed it Gallaudet University. The university campus occupies the site of Amos Kendall's estate in northeast Washington, DC, and has long been referred to as Kendall Green.

In 1864 the U.S. Congress authorized the establishment of collegiate programs as a department of the Columbia Institution. This department was known for many years as the National Deaf-Mute College and, informally, as the College for the Deaf or Gallaudet College. The board of directors changed the name to Gallaudet College in 1894 in honor of Thomas Hopkins Gallaudet, the founder of deaf education in America, although the legal corporate name did not change until 1954, as noted above. After the establishment of the college program, the Columbia Institution continued to operate a school for deaf children. This school was generally known as the Kendall School in honor of Amos Kendall, and it was eventually replaced by two separately authorized schools—the Model Secondary School for the Deaf (MSSD) in 1966, and the Kendall Demonstration Elementary School (KDES) in 1970. All three programs, the university, MSSD, and KDES, are now authorized by a single piece of federal legislation, the Education of the Deaf Act (EDA) of 1986, and the name of the entire corporation is Gallaudet University.

In this book, the word *Institution* generally refers to the corporate body, under any of its legal names. The term *school* generally refers to the Kendall School and its successors; *college* refers to the collegiate program or the corporate body after 1954; and *university* refers to the Institution as it has existed since 1986.

The word *deaf* has both physical and cultural meanings. Throughout this book, *Deaf* refers to cultural entities and concepts, such as Deaf culture, Deaf organizations, and Deaf perspectives, for example. The word *deaf* is used for all other references, including an audiological condition and to individual people.

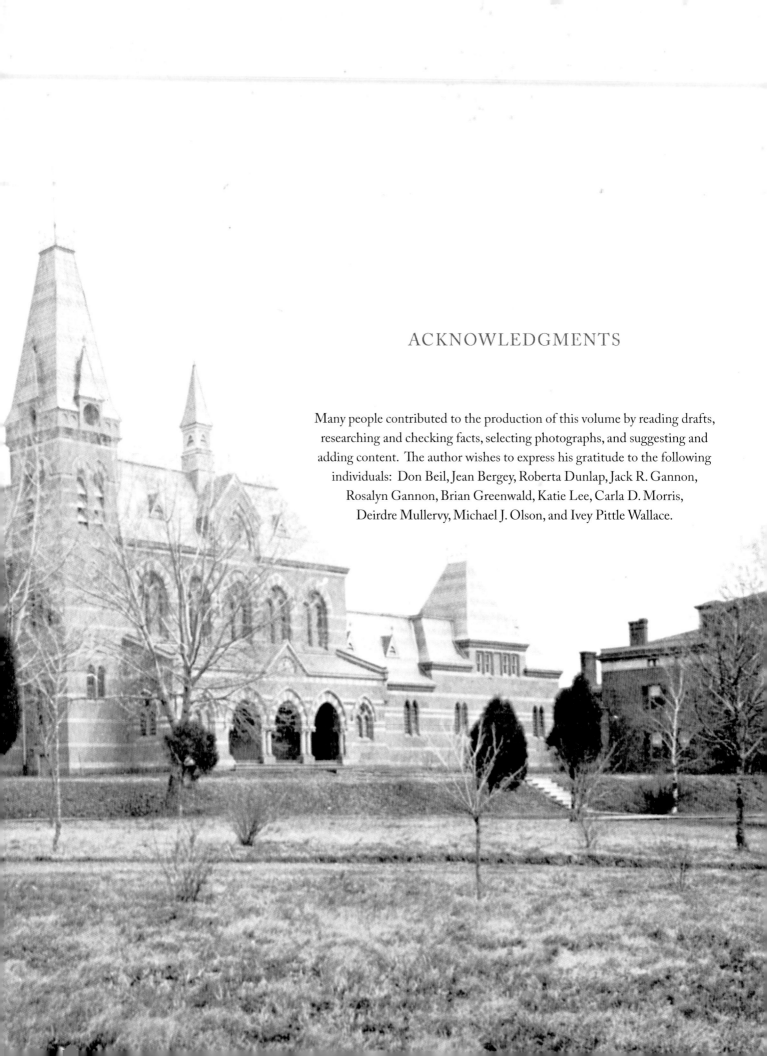

ACKNOWLEDGMENTS

Many people contributed to the production of this volume by reading drafts, researching and checking facts, selecting photographs, and suggesting and adding content. The author wishes to express his gratitude to the following individuals: Don Beil, Jean Bergey, Roberta Dunlap, Jack R. Gannon, Rosalyn Gannon, Brian Greenwald, Katie Lee, Carla D. Morris, Deirdre Mullervy, Michael J. Olson, and Ivey Pittle Wallace.

PROLOGUE

Abraham Lincoln and the Founding of the College for the Deaf

April 8, 1864, was a momentous day for the American Deaf community. On that day President Abraham Lincoln signed the federal legislation, passed unanimously by the United States Congress, authorizing the Columbia Institution for the Instruction of the Deaf and Dumb and the Blind to grant collegiate degrees. As a result, deaf people gained access to higher education for the first time in history, in an environment free of communication barriers. This was at a time of great turmoil for the United States, which was in the third year of what Lincoln would later characterize as "this terrible war." Nine months earlier, in July 1863, a Southern army led by Robert E. Lee had entered the state of Pennsylvania. Although Lee was defeated in a bloody battle at Gettysburg, many in the North feared that the Civil War was not winnable. In November of that year, Lincoln gave the best known of his many celebrated speeches. His brief but memorable remarks commemorated that battle and all the loss of life that the nation had suffered. Lincoln knew full well that he faced possible defeat in the election, but events during the summer and fall of 1864 set the stage for eventual Union victory and ensured Lincoln's reelection. However, when he signed the authorizing legislation for what would become Gallaudet University, Lincoln knew that

things were still very much in doubt. What would have led him to take this step at such a time of crisis?

James McPherson, winner of the Pulitzer Prize and dean of American Civil War historians, writes that Lincoln signed Gallaudet's collegiate charter without comment, but he speculates about Lincoln's possible motivation. McPherson notes that, on July 4, 1861, in Lincoln's first presidential message to Congress, he explained what the North was fighting for in the Civil War: "This is essentially a People's contest. On the side of the Union, it is a struggle for maintaining in the world, that form and substance of government, whose leading object is, to elevate the condition of men—to lift artificial weights from all shoulders—to clear the paths of laudable pursuit for all—to afford all, an unfettered start, and a fair chance, in the race of life." McPherson then suggests that, had Lincoln commented when he signed Gallaudet's collegiate charter, he most "likely would have included some words about lifting weights from shoulders and providing a fair chance in the race of life for students in this first institution for higher learning for deaf students in the world."[1]

The creation of the collegiate program at Gallaudet, as McPherson points out, thus fits into the context of progressive federal legislation designed to unify the nation during a time of

◄ Abraham Lincoln, sixteenth president of the United States, signed the legislation granting authority to the Columbia Institution for the Instruction of the Deaf and Dumb to confer college degrees. Photograph taken February 5, 1865.

▼ The charter authorizing the Columbia Institution for the Instruction of the Deaf and Dumb and the Blind to grant collegiate degrees was signed on April 8, 1864, by President Abraham Lincoln, Vice President Hannibal Hamlin, and Speaker of the House Schuyler Colfax. The date, now known as "Charter Day," is celebrated annually at Gallaudet University. Courtesy of the National Archives and Records Administration.

disunity and crisis. The year 1862 had seen the passage of the Morrill Act that led to the establishment of the system of state land grant colleges, opening the way to mass higher education in the United States. Edward Miner Gallaudet, superintendent of the Columbia Institution, in fact, used the passage of the land grant or Agricultural Colleges Act as the basis of his argument for obtaining federal funding for a national college for deaf students: "I felt justified in asking such action of Congress in view of the liberal grants of land to the states under the Agricultural Colleges Act, from the benefits of which the deaf youth of the country were shut out."[2]

It is likely that the existence of a large network of public higher education institutions influenced the provision of nearly universal access to secondary education to prepare students for college and university studies, and it also allowed for a strong influence on the secondary school curriculum, away from almost total devotion to the classics (especially Greek and Latin) and toward the generalized curriculum that exists today. Edward Miner Gallaudet knew that the establishment of a college for the deaf would have a similar impact on deaf education in general, requiring that more attention be paid to the academic preparation of students. Years later, he reflected on his actions to establish the college.

Writing these lines on the 7th of April 1896—thirty two years, lacking a single day, from the date of approval of the act—and reflecting on the part I took in securing the passage of this law, I can regard my course in asking it as nothing else than an illustration of *monumental cheek*. Pardon the slang—for polite language is inadequate.

I was a youngster of twenty-seven at the head of a little school of deaf and blind children in which no word of Latin, Greek, or any language but English had ever been taught. Arithmetic had not been completed. No higher mathematics had been touched, no science taught.

But the *purpose* to establish and develop a college for the deaf was within my breast, and I felt that the best way of securing the support of Congress and the public for such an institution was to secure full collegiate *powers* at the outset.[3]

It is also important to place the founding of Gallaudet in the context of Lincoln's "fair chance in the race of life." This action reveals that, from the beginning, it was intended to be an *educational* institution designed to prepare deaf people for lives as productive citizens—it was not intended to be an asylum or a charitable institution. Graduates of this unique institution have formed the core of an activist Deaf community that has worked for the common good and that has returned to American society much more than the Institution has been given.

Although Abraham Lincoln did not visit the college while he was alive, his body passed by Kendall Green on its final journey from Washington to Springfield, Illinois.[4] On the morning of April 21, 1865, his funeral train followed the tracks of the Baltimore and Ohio Railroad along what is now West Virginia Avenue, adjacent to the eastern edge of the campus. It is quite likely that Gallaudet students and faculty were among the thousands who lined the tracks to pay their final respects.

CHAPTER I

Establishing a College for the Deaf, 1864–1910

The entire early history of the Columbia Institution revolves around the actions of one man—Edward Miner Gallaudet, the youngest son of Thomas Hopkins (T. H.) Gallaudet and Sophia Fowler Gallaudet. The elder Gallaudet is renowned as the founder, along with Laurent Clerc and Mason Fitch Cogswell, of deaf education in the United States. Together the three men established the Connecticut Asylum for the Education and Instruction of Deaf and Dumb Persons (now the American School for the Deaf), the first permanent school for the deaf, in Hartford, Connecticut, in 1817. The story of T. H. Gallaudet's voyage to England and ultimately France in search of methods for teaching deaf children, and his return to Hartford with Clerc, an experienced deaf French teacher, is well known in the annals of American Deaf history.[1] T. H. Gallaudet's trip was not at all unusual for Americans of that time who traveled to Europe, most often to France, in search of new ideas, especially in science, technology, and the arts. For example, the American painter Samuel F. B. Morse returned to the United States from France in 1832 with the idea for the electric telegraph, after having observed a long-distance system of visual communication in use in France.[2] In 1844, the first long distance telegraphic transmission in history traversed the estate of Amos Kendall,

Morse's business partner. Thirteen years later, Kendall founded the Columbia Institution for the Instruction of the Deaf and Dumb and the Blind, the institution that became Gallaudet University, on his estate in the northeast section of Washington, DC.

The impetus for the school began in 1856 when P. H. Skinner approached Kendall to solicit donations to found a school for deaf and blind children in the area. Skinner had brought five deaf children from New York and recruited several deaf and blind children in Washington. On learning that the children were not receiving proper care, Kendall successfully petitioned the court to make them his wards. He donated two acres of his estate, named Kendall Green, to establish housing and a school for them. The school opened with twelve deaf and six blind students.[3]

At that time, the federal government controlled virtually all public business in the District of Columbia. However, Kendall, a confidant of President Andrew Jackson and former postmaster general, used his political connections to secure the passage of legislation authorizing the establishment of the school, which President Franklin Pierce signed into law on February 16, 1857. Federal appropriations to support the operation of the Columbia Institution began in 1858 (under the

◄ Columbia Institution students, 1860.

◄◄ Laurent Clerc was born December 26, 1785, near Lyon, France. He became deaf when he was a year old, but he did not go to school until he was twelve. He attended the Royal National Institute for the Deaf in Paris for eight years and then became a teacher at the school. In 1816 he traveled with Thomas Hopkins Gallaudet to America, where they and Mason Fitch Cogswell established the first school for the deaf in the U.S. Portrait by Charles Willson Peale, 1822; courtesy of the American School for the Deaf Museum, West Hartford, CT.

◄ Thomas Hopkins Gallaudet was born on December 10, 1787, in Philadelphia, Pennsylvania. He earned both bachelor's and master's degrees from Yale University and became a Congregational minister after studying at the Andover Theological Seminary. He changed his plans to be an itinerant preacher after meeting Alice Cogswell, the deaf daughter of his neighbor. In 1815, Gallaudet traveled to England and France to study the European methods of educating deaf children. Portrait date unknown.

When Gallaudet returned from France, he brought Laurent Clerc with him to establish a school for deaf children in Hartford, Connecticut. The school officially opened on April 15, 1817. Gallaudet married Sophia Fowler, a former pupil, and they had eight children. Their youngest son, Edward Miner, became the first president of the National Deaf-Mute College.

Sophia Fowler was born on March 20, 1798, near Guilford, Connecticut. Deaf from birth, she did not attend school until 1818, when, at the age of nineteen, she went to the newly founded school for the deaf in Hartford. She remained a student until the spring of 1821, and the following August she married Thomas Hopkins Gallaudet. When their youngest son, Edward Miner, became superintendent of the Columbia Institution, Sophia went to Washington, DC, with him to be matron of the school. Daguerreotypes circa 1842.

administration of President James Buchanan) and have continued annually up to the present.[4] All in all, the consistency and longevity of this support indicates an abiding commitment by the government to the deaf citizens of the country. The fact that this support has been given to a private corporation (which Gallaudet has always been) is also testimony to a long-lasting bond of trust that the university would act in the best interests of deaf people and the country at large.

In 1857, when Edward Miner Gallaudet (hereafter EMG) was just twenty years old, Amos Kendall offered him the superintendency of the Columbia Institution. Although both T. H. Gallaudet and EMG were hearing, EMG's mother Sophia was deaf. Not surprisingly, EMG grew up as a native user of what then was known as the Sign Language and later came to be called American Sign Language or ASL. The importance of this fact should not be overlooked as the Institution he presided over was a constant haven for instruction in signed language, even when its use was prohibited or discouraged elsewhere. When EMG accepted Kendall's offer, he was unmarried, but because the standards of propriety called for an adult female presence at the school, his mother accompanied him to serve as matron of the Institution.

Edward Miner Gallaudet (EMG) was born February 5, 1837, in Hartford, Connecticut. After high school, he worked at a bank in Hartford, and a few years later, he enrolled in Trinity College. While still a student, he became a teacher at the American School. He was just twenty years old when Amos Kendall wrote to him about the Columbia Institution in Washington, DC. Photograph circa 1857.

▲ Amos Kendall (August, 16, 1789–November 12, 1869) was a wealthy businessman and philanthropist when he became the guardian of five deaf children in 1856. He used his political connections to convince Congress to pass legislation establishing the Columbia Institution for the Instruction of the Deaf and Dumb and the Blind on his estate in northeast Washington in 1857. Photograph by Mathew Brady, circa 1860 1865; courtesy of the National Archives and Records Administration.

◄ Sophia Fowler Gallaudet served as matron of the Columbia Institution for nine years (1857–1866). She died in May 1877 while visiting EMG and his family, and her loss was mourned by all at the college. She is buried in Hartford next to her husband. Photograph circa 1860s.

James W. Grimes, a Republican senator from Iowa (1859–1869), chaired the Senate Committee on the District of Columbia from 1861 to 1865. In March of 1864, EMG sought his assistance in presenting a bill to the Senate that gave the Columbia Institution the authority to confer collegiate degrees. With Grimes's support, the bill passed, and President Lincoln signed it into law on April 8, 1864.

Soon after assuming the duties of superintendent of the Columbia Institution, EMG became convinced that the establishment of a college for the deaf was possible on Kendall Green, but he knew that federal legislation would be necessary. He began making plans to seek passage of the legislation without first consulting his friend and mentor, Amos Kendall, who was still president of the corporation. EMG described his actions as follows:

By what seemed a special providence, Mr. Kendall, in drafting the Act of Incorporation [in 1857], provided for the admission of deaf and blind children "of teachable age" as beneficiaries of the United States in the institution but set no limit of time or age at which they must be discharged, as is usual in the state schools for the deaf. So with our pupils in the District of Columbia

we had the material for beginning a college, and we were authorized to keep them as beneficiaries of the government as long as we could teach them anything. Thus without intending to do so, Mr. Kendall had secured a very important provision of law for the starting, at least, of a college for the deaf.[5]

Early in 1864, EMG drafted a bill granting the Institution the authority to confer collegiate degrees, and he began working with Senator James W. Grimes of Iowa to enable its passage. The law passed without significant opposition in both houses of Congress, and was signed by President Lincoln on April 8, 1864. After talking to Kendall, EMG became convinced that Kendall was not upset about not being consulted.

When Mr. Kendall learned of the passage of the bill authorizing us to confer degrees, he was pleased but remarked that he hoped I was not going too fast. My reply was, "You must remember Mr. Kendall, I am here to get upstream and move forward; if you think my rate of speed too high, you must put on the brakes….." He laughed and told me that he believed he could trust me. And it was not long before he proved his confidence in me by a proposal that surprised me beyond measure.

It was soon decided by the [board of] directors to inaugurate a collegiate department with suitable public exercises, and Mr. Kendall informed me that he wished to have me inaugurated on this occasion as president of the institution in all its departments, including the corporation and the Board of Directors.[6]

The Inauguration and Organization of the College for the Deaf

On June 28, 1864, the College for the Deaf and Dumb (within the corporate structure of the Columbia Institution) was inaugurated with due pomp and circumstance. Many speakers addressed the crowd, including EMG and Kendall; Congressman James Patterson from New Hampshire; the legendary Laurent Clerc; John Carlin, a well-known deaf poet and artist who had advocated for

Laurent Clerc taught at the American School for the Deaf from 1817 until 1858. In 1821, he took a leave of absence for eight months to be acting principal of the Pennsylvania Institution for the Deaf, where he planned the school's instructional program. Many of his students became teachers and founders of schools for the deaf throughout the United States. Clerc died in 1869, the same year this photograph was taken.

Thomas Gallaudet, born on June 3, 1822, in Hartford, Connecticut, was the oldest son of Thomas H. and Sophia Fowler Gallaudet. Like his youngest brother, EMG, he was active in the deaf community his entire life. He taught at the New York Institute for the Deaf, and, after becoming an ordained Episcopal minister in 1852, he established St. Ann's Church for Deaf-Mutes in New York City, where he conducted services in sign language. In 1885, he founded the Gallaudet Home for Aged and Infirm Deaf-Mutes near Poughkeepsie, NY. Gallaudet often came to Washington, DC, to visit his family at Kendall Green, and he acted as chaplain at several of the college's commencement ceremonies. Photograph circa 1855–1865; courtesy of the Library of Congress.

the establishment of a college for the deaf; and the Rev. Thomas Gallaudet, EMG's brother and rector of St. Ann's Church for Deaf-Mutes in New York City. The college bestowed its first degree, an honorary master of arts, on John Carlin. Clerc may have best summed up the emotions of many deaf people: "In closing, let me express to you, my dear young friend, Mr. E. M. Gallaudet, president-elect of this institution, the earnest hope that in the great work which is before you, you will be blessed and prospered, and receive for your efforts in behalf of the deaf and dumb such proofs of its benefits as will reward you for the glorious undertaking."[7]

Daniel R. Goodwin, provost of the University of Pennsylvania, was unable to attend the ceremony but sent a letter of congratulations that sums up the purpose of the college in terms that EMG must have found extremely gratifying.

The form of your present undertaking is novel, but I have no doubt that experience will prove it to be practicable and wise. Those who are deprived of one of the senses, possess, in general, as great intellectual capacities, as good natural aptitudes, and oftentimes as strong physical powers, and withal, as earnest a desire for knowledge and activity, as those who are blessed with the enjoyment of all the organic functions. It is right that they should have an opportunity to gain a full preparation for the highest employments that may be open before them, and should enjoy the happiness of the largest intellectual, moral, and religious culture.[8]

◀ John Carlin (honorary degree 1864) was born in Philadelphia in 1813 and became profoundly deaf as an infant. He attended the Mount Airy School (now the Pennsylvania School for the Deaf) and graduated in 1825. He later studied painting and became well known for his portraiture work, as well as for his poetry. Carlin raised $6,000 to help establish St. Ann's Church for Deaf-Mutes in 1852. In June 1864 he received the first degree from the Columbia Institution.

▶ Edward Miner Gallaudet at age 27, in 1864 when the college opened.

Almost as soon as the collegiate program was approved, EMG began to prepare for its establishment. At the outset of this process, he and Kendall had the first serious disagreement of their twelve-year association. EMG believed that very few graduates of the existing twenty-four schools for the deaf in the country would be sufficiently prepared academically to directly enter a college-level program, so he proposed that the college offer a preparatory year that most entering students would have to complete before being formally admitted to the collegiate degree program. Kendall objected, worried that the public would be skeptical of the very existence of the Institution if it became known that very few deaf students were actually qualified to enter the college. For some reason that EMG never determined, Kendall eventually withdrew his objection, and the preparatory program was established. It continued to operate until 1995, when the college began to admit students directly to the bachelor's level program, but required them to fulfill basic courses in English, math, or science before they could earn college credits in those subjects. The existence of the preparatory program and the fact that most students entering the college had to complete it influenced the creation of the signs used to refer to students by class standing. The sign for "prep" is made by tapping the open palm of the dominant hand on the pinky of the other hand; "freshman" by tapping the palm on the ring finger of the other hand, and so on, through "senior," indicated by tapping the palm on the thumb of the other hand.

In his detailed history of the first fifty years of the Columbia Institution, EMG described the first students to enter the collegiate program, revealing just how small its beginnings were.

It will be of interest to record the names of those who were the first to enter upon the advanced course of study prepared in connection with the college.

Melville Ballard of Maine, a graduate of the high class of the American School for the Deaf at Hartford in 1860, and who had performed acceptable service as a teacher in our institution from 1860 to 1863, then voluntarily retiring, entered in September 1864 on a special course of collegiate study. He is therefore to be named as the first student in our collegiate course and the only one for the year 1864–1865.

Charles K. W. Strong of Vermont, a graduate of the high class of the New York Institution for the Deaf and Dumb, and employed in the U.S. Treasury Department in 1864, declared his purpose of entering college on a footing similar to that of Mr. Ballard, and his name was entered on our records. But he changed his mind and never became an actual student.

In September 1864 four pupils of our institution— Emma J. Speake, Annie Szymanoskie, John Quinn, and Isaac Winn, all of the District of Columbia—entered upon our advanced course of study under the tuition of Professor Storrs of our college, with a view of entering on the regular collegiate course as soon as they could be prepared therefore.

James Cross, Jr., and James H. Logan, both of Pennsylvania, entered upon a similar course of study with Professor Storrs. It will be seen therefore that seven persons made up the number of those who were regarded as connected with the college as students during the first year of its existence.[9]

According to EMG, Ballard's status as the sole enrollee in the college program was the occasion for much amusement: "As only one of the five young men occupying this [college] building was, strictly speaking, a college student, remarks about him were often facetiously made by his mates, as follows, 'The College has gone to the City.' 'The College has gone to bed.' 'The College is taking a bath.' 'The College has a toothache today.'"[10]

In 1866, Melville Ballard became the first recipient of a bachelor's degree from the college, and he went on to serve as a teacher at the Columbia Institution for more than fifty years. One of the houses on Gallaudet's Faculty Row and a residential complex on the campus are named in his honor. The first regular class of college students received their diplomas in 1869. As patron of the institution, President Ulysses S. Grant signed the diplomas of the three graduates, and every sitting U.S. president has since done likewise. EMG noted that, "the graduation of the first bachelors of arts in a college for deaf-mutes, from what could justly be claimed to be a regular collegiate course of study, excited unusual interest in the educational world."[11]

In 1869, EMG also marked the death of his good friend and mentor, Amos Kendall: "My memory of Amos Kendall is one of particular tenderness. That he should give me the confidence he had when I came to Washington a youth of twenty was a surprise. The internal management of the institution could not have been committed more absolutely to me than it was."[12] Aside from his initial disagreement with Kendall over what became the prep program, EMG noted only one other serious dispute with Kendall—EMG wanted the college diplomas to be written in Latin, as was the frequent custom at the time, and Kendall wanted them to be in English. This may seem to be a trivial argument, but it reflected an underlying tension in American higher education. At this time, there was a growing movement away from "classical" education in the Greek and Latin languages, knowledge

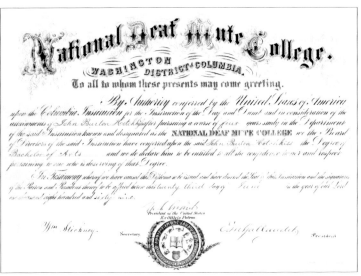

John Burton Hotchkiss, one of three students in the class of 1869, received this diploma on June 23, 1869. It is signed by President Ulysses S. Grant, EMG, and William Stickney, the secretary of the college and Amos Kendall's son-in-law.

of which was a mark of upper-class status, to a more populist, practical education in English, math, science, and other "useful" subjects. Insistence on an English diploma, which the graduates themselves could actually read, was a mark of the latter view. Kendall won the argument—Gallaudet diplomas are written in English.

During the 1865–1866 academic year, the number of students enrolled in the college grew to twenty-five, including two women. They came from throughout the East Coast and the Midwest. The college then became known as the National Deaf-Mute College. Within a few years, students were coming from most of the existing states, and in

JANE MELISSA FESSENDEN GALLAUDET

Jane Fessenden Gallaudet in 1863, when she was twenty-six years old. EMG affectionately called her "Jennie."

Jane Melissa Fessenden was born in Hartford, Connecticut, on October 16, 1837. Her parents, Edson Fessenden and Lydia Worden, owned a hotel, the Trumbull House, and it was there that Jane grew up. Both the Fessenden and Gallaudet families attended the First Church of Christ in Hartford, and they were well acquainted. Coincidentally, Edward Miner Gallaudet's sister Alice and her husband Henry Trumbull lived in the Fessendens' hotel.

During the 1850s, EMG would visit his sister and brother-in-law, and they often invited Jane to join them on their outings. Jane and EMG became engaged in December 1857 and married seven months later on July 20, 1858, in Hartford. Soon after their wedding, the couple moved to Washington, DC, and took up residence in the Stickney House on Kendall Green. Jane's father provided the furnishings for their rooms. Though Jane did not have an official position at the Columbia Institution, she occasionally filled a vacancy as a teacher of the blind students.

Jane and EMG had three children—Katherine Fessenden (June 25, 1861), Grace Worden (December 27, 1862), and Edward LeBaron (November 9, 1864). Young Edward died suddenly in July 1865, and Jane's health deteriorated soon after. In June of 1866, EMG took Jane to stay with her parents in Hartford in the hope that a cooler climate might help her regain her strength. After a few months, he brought their two daughters north to join their mother, and he returned to the college to tend to his administrative duties. Later that fall, EMG received word that Jane had died on November 23; she was twenty-nine years old. She was buried in the Gallaudet family plot at Cedar Hill Cemetery in Hartford.

Katherine and Grace came back to live with their father on the Gallaudet campus. As young women, they traveled frequently and were active in Washington society. In EMG's later years, Katherine became

EMG and his wife Jane had two daughters, Katherine (*right*) and Grace (*left*). The young women grew up on Kendall Green and were well known on campus and in Washington, DC. Here they are shown riding their tandem English tricycle when they were twenty-nine and twenty-eight years old, respectively. An article in the *Washington Post* on October 3, 1887, described them as riding "with perfect ease and grace. They show the possibilities of the tricycles to perfection as they sweep through the streets on noiseless wings."

his companion, living with him at House One and, following his retirement, at their home in Connecticut. Grace graduated from Smith College in 1883 and spent most of her life in New England and Washington, DC. She was married and widowed twice. Katherine died December 13, 1942, and Grace died two weeks later on December 27, 1942.[13]

► The *American Annals of the Deaf and Dumb* began publication in 1847 at the American School for the Deaf. It is the official journal of the Council of American Instructors of the Deaf (CAID) and the Conference of Educational Administrators of Schools and Programs for the Deaf (CEASD) (formerly the Convention of American Instructors of the Deaf and Dumb). When EMG joined the executive committee of CAID, the journal became closely associated with the college. In 1886 the name of the periodical changed to the *American Annals of the Deaf*. The *Annals* is still published quarterly by Gallaudet University Press.

►► Edward Allen Fay (November 23, 1843–July 14, 1923) taught at the New York Institute for the Deaf (Fanwood) before being hired in 1865 as the third professor at the college. Before coming to the college he taught in Morristown, New Jersey. In 1870 Fay became the editor of the *American Annals of the Deaf*. In 1881, he earned his PhD from Johns Hopkins University in Baltimore, MD, and four years later he became vice president of the college. Fay retired in 1920 at the age of seventy-seven.

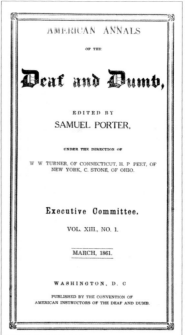

the 1880s the first international students began arriving. Enrollment in the bachelor's program had exceeded one hundred by the early 1900s but did not increase significantly above two hundred before the 1950s. After the college was founded, responsibility for educating blind children was removed in 1865, and the Columbia Institution continued to operate a school for deaf students, primarily the deaf children of the District of Columbia. Throughout the institution's history, this school was generally known as the Kendall School. Eventually the mission of the school was expanded through legislation establishing the Model Secondary School for the Deaf in 1966 and the Kendall Demonstration Elementary School in 1970. The legal establishment of these programs formalized the Institution's national responsibilities in research and development, but the college played a key role in research and scholarship concerning deaf people and their education right from the beginning. The Institution has had a long editorial association with the journal the *American Annals of the Deaf*, which was founded in 1847 and is believed to be the oldest English-language journal for education professionals. Gallaudet professor Edward A. Fay served as editor of the journal from 1870 until 1920. Fay

himself was a pioneer in studies of the Deaf community and the education of deaf students.

Deaf students at the college quickly began to establish literary societies, social organizations, and college customs similar to those of other American college campuses. One of the best known of these customs is the "rat funeral," a tradition whose origins seem to have been lost in the mists of time. The ritual of the rat funeral involves the adoption and eventual execution and burial of a rat by each entering undergraduate class. The graves are marked by a headstone that became emblematic of each particular class. Because of concerns about animal cruelty, live rats have been replaced by rubber ones in recent years.

The predecessors of Greek fraternities date from the beginning of the college. The secret society for men, known by the initials H.O.S.S., was founded in 1864 and renamed Xi Phi Sigma in 1894. In 1901, it assumed its current name, Kappa Gamma, and many of Gallaudet's faculty and other leaders through the years have been members. Female students, who had been excluded from the college for two decades, quickly began to form similar societies when they were readmitted in the late 1880s. The first alumni reunion took place in 1889

Gallaudet's football team, originally called the "Kendalls," had a reputation for being fierce competitors. Paul D. Hubbard, the quarterback in the early 1890s, is seated in the center of the first row. Photograph 1894.

▲ The men's gymnastics "Indian club" drill team practicing in front of the gymnasium (now called Ole Jim). Photograph circa 1885.

◄ In the 1880s the male faculty and students of the college formed the Kendall Green Bicycle Squad. Pictured left to right: Arthur D. Bryant, Amos G. Draper, John W. "Jack" Chickering, N. Field Morrow, John B. Hotchkiss, James Denison, Edward A. Fay (on tricycle), Cadwallader L. Washburn, Albert F. Adams, Olof Hanson, Henry L. Stafford, and Edson Gallaudet (EMG's son, age 14). Photograph 1885.

and an active alumni association was founded at that time. The college also participated in intercollegiate athletics—it fielded a football team as early as 1883, just fourteen years after the first American intercollegiate football game was played between Rutgers and Princeton in 1869. An enduring bit of Gallaudet and Deaf folklore holds that the football huddle was invented at Gallaudet. According to the 1974 *Gallaudet Almanac,*

The football huddle, which is universally used today, was invented by a Gallaudet College football team. Paul D. Hubbard, quarterback for the "Kendalls"

forerunners of the "Bisons," is credited with originating this system in the 1890's to prevent other teams from reading his signs when he called signals. The position proved such a practical and quick way of getting the team together on the field to discuss the next play that soon one college after another adopted the method.[14]

Female students also participated in athletic competition early in the college's history. The first women's basketball team began playing in 1896. (See chapter 2 for more information on Gallaudet's student organizations and athletic traditions.)

▲ The men's baseball team competed against collegiate teams from the District, Maryland, and Virginia. The team's name is printed on their equipment bag. Photograph 1886.

▶ Male students circa 1885 in front of Kendall Hall. A student is pretending to feed the "Iron Dog" on the second step.

The 1896 women's basketball team in Ole Jim, wearing their uniforms.

The women students on their safety bicycles. Photograph circa 1897.

The 1899 football team on the western steps of College Hall.

After the board of directors changed the name of the Institution to Gallaudet College in 1894, the baseball team added a G to their uniforms. Photograph 1898.

THE ALUMNI ORGANIZE

As the number of graduates grew, the alumni became more involved in and concerned with the reputation and performance of the college. In 1889, a group of alumni attending the third convention of the National Association of the Deaf (NAD), held in Washington, DC, met on June 27 to form the Gallaudet College Alumni Association (GCAA; now the Gallaudet University Alumni Association or GUAA). Its purpose was "to preserve and increase the influence and prestige of the College; to extend the sphere of its benefits among those for whom it was established; to oppose all influences tending to restrict those benefits; and secondarily, to perpetuate the friendships formed in College, and to promote relations between alumni of different college generations."[15] John B. Hotchkiss (BA 1869) chaired the organizational meeting, and Melville Ballard (BA 1866), the first person to receive an undergraduate degree at Gallaudet, was elected the first president. The first group of officers also included Hotchkiss as vice-president, George W. Veditz (BA 1884) as secretary, and Amos G. Draper (BA 1872) as treasurer. Thirty-one people paid the one dollar initiation fee that day to become charter members, and each year they paid $.50 annual dues.[16]

As its membership grew, the GCAA became involved in and concerned with the college's relations with the federal government. In 1890, the alumni objected to a measure adopted by Congress that would have restricted free tuition to only certain students. The GCAA conducted a writing campaign and, along with the efforts of the college administration, was successful in persuading Congress to repeal the measure.

In 1895, alumni living in Minnesota established the first GCAA chapter. At that time, the chapters were called "branches," and in the following years, new branches formed in cities and states around the U.S. Most of the chapters were established in cities with a significant number of alumni or a residential school for deaf students. These chapters perpetuated

The charter members of the Gallaudet College Alumni Association sat for this photograph on the steps of Chapel Hall in July 1889.

Melville Ballard (July 31, 1839–December 15, 1912) enrolled in 1864 as the first student in the collegiate program, and in 1866, he received the first bachelor's degree. He had a long and distinguished career as a teacher at the Kendall School.

Amos Galusha Draper (1845–1917) attended the American School for the Deaf with John B. Hotchkiss. He worked as a newspaper editorial writer during and after the Civil War. In 1868, he enrolled in Gallaudet and, after graduating, he became a professor of Latin and mathematics at the college.

John Burton Hotchkiss (August 22, 1845–November 3, 1922) attended the American School for the Deaf before coming to Gallaudet. After he received his BA in 1869, EMG hired him as a professor of English, history, and philosophy. He is credited with introducing football at the college, and the football field is named in his honor.

George W. Veditz (August 13, 1861–March 12, 1937) went to the Maryland School for the Deaf (MSD) when he was fourteen. He received both his bachelor's and master's degrees from Gallaudet and then became a teacher at MSD and later the Colorado School for the Deaf.

friendships among Gallaudet graduates, encouraged young deaf students to attend Gallaudet College, and took on projects in support of the college and alumni association. They also raised funds for student loans, scholarships, and other awards; athletic uniforms; and additional college needs.[17]

At the 1896 meeting, the alumni asked that deaf graduates be admitted to the Normal Department (the graduate school). In 1907, they passed a resolution to admit graduates of the Normal Department to membership in the GCAA. The members also adopted a resolution protesting a civil service ruling that denied deaf people the right to take the civil service examination, thereby excluding them from most federal government jobs. President Theodore Roosevelt reversed the ruling by executive order. At this same meeting, the members launched a drive to raise $50,000 for a memorial to Edward Miner Gallaudet; and in 1908, the association was incorporated.

The importance of student organizations cannot be overestimated in the formation of a well-organized and effective leadership group for the American Deaf community. William C. Stokoe, Russell Bernard, and Carol Padden have described the impact of these activities as follows:

> What happens is that age and the associations afforded by this unique institution work together to provide strong bonds indeed. . . .
>
> A few in each subgroup, as classmates, have shared both sides of the initiatory rites of hazing and all the rest of class rivalry and other college activities. Many have been in close touch since sharing one to five years in college. These then are more than cognitively and communicatively linked subgroups of deaf individuals; they are "cohorts" proceeding through life in a social formation that resembles the age-sets described in classic anthropological studies.[18]

From fairly early in its history, the college administration felt a responsibility to report on the post-college careers of its alumni, especially with respect to the kinds of employment they found. In 1890, alumnus and professor Amos Draper prepared such a report on the occupations of alumni, titled "Some Results of College Work." Following is a summary of his findings:

> One foreman of a daily newspaper, one assistant postmaster of a city, one clerk to a recorder of deeds, one official botanist of a state, one deputy recorder of deeds in a leading city, thirty-four teachers, one principal of a leading institution, five teachers and founders of schools for the deaf, four teachers and editors of schools for the deaf, two assistant professors in the College, one patent examiner, four teachers and clerks in the U.S. Departments, one clerk to the Librarian of Congress, eight clerks in U.S. Departments, custom houses and post offices, two editors and publishers of county newspapers and general printers, one bank clerk, two farmers and teachers, one ranchman, one teacher and fruit grower, one insurance clerk, one expert in the finishing of lenses, one publisher of a paper for a Methodist educational society, three teachers and

The Cremation of Mechanics

The Cremation of Mechanics (also known as Burning of Physics, Burning of Mechanics, or Burning of Analytics) was a popular tradition at many universities during the 1800s. Most colleges required students to pass a series of rigorous mathematics courses, including algebra, plane geometry, solid and spherical geometry, analytic geometry, and trigonometry. When students completed their final mathematics course, they would hold a mock funeral and cremate an effigy representing mathematics.

At the National Deaf-Mute College, the students completed the mathematics requirements in their junior year, and they would hold the cremation ceremony at the end of the spring semester. They often gave the effigy a humorous name, such as *Anna Lytics*. Ushers, pall-bearers, an undertaker, and a minister or master of ceremonies performed the last rites and other formalities. "Mourners" or "wailers" would weep for the "departed," inducing tears by rubbing onions under

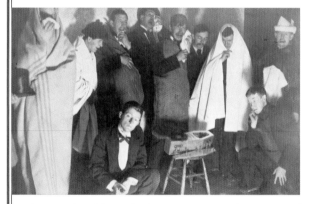

The Cremation of the Mechanics ceremony occurred in the spring of the students' junior year. One of the earliest student ceremonies performed at the college, it was a precursor to other traditions such as the rat funeral. Photograph 1892.

The Hare and Hounds Chase, an annual race. The hares (*left and right*, holding bags of paper scraps) run ahead of the hounds, releasing paper to mimic the hares' scent. The hounds follow the paper trail and attempt to catch the hares before they reach the finish line. Photograph 1888.

The annual weeklong camping trip to Great Falls during the Easter holiday. Photograph 1908.

their eyes. The class of 1898 was the last junior class to perform this ceremony at the college, which may have been the result of a changing curriculum or an indication of changing attitudes on campus.

Hare and Hounds

The Hare and Hounds (also known as a Paper or Chalk Chase) is a traditional cross-country racing game. The game had been played for centuries, but it gained greatest popularity in the U.S. between the late 1800s and early 1900s. In the game, one person was designated as the *hare* and all other players were the *hounds*. The hare started ahead of the other players, dropping bits of paper to leave a trail for the hounds to follow. After a set amount of time the hounds would begin to follow the trail, chasing the hare in an attempt to catch him before he reached the finish line. The annual Hare and Hounds race at Kendall Green began and ended on its 99 acres, which at the time included the college buildings, farmland, and back-

woods. Racers also covered miles of land through the eastern portion of Washington, DC.

Camping at Great Falls

In the early years of the college, the students and faculty began taking an annual camping trip to Great Falls, Virginia, in the area that later became Great Falls National Park. During the Easter recess, the male students would journey out to the camp-grounds with wagonloads of provisions, including food and tents. The men would stay for an entire week, while the female students would come out on Saturday and Sunday to join them for their "Ladies Day Camp." Students and faculty activities included swimming, hiking, and playing games. The tradition continued into the twentieth century; however, the latest photo of this event is from 1910, suggesting that interest in the camping trip waned and it fell out of practice. Curiously, the trips ended the same year that EMG retired.[19]

Amos G. Draper (BA 1872, MA 1877, honorary degree 1904), taught at Gallaudet for 44 years. He was well liked and well respected by students and faculty.

missionaries among the deaf, one architect's draftsman, one architect, two practical chemists, and one partner in a wholesale floor milling business.[20]

The concentration of graduates in educational institutions and public agencies has continued into the present.

In 1894, the board of directors voted to change the name of the collegiate department from "National Deaf-Mute College" to "Gallaudet College," an idea proposed by the alumni to honor Thomas H. Gallaudet. EMG noted that

the alumni and students had often during a number of years expressed their dislike of the words *deaf-mute* in the name of the college, and they felt it to be a misuse of terms to apply those words to the college which certainly was not a deaf-mute. . . .

In regard to this matter I naturally had a good deal of feeling lest some might think I was anxious that the college should have *my* name. Some of my friends and members of my family thought the name should not be given to the college while I was its president. But I wish to record here that my wish was to have the name given with the clear understanding that it was *in no way* in honor of me, but solely to honor my father who richly deserved such an honor.[21]

Relations with the Federal Government

Although Kendall and EMG were able to secure appropriate authorizing legislation for the Columbia Institution and its collegiate program, relations between the Institution and the federal government were not always smooth. In general, before an agency or a program can receive federal appropriations, it must be established by separate legislation that defines its purpose and authorizes its receipt of funds. Once funds are appropriated, oversight mechanisms ensure that the funds are used for the purposes for which they were appropriated. Both Congress and the executive branch may exercise oversight; in Gallaudet's case, the Department of the Interior initially provided this oversight (the Department of Education did not exist at this time). During the late 1800s the Interior Department had responsibility for overseeing a diverse array of domestic programs, including the schools for American Indians being established at this time by the Bureau of Indian Affairs. Gallaudet has also received oversight from congressional committees, including the appropriations committees of both houses, and by members of Congress who have served as voting members of its board of directors. For example, Senator Henry Dawes of Massachusetts sat on Gallaudet's board for more than thirty years, from 1869 to 1903. Gallaudet's current authorizing legislation specifies that the board include two representatives and one senator and that the Department of Education provide executive branch oversight.

There can be little doubt that EMG was a skilled and persistent lobbyist in support of funding and favorable treatment for the Institution. He was quite literally a lobbyist—he once waited in the cloakroom of the Senate in order to confront senators whose support he needed. EMG faced several early threats to the Institution's funding from members of Congress. The following account of an encounter with Representative Benjamin Butler of Massachusetts in 1867 is but one example.

I remember appearing on one occasion before the Appropriations Committee of the House when General

Henry L. Dawes was a Massachusetts state representative (1857–1875) and senator (1875–1893). After succeeding E. B. Washburne as chair of the Committee on Appropriations in 1869, Dawes became a supporter and advocate of Gallaudet; he later joined the college's board of directors. In 1910, the boys' dormitory was named Dawes House in the senator's honor. Photograph circa 1860–1865, courtesy of the Library of Congress.

Benjamin F. Butler was a Massachusetts state representative (1867–1879), the thirty-third governor of Massachusetts, and a member of the U.S. House of Representatives Committee on Appropriations. Photograph circa 1860–1865, courtesy of the Library of Congress.

B.F. Butler was a member of the committee. As the interview proceeded General Butler asked me in rather a sneering tone if I would tell the committee on what ground I would urge their appropriating money for the training of persons so deficient as the deaf and dumb were. "Why would it not be better," said the general "if Congress wished to spend money for educational purposes, to give it to those who had all their faculties."

I replied, "I ask aid for the deaf, with confidence that it will be given, because I believe that every generous man giving help to others likes to feel that it is bestowed where it is most needed." The committee gave me all I asked for, but General Butler opposed the appropriation in the House and in the course of his speech said when a deaf-mute had received all the education that could be given him, he is at the best no more than "half a man."

This expression roused the ire of one of our students, Joseph G. Parkinson (BA 1869) by name, who came to me to ask if I thought harm would come from his calling at General Butler's and sending in his card with the following written on it. "Half a man desires to

see the Beast." Some will remember that during Butler's administration of the municipal government of New Orleans during the Civil War, the people gave him the soubriquet "Beast Butler."[22]

A similar incident occurred in 1868, this time involving Congressman Elihu B. Washburne of Illinois, who opposed funding for the Institution. During lengthy hearings, Washburne presented information on enrollments and expenses at the Institution and claimed that there had been extravagant and inefficient use of public funds. EMG succeeded in defeating this attempt to block the appropriation, but he was left with Washburne's continuing animosity. According to EMG, "Mr. Washburne spoke of me with bitterness ... declaring that he would yet 'get even with that d---d little Frenchman'" [the Gallaudets were descended from French Huguenots].[23] There is a double irony here. Despite his apparent lack of affection for the French, within a few years Washburne would win praise for

Susan Skinner Denison was born January 24, 1847, in Royalton, VT, to Dr. Joseph A. Denison and Eliza Skinner, the tenth of eleven children. Her second oldest brother, James, was deaf. He graduated from the American School for the Deaf, taught at the Michigan Institution for the Deaf, and became the first teacher at the Kendall School in 1857. He and Edward Miner Gallaudet were the same age and they became close friends. In the summer of 1864, EMG traveled to Vermont to visit James, and there he met Susan for the first time. In July of 1868, EMG, who was now a widower, again went to Vermont to stay with the Denisons, and by the time he returned to Washington, he and Susan were engaged. They married on December 22, 1868. When they arrived in Washington, Susan took on her new role as stepmother to EMG's two daughters, Katherine and Grace (ages 7 and 6 at the time), and as the president's wife she began running the household and his social affairs. In 1869 they moved into the newly built president's house (House One).

EMG and Susan's first child, a son named Denison, was born on April 1, 1870. The following year their second son, Edson Fessenden (named after the father of EMG's first wife), was born. The couple's daughter, Eliza (named for Susan's mother) was born in June of 1874, but she died fourteen months later due to whooping cough. Their third son, Herbert Draper, was born in 1876, and their youngest child, a daughter named Marion Wallace, was born in 1879.

Susan maintained the family home and raised their six children while being actively involved in the social life of the campus and in Washingtonian society. She gave birthday parties for the children in Kendall School, held receptions for the older students and faculty, and entertained public officials and politicians and their wives.

After suffering from various ailments, including headaches and abdominal pain, Susan died on November 4, 1903. She was buried in the Gallaudet family plot at Cedar Hill Cemetery in Hartford.[27]

EMG and his second wife, Susan Denison, with EMG's two daughters Katherine (age seven) and Grace (age six), and Susan's nephew Will Denison (age eleven, the orphaned son of her eldest brother George). Photograph by Mathew Brady, 1868.

By 1869, construction of the residence for the college president and his family had been completed. EMG and Susan lived there for many years with their six children. *Left* to *right*: Herbert (standing), Marion (seated), Susan (seated), Katherine (standing), Grace (seated), EMG (standing), Edson (standing), and Denison (seated). Photograph circa 1885.

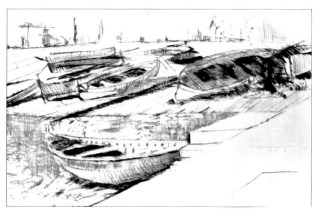

◀ Cadwallader Lincoln Washburn (BA 1890, honorary degree 1924) received his bachelor's degree from the college and then studied at the Art Students League in New York City. He later traveled to Spain and France to study art and exhibit his work. Washburn also worked as a war correspondent, reporting on the Russo-Japanese War and the Mexican Revolution. He is well known as a dry point etcher and an oil painter. The Washburn Arts Building on the Gallaudet campus was named in his honor in 1969.

▲ Washburn became internationally known for his printmaking.

his heroic actions as the U.S. minister to France during the Franco-Prussian War and Paris Commune of 1870 and 1871.[24] Upon learning of Washburne's appointment to the post, EMG remarked: "I need not say that the action of President Grant in sending Mr. Washburne to that glorious city where all good Americans like to go, met with the hearty approval of the friends of our college."[25] Later, in 1890, Washburne's own nephew, Cadwallader L. Washburn (spelled without the final *e*), graduated from the college. Cadwallader Washburn became one of the Institution's most illustrious early graduates, gaining fame as an artist. EMG could not resist a final dig: "Mr. E. B. Washburne was not living at the time of his nephew's graduation, but he lived long enough to know that he *had* a nephew in the college he had tried to break down."[26]

EMG's skill as a lobbyist can also be seen in his efforts to secure congressional support for full scholarships for the undergraduate students.

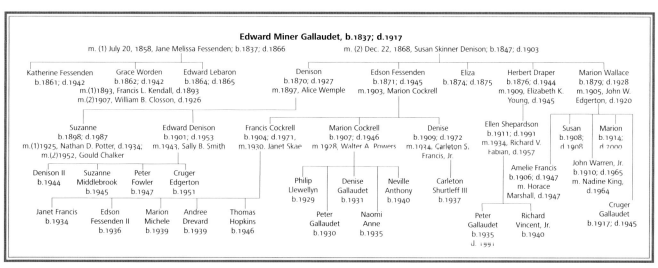

Adapted from Boatner (1959), p. iv.

During 1898 and 1899, I made efforts in Congress to secure an increase in the number of free scholarships in the college, the number allowed by law, sixty, having been reached.

The law increasing the number of free scholarships from forty to sixty was carried through chiefly by the friendly cooperation of Hon. Joseph G. Cannon, then chairman of the Committee on Appropriations. Mr. Cannon wrote the paragraph in his own hand and said, when I remarked that the limit of sixty might be reached in a few years, that it would be easy to increase the number allowed. This law was passed on August 30, 1890 and the limit of sixty was reached in 1898.

Greatly to my surprise he declared himself opposed to any increase. I got my friends in the Senate to give the increase, but Mr. Cannon opposed the measure successfully. In 1899, I made a second attempt, with a similar result.

In 1900 it happened that five applicants for admission to the college from Iowa could not be received because of the limitations of existing law. I laid the matter before Speaker [David] Henderson who was from Iowa and who had been a good friend of the college for many years.

I had recommendations from five members of Congress from Iowa, asking for the admission of the five young people. General Henderson was naturally *for Iowa* as well as for the college. He advised me to get the provision for one hundred put on in the Senate and said he would do all he could to carry it in the House.

The provision was agreed to by the Committee of Conference, and I was told that Mr. Cannon, making use of language more emphatic than elegant said, "With the Senate and the Speaker against me, what in ------ could I do?"[28]

EMG also had occasional clashes with officials of the Department of the Interior. Late in 1897, an Interior official asserted the right to control all expenditures by the Institution, a development that would have made management by EMG and the board of directors extremely difficult. Going again to his friends in Congress, EMG managed to defeat this effort.[29] Disagreements with federal officials about how to control programs and expenses at the college continue up to the present, as will be seen throughout this book. For a period of time, for example, the federal General Services Administration contracted for all construction on the campus, with less than architecturally pleasing results. It is, however, fair to say that the federal government has rarely attempted to involve itself in policy issues concerning modes of instruction, especially with respect to how language is used in the classroom.

During the early years of the college, U.S. presidents were fairly frequent visitors to Kendall Green, and EMG clearly understood the importance these visits lent to the visibility of the college. President Grant attended the dedication of Chapel Hall (the central building of the original campus) in 1871. In May 1874, the college began the practice of holding a "Presentation Day" for the degree candidates in that year. EMG reasoned that the weather was still likely to be cool, and the professors and students less tired than they would be at the end of the academic year in June. At this ceremony, the candidates for degrees were "presented" to the public. Presidents Grant, Hayes, Garfield, Arthur, Cleveland, and Harrison all attended these ceremonies between 1874 and 1889. President Garfield, in particular, made several visits to the college both as a member of Congress and as president. He was assassinated shortly after attending Presentation Day in 1881. Very near the end of EMG's tenure as president, Theodore Roosevelt attended Presentation Day in 1906, where "the young men of the college greeted him with the college 'yell,' surprising him with the noise of the voices of those whom he expected to find *mute*."[30]

Growth of the Sign Language

Instruction in sign language, especially at the collegiate level, was central to the character and spirit of the Institution right from its founding. At this time, most residential schools for the deaf in the United States used sign language for instructional purposes, and many educated people accepted it as a real language, although different in some respects from spoken languages. In addition,

◀ James A. Garfield became the twentieth president of the United States after completing nine consecutive terms in the House of Representatives and serving as chair of the House Committee on Appropriations. He was a great supporter and advocate of the college and a close friend of EMG. Three months before his assassination in 1881, he spoke at the college's commencement. The alumni association later commissioned a bust of his likeness, which has been on display in Chapel Hall since 1883. Photograph circa 1870–1880, courtesy of the Library of Congress.

▶ President Theodore Roosevelt arriving at the front steps of Chapel Hall to preside over the college's commencement in May 1906. He was the last U.S. president to attend commencement ceremonies at the college until 1966.

scholars had long speculated that some form of gestural language might have preceded speech in human history. In his 1864 address at the inauguration of the college, Amos Kendall expressed the underlying ideas in terms that would have been familiar to many educated people at that time.

It is a great mistake to suppose that deaf-mutes are in general inferior in capacity to children having all their senses in perfection. The inferiority is not in the want of capacity, but in the want of its development. We wish to supply that want . . .

If the whole human family were destitute of the sense of hearing, they would yet be able to interchange ideas by signs. Indeed, the language of signs undoubtedly accompanied if it did not precede the language of sounds. . . . We read that Adam named the beasts and birds. But how could he give them names without first pointing them out by other means? How could a particular name be fixed upon a particular animal among so many species without some sign indicating to what animal it should thereafter be applied? . . . If a company

of uneducated deaf-mutes were, for the first time, brought into contact with an elephant, without knowing its name, they would soon devise a sign by which he should be represented among themselves. So, were it possible for a company of adults with their senses entire to be placed in a similar situation, they would probably point him out by a sign accompanied by some exclamation, and the exclamation might become the name of the animal. Thenceforward the perfect man would convey the idea of an elephant by sound, while the deaf-mute could only do it by a sign . . . .

It is our function to teach, improve, and enlarge the sign-language; make it co-extensive with the language of sound, and through its instrumentality open the minds of deaf-mutes to the wonders of creation and the secrets of science and art.[31]

Many of the hearing people in the audience would not have been surprised by the assertion that sign language may have preceded speech in human history or that signing was somehow more "natural" than speech. Prior to the rise of oralism in deaf education, most would not have been surprised by the idea that education, including higher education, could be carried out in sign language, or that sign languages were, in fact, languages. Scholars at this time were interested in understanding how sign languages worked, including the sign languages used by members of American Indian tribes (in this case, hearing people). Garrick Mallery of the Smithsonian Institution, author of a major study of Plains Indian Sign Language, gave the following account of a visit to the college.

On March 6, 1880, the writer had an interesting experience in taking to the National Deaf-Mute College at Washington seven Utes (which tribe, according to report, is unacquainted with [deaf] sign language), among whom were Augustin, Alejandro, Jakonik, Severio, and Wash. By the kind attention of President GALLAUDET a thorough test was given, an equal number of deaf-mute pupils being placed in communication with the Indians, alternating with them both in making individual signs and in telling narratives in gesture, which were afterwards interpreted in speech by the Ute interpreter and the officers of the college. Notes of a few of them were taken, as follows:

Among the signs was that for *squirrel*, given by a deaf-mute. The right hand was placed over and facing the left, and about four inches above the latter, to show the height of the animal; then the two hands were held edgewise and horizontally in front, about eight inches apart (showing *length*); then imitating the grasping of a small object and biting it rapidly with the incisors, the extended index was pointed upward and forward (*in a tree*).

This was not understood, as the Utes have no sign for the tree squirrel, the arboreal animal not being now found in their region.

Deaf-mute sign for *jack-rabbit*: The first two fingers of each hand extended (the remaining fingers and thumbs closed) were placed on either side of the head, pointing upward; then arching the hands, palm down, quick, interrupted, jumping movements forward were made.

This was readily understood.

The signs for the following narrative were given by a deaf-mute: When he was a boy he mounted a horse without either bridle or saddle, and as the horse began to go he grasped him by the neck for support; a dog flew at the horse, began to bark, when the rider was thrown off and considerably hurt.

In this the sign for *dog* was as follows: Pass the arched hand forward from the lower part of the face, to illustrate elongated nose and mouth, then with both forefingers extended, remaining fingers and thumbs closed, place them upon either side of the lower jaw, pointing upward, to show lower canines, at the same time accompanying the gesture with an expression of withdrawing the lips so as to show the teeth snarling; [pg 322] then, with the fingers of the right hand extended and separated throw them quickly forward and slightly upward (*voice* or *talking*).

This sign was understood to mean *bear*, as that for *dog* is different among the Utes, *i.e.*, by merely showing the height of the dog and pushing the flat hand forward, finger-tips first . . . .

It will be observed that many of the above signs admitted of and were expressed by pantomime, yet that was not the case with all that were made. President GALLAUDET made also some remarks in gesture which were understood by the Indians, yet were not strictly pantomimic.

The opinion of all present at the test was that two intelligent mimes would seldom fail of mutual understanding, their attention being exclusively directed to the expression of thoughts by the means of comprehension and reply equally possessed by both, without the mental confusion of conventional sounds only intelligible to one.

A large collection has been made of natural deaf-mute signs, and also of those more conventional, which have been collated with those of the several tribes of Indians. Many of them show marked similarity, not only in principle but often in detail.

The result of the studies so far as prosecuted is that what is called *the* sign language of Indians is not, properly speaking, one language, but that it and the gesture systems of deaf-mutes and of all peoples constitute together one language—the gesture speech of mankind—of which each system is a dialect.[32]

▲ Alexander Graham Bell, though a strong proponent of oralism, received an honorary degree from Gallaudet in 1880.

◄ EMG attended the Second International Congress on Education of the Deaf in Milan, Italy, accompanied by his brother-in-law James Denison, his older brother Reverend Thomas Gallaudet, Isaac Lewis Peet, and Charles A Stoddard. Photograph by Mathew Brady, circa 1870–1880, courtesy of the Library of Congress.

Later linguistic studies would show that this conclusion is not warranted—the signed languages of Deaf people and hearing people such as Plains Indians are, in fact, quite distinct from each other. However, they share mechanisms for sign creation and formation that depend upon iconicity or resemblances of many signs to the things they refer to. As a result, people who are unfamiliar with each other but are used to communicating either in formalized signed *languages* or less formalized gestural systems may find it easier to develop mutually intelligible ad hoc signs.

The year 1880 is particularly important in the history of ASL and deaf education in general. The International Congress of Instructors of the Deaf held that year in Milan, Italy, voted to support oral education of the deaf to the exclusion of sign-based methods. The passage below is the first of several resolutions that the congress approved overwhelmingly.

The Convention, considering the incontestable superiority of articulation [speech] over signs in restoring the deaf-mute to society and giving him a fuller knowledge of language, declares that the oral method should be preferred to that of signs in the education and instruction of deaf-mutes.[33]

EMG attended the Milan Congress and voted against the resolutions, and he gives the following account of what happened:

The Milan Congress was a partisan body, a majority of its voting members being from the Italian Schools. Out of 164 members only 21 came from countries outside of Italy and France. The Congress was, therefore, not really international in its character nor was its composition representative. It is not improper to say that its pronunciamento in favor of the oral method was the expression of little more than local opinion in Italy and France.[34]

Oral education programs existed in the United States and Europe before this congress; however, this vote was to prove influential in eliminating signed-based education in Europe and restricting it severely in the United States. Historian Douglas Baynton points out that as oralism prevailed and signing declined, there was a chilling effect on the scholarly study of sign languages and their acceptance by the public as legitimate forms of communication.[35] The best known and most influential of the American oralists was Alexander Graham Bell.

Following the establishment of the Normal Department in 1891, hearing men and women enrolled in the two-year graduate program. Pictured here are the instructors and students of the second Normal class, during the 1892–1893 academic year.

A. G. Bell was married to a deaf woman and considered himself a teacher of the deaf. He founded the Volta Bureau in Washington, DC, to promote the ideals of oral education, and, in doing so, he had a significant impact on the development of the National Deaf-Mute College.

Establishment of the Normal School

The idea for a normal department at the college to train teachers of the deaf came from Mr. L. S. Fechheimer of Cincinnati, Ohio. Fechheimer had a deaf son and was a strong supporter of oral instruction. Despite this, EMG requested funds from Congress to establish a new program "in which young men and women, having all their faculties, could be thoroughly trained to be teachers of the deaf," in both methods then in use—oral and manual. He also told A. G. Bell about his plan and invited Bell to be a lecturer. The House Appropriations Committee held hearings to consider funding the department in January 1891. A few days before the hearings, EMG discovered that Bell planned to block passage of the appropriation. Bell was extremely influential both as the inventor of the telephone and as a staunch oralist. EMG went to Bell and explained

that he planned to restrict admission to the normal department to hearing students. Bell replied that he opposed the establishment of the normal school because he believed that deaf students would be admitted. EMG then told him

plainly that he was entirely mistaken in this idea, that no deaf persons would be admitted to our normal class, and that all its members would be thoroughly trained in the oral method of teaching the deaf. And yet on the very next day Professor Bell appeared before the Appropriations Committee and spoke for forty-five minutes, asserting flatly that our purpose *was* to train deaf teachers of the deaf and opposing the plan mainly on that ground.[36]

EMG succeeded in getting the appropriation passed, although it was less than he had hoped for, and it was to be used specifically to pay articulation teachers. Nevertheless, the college established the normal department as it had originally planned. The first students graduated from the program in 1892, and all seven were hired by schools for the deaf. As for his feud with Bell and its eventual settlement, EMG wrote in his diary, "The hatchet is buried, but I know where it is."[37]

Development of the Campus on Kendall Green

In planning the Kendall Green campus and allowing for its growth, EMG tended to hire the most renowned experts of the day in whatever art form might be involved. His motivation may have been partly to draw positive attention to the Institution. In 1866 he engaged Frederick Law Olmsted, generally considered to be the founder of landscape architecture in the United States and still its best known practitioner, to design the campus. EMG had known Olmsted in Hartford, and Olmsted had gained national fame as the designer of Central Park in New York City. EMG also hired well-known architects to design the buildings on the campus.

The campus was located on what had been Amos Kendall's farm in the northeastern quadrant of the District of Columbia, on what was then known as Boundary Street (now Florida Avenue). It retained much of the flavor of its agricultural

Frederick Law Olmsted was commissioned as the architect and designer of the Institution's campus. Olmsted Green is named in his honor. Engraving made and photograph taken in October 1893, courtesy of the Library of Congress.

▼ A view of Kendall Green in 1866 with the Rose Cottage (*right*) and the newly built east wing of College Hall (*left*), which was designed by Emil S. Friedrich.

▼ ▼ The east wing of College Hall (*left*), and Chapel Hall (*center*), which was completed in 1871. A portion of the shop building can be seen between the college building and Chapel Hall, along with the "old" Fowler Hall (*right*). Photograph circa 1875.

In planning the Gallaudet campus, Olmsted

organized the college and Kendall School buildings so that they backed onto a shared service yard with spaces for the kitchen yard, boys' playground, and the mechanic shop. Kendall School faculty housing faced the service yard as well, making this area a lively outdoor space on the campus. The formal entry to the academic buildings in this cluster faced outward to the campus grounds bounded to the west by Faculty Row, a line of five brick houses for faculty and the president's house. These campus grounds were designed as a park-like "naturalistic" setting where pathways meandered through groves of shade trees and open fields offering a variety of spatial and sensory experiences. Within the informal campus quad between College Hall and Faculty Row, students and faculty alike had many choices of places to either seek social interaction or solitude along the paths, where one could linger within the shaded groves and gaze across the open fields. One can still experience this sublime campus experience by walking along the original pathways that surround the historic Olmsted Green [the heart of the original campus, later named in Olmsted's honor].[38]

Gallaudet alumnus and professor, BENJAMIN BAHAN, and Campus Architect, HANSEL BAUMAN

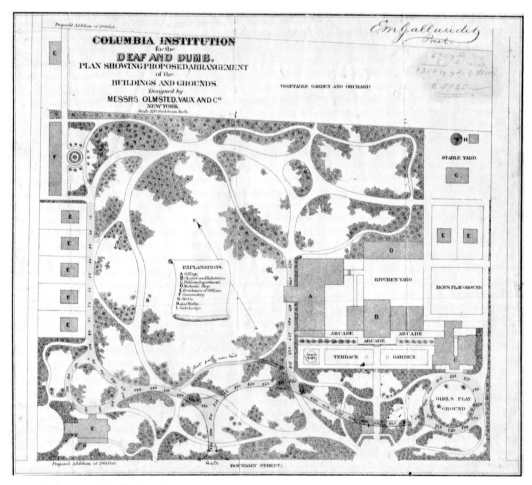

The original proposed plan for the Columbia Institution campus, designed by Olmsted in 1866 and approved by EMG.

▲ Olof Hanson (BA 1886, MA 1889, honorary degree 1914) graduated from the Minnesota School for the Deaf in Faribault and then attended Gallaudet. Following graduation from the college, he worked in an architecture firm. He is perhaps best known at Gallaudet for his design of the boys' dormitory (now Dawes House). Hanson married fellow alumna, Agatha M. A. Tiegel. Photograph circa 1890s.

▶ The boys' dormitory for Kendall School (Dawes House), soon after construction of the building was completed in 1895.

origins, including orchards and pastureland. For many years, the college maintained a working farm, and students could take agriculture courses. An alumnus, Harley Drake (BA 1904), taught agriculture and managed the farm for many years.

Olmsted's task was to turn Kendall's estate and farm into a college campus. The part of the Kendall estate that Olmsted had to work with in 1866 was only a small portion of the eventual ninety-nine acres currently owned by Gallaudet University An additional eighty-one acres of Kendall's land was purchased by the Institution in 1870–71. Olmsted's design not only included the placement of buildings but also allowed for walkways, lawns, and ornamental gardens.

A number of the buildings located within the original area designed by Olmsted are still standing, including College Hall; Chapel Hall; the original gymnasium (Ole Jim); four of the Faculty Row houses, including the president's residence; the Gate House; the original Kendall School building; and Dawes House.

Dawes House, named for U.S. representative, senator, and college supporter Henry L. Dawes of Massachusetts, is particularly noteworthy. Built in 1895, it was the last of the historic buildings constructed during EMG's presidency, and it was designed by Gallaudet alumnus and practicing architect Olof Hanson (BA 1886) of Faribault, Minnesota. EMG was highly satisfied with his work.

Mr. Hanson drew up complete specifications for this building and made careful estimates of its probable cost. It was to his credit and greatly to our satisfaction that the expense of constructing the building fell a few hundred dollars [a significant amount in 1895] short of the estimates. The building is a dormitory for the boys of the Kendall School, is well adapted for the purpose, and has no little architectural beauty.[39]

The location of Kendall Green, within about one mile of the U.S. Capitol, had great strategic significance for a lobbyist as adept as EMG. He was a regular visitor to the Capitol, as have been all

On the morning of February 6, 1910, a fire burned through the upper levels of College Hall. Onlookers, including students, faculty, staff, and neighbors of the College, watched the action from Olmsted Green while firefighters with a horse-drawn fire engine (*foreground*) battled the blaze.

subsequent Gallaudet presidents, and he frequently invited members of Congress to visit the campus. In 1891, EMG had to use his lobbying skills once again to preserve the integrity of the campus. The Baltimore and Ohio Railroad had a bill introduced in Congress to give the company a right of way to lay tracks across the Institution's grounds. The placement of the tracks would have made Kendall Green unfit for use by an educational institution and would have severely depreciated the value of the property. EMG gave the following account of his efforts to defeat this measure:

Our directors in Congress, Senators Hawley and Dawes and Representatives Hitt and Hemphill, gave me much valuable aid, and the result was that a signal triumph was won for the institution. I hope I may be pardoned for quoting from my diary a remark I find recorded there from Senator Dawes under the date of January 30, 1891: "Senator Dawes, when I told him of the surrender of the B & O Railroad, said, 'You are bigger than Congress for they can't beat a great railroad which you have done.'"[40]

On February 6, 1910, shortly before EMG retired, one final dramatic event took place on the historic campus. During the morning, a fire broke out in College Hall where the male students lived. The fire spread to the roof of the building, a location that made it particularly hard to put out. College students and faculty fought the fire until firemen arrived, averting catastrophic damage and injury. Because it was bitter cold, the water pumped by the fireman froze and encased much of the building in ice. It also flooded the lower floors. The next day, the *Washington Evening Star* reported on the aftermath of the fire.

Dr. Gallaudet was not present at the time. Acting President Fay quickly straightened out the situation, and saw that the boys got comfortable beds for the night. The work of cleaning out the debris began Monday morning, the college boys and younger members of the faculty volunteering, and all worked with a will that the re-construction might speedily begin. As is the rule with government buildings, no insurance was carried. Dr.

Gallaudet will shortly go before Congress and ask for a special appropriation to cover the cost of the repairs. With favorable weather it will take about two months to put everything back in first-class order.

Controversy on the Campus

During EMG's tenure as president of the college, several issues arose that prompted actions deemed acceptable at the time, but that are questionable in hindsight. One particular incident involved the Deaf community's opposition to EMG's actions in a decision they believed rightly belonged to them. It all began in 1883 at the second convention of the National Association of the Deaf (NAD). C. K. W. Strong proposed that the NAD commission a bronze statue to honor the one hundredth anniversary of Thomas Hopkins Gallaudet's birth, which would be in 1887. The statue would be unveiled in 1888 on the grounds of the National Deaf-Mute College. The resolution passed and the NAD formed a committee of fifteen members to manage the project.[41]

A number of controversies arose over fundraising and selection of a sculptor, but the controversy that is significant here involves convincing evidence that EMG exerted undue influence in the selection of Daniel Chester French, a hearing person, as the sculptor. French was already well known at the time of his selection, but he achieved lasting fame for his monumental sculpture of a seated Abraham Lincoln for the Lincoln Memorial in Washington.

Problems began to surface early in 1886 when Theodore A. Froehlich, chairman of the NAD committee, announced that he had asked French to submit a design for the statue. However, Michael J. Olson, the Gallaudet archivist, has found evidence that French went to Washington to meet with EMG and to select an appropriate spot for the statue on November 18, 1885.[42] Several articles appeared in Deaf newspapers questioning Froehlich's apparently unilateral decision. EMG also noted in his diary on February 24, 1887, that

Daniel Chester French (*left*), the sculptor, and Henry Bacon (*right*), architect of the memorial, stand beside the Abraham Lincoln Memorial statue. Many deaf people believe that the hands of the statue form the manual alphabet letters "A" and "L." French began working on the statue in 1915, some twenty-six years after he created the Thomas H. Gallaudet/Alice Cogswell statue on the Gallaudet campus. In that work, both Gallaudet and Cogswell are forming the letter A, which indicates that French knew of the manual alphabet.[43] Photograph circa 1921–1922, courtesy of the Library of Congress.

Froehlich told him the committee planned to offer French a commission in the spring.[44]

Froehlich placed an announcement in the *Deaf-Mutes' Journal* on April 14, 1887, stating that a five-member committee would select an artist, and he encouraged artists to submit their designs by May 2nd. The committee met on May 3, 1887, and awarded the project to French. Protests arose immediately among members of the Deaf community, which had been responsible for raising the funds to construct the statue. Olson writes that a mass meeting took place in New York on May 9, 1887, where "deaf people protested against the committee for awarding the contract to a hearing sculptor They argued that experienced deaf artists would do the job for only $8,000 to $10,000, including the pedestal, whereas French charged $10,000 for a bronze statue without a pedestal. They also complained that one member of the committee was afraid to give the job to a deaf artist because he thought that a deaf artist could not do the task."[45]

The deaf artists mentioned as capable of creating the statue included Albert Ballin, J. F. J. Tesch, and Douglas Tilden. Ballin and Tesch both submitted proposals during the selection process. In June, Tesch wrote to Amos Draper, the chairman of the fund-raising committee, complaining that French was "a *pet friend* of yours and Gallaudet."[46] Nevertheless, EMG and the fund-raising committee stood firmly behind their selection of French, and the controversies eventually died down. French's statue of T. H. Gallaudet and Alice Cogswell now stands in front of Chapel Hall on the

The memorial statue of Thomas Hopkins Gallaudet and Alice Cogswell, also designed by Daniel Chester French, was unveiled in 1889. The NAD commissioned French, who was well known as a capable and professional artist, in 1887 to design the statue. Photograph circa 1930s.

SELECTING A SITE FOR THE GALLAUDET STATUE

How the statue wound up in its current site is a frequently told piece of Gallaudet lore. After visiting the campus, French suggested the site in front of Chapel Hall. However, an old apple tree where EMG's daughters had played as children stood on the site, and they objected to its removal. Even after a storm had destroyed much of the tree, his daughters still objected. EMG, who occasionally saw the hand of Providence at work in the college's history, wrote to French describing what happened next:

What will you say when I tell you that a miracle has happened? Behold! Another storm has come and gone, and the other branch has been torn away, and even my unreasonable offspring do not insist that the bare stump be left standing. The statue can stand where you and I want it, and where it should stand.[47]

Kendall Green campus. The dedication took place on June 26, 1889, with prominent members of the Deaf community, Alexander Graham Bell, and U.S. President Benjamin Harrison in attendance.

In 1905, EMG took steps to move the few African American students attending Kendall School to the Maryland School for Colored Deaf-Mutes in Baltimore. It appears that EMG bowed to pressure from parents when he instituted this policy.

Important legislation was enacted by Congress in regard to the education of the colored deaf-mutes of the District [of Columbia]. From the very early days of the institution we have had colored pupils. But the number was so small for many years as to occasion no particular difficulty. We had separate sleeping rooms and separate tables for them with the white pupils in the classrooms. Within the past few years the number of the colored increased until we had fourteen. On a good many occasions we had complaints from the parents of white children and protests against the mixture of the races in our school. Some difficulties also arose, growing out of the treatment of the colored by the white. Other considerations made it seem best, on the whole, that there should be a separation. Senator Cockrell [of Missouri] rendered very important aid in securing the necessary action of Congress authorizing the transfer of the colored deaf children of the District to the Maryland School for Colored Deaf-Mutes in Baltimore.

The transfer was successfully made in September 1905, and the new arrangement works well in all respects. The principal of the school in Baltimore is a graduate of our normal department, and two of the teachers were graduates of our college.[48]

This is apparently all the justification that EMG offered for moving the African American students. If he had felt the need to elaborate, he would probably have pointed out that Jim Crow was the order of the day and that the District of Columbia public schools were also segregated. He might also have asserted that his overriding goal was to ensure the survival of the college and that he did not want to anger Southern senators and congressmen. However, other models of how to deal with legalized segregation were available, and it can be seen as a failure of the Institution (and EMG personally) that it dismissed African American parents and their deaf children in this way. No record exists that the children themselves or their parents felt that this arrangement worked "well in all respects." In fact, dissatisfaction with the arrangement finally led to the return of deaf African American students to the Kendall School almost fifty years later (see chap. 2).

Although the college never had a specific policy against admitting African Americans, records exist for only two African American students in the nineteenth century. James Gilbert, Jr., entered as a preparatory student in September 1880 at the age of nineteen. He left Gallaudet after his first year of study, possibly because of the treatment he received from other students. In September 1883, sixteen-year-old Ennal Jerome Adams, Jr., was admitted as a preparatory student. Three months into his freshman year, he left the college and returned home to Baltimore. There is no clear account of why he left, but the minutes from a faculty meeting state that he was "allowed to withdraw."[49]

It was not until 1954 that African American students received a Gallaudet degree. In that year, Andrew Foster got a bachelor's degree and Hylda Purce obtained a master's degree. Gallaudet archivist Michael J. Olson has found evidence that a perception may have existed that the college would not accept black students. In December 1897, EMG received a letter from William J. Blount of the Colored Division of the Kentucky School for the Deaf. In it, Blount makes this request:

The information came to us to the effect that you will not accept a negro deaf mute into your college—hence this letter to you for the confirmation or denial. If such is the case, we deplore it greatly as we have an unusually bright colored boy, named Lee Bates, aged 15 years. He is a semi-mute, having lost his hearing at the age of about 7 years. We are more than anxious to send him to your college upon his graduation. So is Supt. Rogers [of the Kentucky School for the Deaf as a whole].[50]

Olson has been unable to find a response from EMG in the Gallaudet Archives, and no one named Lee Bates enrolled in the college. There is no record of organized faculty or student protests against the racial policies during this period and no evidence that white deaf people at Gallaudet felt a sense of solidarity with deaf African Americans.

Just as societal views on race apparently out-weighed solidarity on the basis of shared deafness, so did the views on women. Although female students were among the first admitted to the college, none made it beyond the preparatory year, and no more were admitted until 1887, when six arrived at Kendall Green. They lived on the upper floors of EMG's residence, known as House One.

Female students were admitted to the college in the fall of 1887. The members of this first class included Alto M. Lowman (BS 1892), Anna L. Kurtz (class of 1892), Annie E. Jameson (certificate 1892), Ella F. Black (class of 1892, attended one year), Georgia Elliott (class of 1892, attended two years), Hattie A. Leffler (class of 1892), Margaret Ellen Rudd (class of 1892), and Agatha Mary Agnes Tiegel (BA 1893). Photograph taken near the Gate House, 1888.

▲ May Stafford (née Martin, BA 1895, MA 1900) attended the New York School for the Deaf (Fanwood), graduating in 1891. As an undergraduate at the college, she was a founding member of the O.W.L.S. and founder of the Jollity Club; she also worked for Vice President Edward A. Fay and assisted him with the editing of the *American Annals of the Deaf.* Following her graduation, she became the first female faculty member at the college. In 1900, she stepped down from her position to marry fellow alumnus Henry Lathrop Stafford (BA 1893, MA 1908).

◄ Agatha Mary Agnes Tiegel Hanson (BA 1893) attended Western Pennsylvania Institute for the Deaf and Dumb until the age of fifteen, when she was admitted as a preparatory student at the college. As an undergraduate, Hanson was a founding member of both the O.W.L.S. and the *Buff and Blue*. She married fellow alumnus Olof Hanson. Photograph taken on May 13, 1893.

EMG was reluctant to admit them because of his general opposition to coeducation, although he gave no real explanation for it. After the first year, though, he wrote that the experience "was so much more so than I had expected that I felt disposed to continue the experiment, and I am compelled to say at the date of the present writing, November 1899, that my apprehensions have not been realized. On the whole I feel that the presence of young women in the college has had a favorable influence."[51]

At first, the male students subjected the women to hazing and harassment. An article in the *Buff and Blue* (the student newspaper) in 1895 reported that "when the girls went to and from recitations in the college halls, all the [male] students would line up in rows and thus compel them to run a daily gauntlet of masculine curiosity." They were also frequently denied membership in student organizations, including the prestigious literary society. In response, thirteen of the women established their own society, the "O.W.L.S.," on January 9, 1892. The founding members included Lily Bicksler, Bertha Block, Laura Frederick, Mary Agnes Gorman, Lulu Herdman, Augusta Kruse, Alto Lowman, Margaret Magill, May Martin, Hannah Schankweiler, Agatha Tiegel, Christina Thompson, and Bertha Whitelock. The society, whose name is "an acronym whose definition is still a tightly held secret," held open literary discussions and dramatic productions, as well as other social programs. In 1893, Agatha Tiegel, the first president of the O.W.L.S., became the first woman to receive a bachelor's degree from the college.[52]

EMG's Legacy

Edward Miner Gallaudet served a total of fifty-three eventful years as head of the Columbia Institution—seven years as superintendent of the original school, and forty-six years as president of the college. He retired as president in 1910, and he lived only seven more years. In the benediction at the end of his *History of the College for the Deaf*, he writes, "My prayer is that the blessing of heaven may ever attend the institution, and all who have, or

In 1904, EMG celebrated his fortieth year as president and his sixty-seventh birthday. Photograph 1909.

may in the future have, any connection with it."[53] There can be little doubt that EMG was a strong-willed and tenacious visionary who was willing to do whatever was needed to ensure the survival of the Institution. But, in what ways did he succeed? Did he have failings? Was he really the "voice of the deaf," as his biographer would have it?[54] It is always difficult to evaluate the ethics and morality of the actions taken by people who lived in times that were quite different from ours. So, in assessing EMG, we should look not only to our values but also to those of the time in which he lived.

It is clear that, in general, EMG held deaf people in high regard, and he respected their abilities and their language. It is also clear, however, that when he felt it was necessary or expedient in some way, he could ignore their interests. The exclusion of deaf students from the normal school is a glaring omission, one that continued until 1960. There is no indication that EMG ever seriously considered the possibility that he might be succeeded as president by a deaf person. The idea that it was acceptable for hearing people to manage the affairs of the Institution at the levels of the presi-

In May of 1910, EMG announced his retirement as president of the college. His chosen successor, Percival Hall (MA 1893, honorary degree 1935), took over the office the following September. In the company of his eldest daughter, Katherine, EMG left Kendall Green to reside at their house in Connecticut, where he lived until his death. Photograph 1915.

dency and the board persisted late into the twentieth century and led to one of the pivotal events in Deaf history.

The removal of African American students from Kendall School during EMG's tenure is a mark of shame both on his record and that of the Institution and its board. It is not enough to say that this policy was typical of the time and place. The Fourteenth Amendment to the Constitution (1868) requires equal protection under the law for all Americans, but the Supreme Court decision in *Plessy v. Ferguson* (1896) established the doctrine of "separate but equal." This cleared the way for the passage of Jim Crow laws in many states and the District of Columbia. The Columbia Institution received substantial support from all U.S. taxpayers, and it was the only institution of its kind—no comparable separate facility was ever offered to deaf African Americans. So the Institution's actions failed even the meager test of "separate but equal." Had the Institution actually been legally compelled

This western view of Kendall Green shows College Hall (*left*, completed 1877), Chapel Hall (*center*, completed 1871), and "old" Fowler Hall (*right*, completed 1859). Both Chapel Hall and the west wing of College Hall were designed by Frederick C. Withers. The east wing of College Hall was originally called the "Friedrich building" (for its architect) and "the college building." Photograph circa 1888.

to exclude African American students (which it was not), it could have followed the example of Berea College. When, in 1904, the Kentucky legislature passed a law requiring racial segregation, Berea raised funds to support a separate college for black students.

The treatment of female students, while not as egregious as that of African Americans, also raises serious questions of fairness. Again, Gallaudet was the only institution of its kind in the world, yet it excluded half of the deaf population from the college program for two decades. When Gallaudet College was founded in 1864, it was no longer unusual for women to obtain higher education. Several women's colleges existed at this time, as did several coeducational institutions, including Oberlin College, which began admitting women in 1837, and the University of Iowa, which did so in 1855. Cornell University had female students as early as 1870, and the University of Pennsylvania admitted its first women students in the mid-1870s. Even though, as EMG said, coeducation might present certain problems, he could have followed the policies in place at other colleges. Finally, there is no evidence that EMG tried to arrange for the higher education of deaf women in some other institution when he was unwilling to have them at the college.

On balance, and despite the blemishes on his record, EMG's achievements were great and far-reaching. Against all odds and at a time of enormous crisis in the country's history, he managed, through his own skill and tenacity, to create and keep alive a completely unique institution that has come to occupy a special place in the hearts of deaf people throughout the world. One hundred and fifty years later, no other country on Earth has created an institution like Gallaudet, and it is unlikely that one ever will.

CHAPTER 2

GROWING INTO A NEW CENTURY, 1910–1957

The Gallaudet Board of Directors appointed Percival Hall, a graduate of Harvard College and a professor at Gallaudet, to succeed EMG as president, and he took office in September 1910. According to Albert Atwood, who was chairman of the board from 1946 to 1968, the directors would have offered the position to Edward Allen Fay, EMG's vice president, but they knew that he would not accept the appointment.[1] Fay was seventy-seven years old, had already served Gallaudet for forty-five years, and was nearing retirement. In fact, he stayed for another ten years, and he received an honorary doctorate from the college in 1916.

Hall was born September 16, 1872, and he grew up in Washington, DC. His father, Asaph Hall, was a well-known astronomer who worked at the Naval Observatory. Because he had spent his childhood in Washington, Percival Hall was probably quite familiar with Gallaudet College. His roommate at Harvard had been Allan B. Fay, the son of Edward Allen Fay, and it was after visits to Kendall Green as a college student that Hall became interested in deaf education. Following graduation from Harvard in 1892, he enrolled as a student in the normal school at Gallaudet and then taught for several years at the New York School for the Deaf, before returning to teach mathematics at the college. He later became EMG's secretary and the head of the normal school for a time. He was, of course, hearing.

Percival Hall married Carolyn Clarke in June 1895, but she died on January 21, 1896. In June 1900, he married Ethel Taylor, a deaf Gallaudet graduate who had received her BA shortly before their marriage. In 1910, Ethel Taylor Hall thus became the first deaf first lady of Gallaudet College. They had three children—Percival Hall, Jr. (MA 1935), Marion Hall Fisher, and Jonathan Hall (MA 1938)—and both sons were professors at the college.[2]

As an indication of what was expected of Gallaudet students (at least the men) at the time, the catalog for 1913 contained the following rules of conduct as "The General Principles of Order":

As the super structure upon which every well-built character must rest, students are enjoined to cherish reverence to God and respect His laws; in particular to have a strict regard to truth, avoiding as mean and unmanly all subterfuges and prevarications; to practice temperance in all things, and total abstinence in those that plainly work harm to the man; to be chaste of thought, word, and action; to be faithful in the performance of duty; to show a due regard to the rights and property of others; to be courteous to all persons and

◄ Chapel Hall, 1950.

The college faculty in 1907–1908. Seated, *left* to *right*, Amos G. Draper, Edward A. Fay, EMG, Percival Hall, and John B. Hotchkiss. Standing, *left* to *right*, Charles R. Ely, Annie E. Jameson, Allan B. Fay, Elizabeth Peet, Herbert Day, and Isaac Allison.

EMG (age 74) and Percival Hall (age 38), at the nineteenth meeting of the Convention of American Instructors of the Deaf in Delavan, Wisconsin, July 1911.

The Hall family on the steps of House One in 1913. From *left* to *right*: Ethel, Marion, Percival, Jonathan, and Percival, Jr. Jonathan was the last person born in House One.

prompt in the manifestation of respect to those, who, by reason of age, position or sex have a right to expect them.

The catalog also said that students were "not allowed to walk on the railroad tracks, nor use tobacco, nor use intoxicating liquors, except on a permit from the President on a doctor's prescription, or use firearms or engage in hazing."[3]

The admonition against walking on the railroad tracks had to be taken particularly seriously. As Gallaudet alumnus Jack R. Gannon points out in

Deaf Heritage, at a time when paved roads and sidewalks were few, many people chose to walk on railroad tracks, and deaf people were especially prone to being hit from behind by locomotives. According to *The Silent World*, "in the states that provide punishments for attempts at suicide, every deaf man found walking on the railroad should be arrested and given the full extent of the law."[4]

Following EMG's victory over the B & O Railroad in 1891 that kept the tracks off the Kendall Green campus itself, there was a period of continuing controversy over the eventual placement of the tracks for both the B & O and the Pennsylvania Railroads. By 1913, the tracks for both railroads had been located to the route currently used by Amtrak, originating at Union Station near the Capitol building, and running to the west of the Gallaudet campus next to New York Avenue. West Virginia Avenue had been extended to the east of the campus, and a new residential area, known as the Trinidad neighborhood, developed along the avenue. The city of Washington was experiencing a period of growth that transformed the area around Kendall Green from rural to urban—Kendall Green, however, remained a green enclave within this city landscape.

While the city expanded around Gallaudet, little changed in the size or scope of the college during Percival Hall's tenure as president. Only two new buildings were erected, a dairy barn and a women's dormitory. The dairy barn, completed in 1911 during the first year of Hall's administration, was torn down long after the college went out of the farming business. The 1974 *Gallaudet Almanac* gives the following description of the building:

The Dairy was built to accommodate 30 cows… The "Cow Barn" as it was known had a lively history before it too fell to the wrecking crew early in 1964. It was the home of Thompson Clayton's wrestling teams which at one time (1950–'56) chalked up 36 consecutive Mason Dixon conference victories.[5]

Harley Drake (BA 1904) was appointed the Institution's farmer in 1911. In 1919 his title changed to Farm Manager, and he served in that position until 1925. The last person to hold the position was George R. Stuntz, and he managed the farm from 1931 until the college sold the livestock and closed down the farm in 1945.[6] The women's dormitory, named Sophia Fowler Hall in honor of EMG's mother, is the current Fowler Hall, a classroom and administrative building used primarily by the graduate programs in education and counseling. It was completed in 1918.

The original Sophia Fowler Hall, or "Old Fowler Hall" in 1914. The building was demolished in 1916 and replaced with the present-day Fowler Hall on the same location.

The era of Percival Hall was also the era of the legendary Elizabeth Peet, a member of the faculty for fifty years (1900–1950), and twice dean of college women (1910–1918 and 1928–1950). Peet, a hearing woman, was the daughter of Isaac Lewis Peet and the granddaughter of Harvey Prindle Peet, both of whom served as principal of the New York School for the Deaf. Her mother, Mary Toles Peet, was deaf. In the words of Percival Hall, Miss Peet was a "model of dress, manners, speech, writing, and all social activities for the American girl or woman."[7]

Harley D. Drake in 1904. Drake married fellow alumna Lillian Swift (BA 1905).

The Gallaudet College farm grew food for the students and faculty. The farm house (*left*) was torn down in 1964 to build West Ballard Hall. Hanson Plaza replaced the barns.

At this time, administrators at American colleges acted *in loco parentis* to their students, and the deans of women and deans of men had quite broad authority. Tales of male students making their escapes from women's dormitories through trapdoors and upper-story windows were commonplace on college campuses. As President Hall's comment suggests, a large part of Elizabeth Peet's role and influence on the women students was in the area of what might be called comportment. This was a time during which female students in American colleges were routinely expected to discontinue their studies if they got married, and many left school before completing their degrees.

In the 1974 Gallaudet *Almanac*, Elizabeth Peet was described as "a leading authority of the language of signs and is remembered as the last of the 'classic signers.' She was the only faculty member to have served under [the first] three presidents—Dr. Gallaudet, Dr. Hall and Dr. Elstad."[8] She retired in 1950, and in 1957 the college named a new residence hall in her honor.

The enrollment at the college did not change much during Hall's presidency. By the end of his administration total enrollment of Kendall, undergraduate, and normal students hovered at around 250. In addition to the traditional academic courses, the college offered courses in agriculture, printing, advanced mechanical drawing, library management, domestic science, and domestic art.[9] These options reflected societal views on the appropriate future careers for deaf adults, yet many of the existing land grant institutions offered the same courses. During the 1920s, President Hall began to discuss an issue that became one of the recurring themes in the college's academic history—the poor academic preparation of many applicants taking the entrance exam.

Kendall Green in 1922. Large expanses of field and lawn comprised a majority of the landscape. House 7-8 (also known as Drake House) is just north of Ole Jim. The woods, farm house (previously called Kendall Mansion), and cow barn are at the northern end of the campus.

Elizabeth Peet in 1900, the year she arrived at Kendall Green.

Elizabeth Peet in 1914 on Nantucket Island.

Peet at her 75th birthday party in 1949 with Elodie Berg (BA 1949), Ruth M. Taubert (BA 1949), and Aileen C. Hoare (BA 1949).

Even with our moderate standards of admission, many fail, 608 in the past five years, 177 in arithmetic, 164 in reading, 132 in algebra, 160 in grammar and 113 in composition. Only one-half of those who took the examinations were admitted.

Our college should not be a trade school. We may need more technical courses, but the students must have a good foundation.[10]

The faculty and administration had similar complaints about the abilities of those students who were admitted. At the 1923 meeting of the American Instructors of the Deaf, the attendees were told that "lots of students are dropped the first or second year and only half who enter graduate. Admission is probationary. Students come who can't even find any given article in an encyclopedia, who can't even find the article on the Amazon."[11] These kinds of comments have reappeared repeatedly during the college's history, but they did not have serious consequences until 2006. Assigning responsibility for this state of affairs has also been an ongoing issue in deaf education, and the question remains of whether the problems faced by many deaf students are due to inadequate K–12 schools, poor preparation of teachers, use of particular instructional methods, or any of a host of other factors, some of

them inherent to the condition of deafness itself. This question has never been resolved.

In 1931 the college administration surveyed graduates and former students "to discover if the education at the College did what it was supposed to do." They received 721 responses representing "82 different kinds of work, ranging from one film inspector to 156 teachers. Printing accounted for 74, farming for 34, clerking 34, machine operators 24, ministers to the deaf 19, supervisors in schools for the deaf 18, laborers 16, chemistry 13, photography 8, drafting 6, and library 5. Two hundred and ninety-

Percival Hall in 1912.

THE *BUFF AND BLUE*

In the early 1890s, Agatha Tiegel, May Martin, along with other members of the O.W.L.S. and some of the male students, convinced EMG to allow them to publish a college newspaper.[13] The inaugural staff included Harvey DeLong (BA 1893), Louis Divine (BS 1894), Jay Cooke Howard (BA 1895), John McIlvaine (BA 1893), Agatha Tiegel (BA 1893), Charles Seaton (BA 1893, MA 1920), and James Stewart (BA 1893, honorary MA 1923). The laboratory building housed a print shop, and there the students hand set the metal type for the first issue of the *Buff and Blue* in the fall of 1892.

The publication began as a journal, and in 1934 the student staff added a newspaper version that was printed simultaneously with the journal. They continued to print both versions until 1962, when they stopped the journal, but the newspaper continued the original numbering system. Beginning in the 2009–2010 school year, the *Buff and Blue* began posting articles online, and by 2013 it had stopped printing a paper version.[14]

The inaugural staff of the *Buff and Blue* in 1892–1893, which included Agatha Tiegel, Jay C. Howard, Harvey D. DeLong, Charles D. Seaton, John A. McIlvaine, Louis A. Divine, and James M. Stewart.

one owned their own homes, and three hundred and thirty-three owned and drove cars. The average salary earned was $150 per month [about $27,000 per year in today's dollars]."[12] This report does not separate normal school graduates from those seeking bachelor's degrees. Although the number of hearing master's degree recipients in the population surveyed was small—during the forty-year existence of the program, an average of only five master's degrees had been awarded annually—it is likely that many of the teachers who responded to the survey were former normal school students.

Although not much overt change occurred during Percival Hall's tenure, Gallaudet's deaf alumni began to exert growing influence in the affairs of the college. They recognized the need for improvements in the Institution itself and questioned the opportunities open to its deaf graduates, not just with respect to employment at Gallaudet but in the world of professional work generally. If the college was, in fact, doing its job, they wondered why no deaf alumni served in the upper levels of the administration, including the presidency. They could see that deaf people were being denied desirable and important jobs at the Institution while hearing people of less than first-rate ability were being hired and promoted.

In general, Gallaudet students have had a strong tradition of writing and publishing while at the college. The college newspaper, the *Buff and Blue*, commenced publication in 1892 as a literary magazine and became a newspaper by the 1930s. The student yearbook, *The Tower Clock*, was first published in 1941. There is no question that deaf people had a long and distinguished tradition of employment in the printing trade and of writing and publishing their own newspapers and other periodicals, but as time went by, some began to question the concentration of deaf college graduates in trades and in employment not generally at the professional level.

According to Ronald Sutcliffe (BS 1959), few deaf people who held good jobs were willing to rock the boat and risk their own careers by agitating for better conditions for deaf professionals.

The GCAA's 1932 reunion. President Hall is seated in the center of the front row with the Iron Dog.

Such paternalistic and subservient attitudes might be incomprehensible to many today, but it is worth noting that even Percival Hall. . . . commented to a young deaf man who wanted to earn a doctorate degree, "Oh you cannot. It is hard enough to earn a bachelor's degree." Despite these beliefs, attitudes, and barriers, many Gallaudet graduates had successful careers, which at that time were limited mostly to teaching, serving as dormitory house parents, and printing. The latter two did not require college training, although printing offered better pay than the other professions. Few deaf graduates worked in the scientific or business arena, as a consequence of their low expectations for success and limited career prospects.[15]

Deaf alumni, however, were organizing to support the growth of the college and their own influence over its future development.

Growth of the Alumni Association

The GCAA continued to grow in the early years of the twentieth century. By 1907, it had five branches and many more members spread across the U.S. At a meeting in 1907, the members voted to establish the Edward Miner Gallaudet Fund on the occasion

Boyce R. Williams, the first alumnus to serve on the Gallaudet Board of Directors. Photo circa 1958.

of EMG's seventieth birthday and the fiftieth year of his work at Kendall Green. Their efforts resulted in the presentation of a full-length oil portrait costing $1,000 and a bust of EMG to the college at their reunion in 1914, held during the fiftieth anniversary of the college's founding.

In 1939, the alumni association formally presented the sum of $50,000 to the college during its seventeenth reunion, and this money formed the basis of a fund used to construct a library on campus. The amount grew to over $100,000, and the Edward Miner Gallaudet Memorial Library was erected in 1956 when sufficient additional funds were appropriated by Congress. Also in 1939, the GCAA established the Percival Hall Endowment Fund "as a fount for the activities of the Association which, in turn, is dedicated to the preservation of the traditions and

David Peikoff and Pauline Nathanson on their wedding day, November 6, 1932.

ALUMNI MARRIAGES

A great deal of the social fabric of the Gallaudet community has been woven from the relationships that undergraduates established during their years at the college. And, as at other colleges, many student romances led to marriage. Some of these couples have made substantial contributions to Gallaudet as faculty, administrators, volunteers, or alumni leaders. The list includes Olof and Agatha Tiegel Hanson, Henry L. and May Martin Stafford, David and Pauline Nathanson Peikoff, Frederick and Regina Olson Hughes, Alan B. and Florence Bridges Crammatte, Leon and Hortense Henson Auerbach, Richard and Ruth Davis Phillips, William and Barbara Myer Stevens, Donald and Agnes Minor Padden, Jack and Rosalyn Lee Gannon, Herbert and Roslyn Goodstein Rosen, Harvery and Astrid Amann Goodstein, and many others.

promotion of the ideals of Alma Mater."[16] In 1949, the association became actively involved in persuading Congress to place Gallaudet employees under the Civil Service Retirement Act. During the next year the GCAA sent a resolution to the board of directors requesting alumni representation on the board. As a result, in 1951 Boyce R. Williams (BA 1932) became the first deaf alumni representative on the Gallaudet College Board of Directors.[17]

One of the most influential of Gallaudet's alumni to graduate during this period was David Peikoff, who received his BA from the college in 1929. Peikoff and his family emigrated from Russia to Winnipeg, Canada, after he became deaf at the age of five. He attended the Manitoba School for the Deaf and after graduation, he worked as a linotypist. He came to Gallaudet at the age of twenty-four and worked nights at the *Washington Post* newspaper.[18] Peikoff was the president of the GCAA in the early 1960s, and he organized the drive to raise funds for the Gallaudet centennial in 1964. In all of these activities, he worked closely with his wife Pauline "Polly" Nathanson Peikoff who had attended the college during the 1930s.

Institutions of American higher education have a long history of soliciting donations from alumni to support the growth and development of their alma maters. In the case of Gallaudet, the alumni population does not include many people of great wealth, but there have been significant alumni campaigns to support the Institution—including the EMG Memorial Fund and the Centennial Fund, both of which resulted in new building and renovation on the campus.

Sign Language at Gallaudet College

Despite the ascendancy of oral education during the last few decades of the nineteenth century and the first half of the twentieth, ASL remained central to the instructional program and the cultural identity of the college. Ted Supalla, a deaf linguist, has done extensive research to identify the form of ASL used at the college in this period. The Deaf community generally referred to it as the *Gallaudet Sign Lan-*

Winfield Marshall (BA 1904) signed an ASL version of "Yankee Doodle" for the NAD film series.

John B. Hotchkiss learned to sign from Laurent Clerc and other teachers at the American School for the Deaf. In "Memories of Old Hartford School," he described his experiences at the school.

Frederick H. Hughes was a student when he appeared in the NAD film "The Story of Gallaudet" in 1914.

guage, and Supalla points out that it could be called a "prestige register" in that it was considered "proper" signing by educated Deaf people. His attempts to reconstruct this form of sign language have been greatly aided by a series of films that the National Association of the Deaf (NAD) produced to preserve a record of this form of "proper" signing at a time when its use was under threat in schools for the deaf. Beginning in 1910 with a lecture by EMG, and ending in 1920, a total of fifteen films of the best signers, deaf and hearing, of the time were made.

Supalla divides the signers in the films into three generations: (1) older signers who were all Gallaudet alumni and/or faculty members, (2) a group of intermediate age, (3) a younger cohort of signers. He considers the first group of signers to be second-generation users of ASL who learned directly from Laurent Clerc and other faculty at the American School for the Deaf in the first half of the nineteenth century. This first, older group includes EMG himself, Amos. G. Draper (BA 1872, faculty 1872–1917), John B. Hotchkiss (BA 1869, faculty 1868–1922), and Edward A. Fay (hearing faculty member 1866–1923). All were well known to the Gallaudet community and the U.S. Deaf communi-

nity generally. The second group, or third generation, including George Veditz, had been early students at the college and had become teachers, NAD leaders, and community leaders, while the youngest group included students and graduates of the college during the early years of the twentieth century.[19] The younger signers included Harley Drake (who graduated in 1904 and served on the faculty from 1912 to 1949) and Frederick Hughes (BA 1913; faculty 1915–1956). Winfield Marshall, another member of the class of 1904 appeared in one of the films, as did Mary M. Williamson Erd (class of 1903, but she did not graduate) and Edith Ruth Knox (BA 1914). Erd and Knox both worked at the Michigan School for the Deaf.

Supalla asserts that the signing of the second generation included a great many compound signs, or signs composed of short phrases of semantic elements. Then, the signing of the third and fourth generations increasingly became influenced by English, especially through the practice of initialization. By examining the signing of these three generations, he has shown that ASL has evolved in ways similar to what happens to spoken languages over time—complex forms become reduced

◄ "As long as we have deaf people on earth, we will have signs. And as long as we have our films, we can preserve signs in their old purity. It is my hope that we will all love and guard our beautiful sign language as the noblest gift God has given to deaf people." George W. Veditz, from *Preservation of the Sign Language*, 1913.

▼ Amos G. Draper, a professor of Latin and mathematics at Gallaudet College, presented a lecture titled "The Signing of the Charter of Gallaudet College" in 1913 for the NAD film series.

NAD at the time the film project began. In 2001, Gallaudet Archivist Michael J. Olson discovered and arranged for the purchase of an English translation of the speech that Veditz had written himself. The following passage reveals the major argument in Veditz's filmed speech:

The French and German deaf look upon the American deaf with envious eyes. They look upon us as prisoners bound in chains look upon those who walk about free in God's open air. They confess that the American deaf are their superiors in mind, in spiritual development, in happiness, in material success. And they all say that it is because the language of signs is permitted in our schools. While they confess their inferiority, they place the blame on the oral method that forbids the sign language and permits speech alone.

But we are fast approaching a crisis in American deaf-mute education. False prophets have arisen who say that the American way of teaching the deaf is a mistake. They ignore the truth that the American deaf now lead the world and that this success is due to the Combined System [instruction in sign language combined with oral training]. They deceive the public and try to make them believe that the oral method is the best when we know, as the French deaf know, as the German deaf know, that it is the poorest.[21]

With preservation of the old way of signing as one of their central purposes, some of the third-generation signers did not approve of the signing of their younger fourth-generation colleagues in the films, let alone the signing of the "deaf man on the street." According to Carol Padden, Veditz approved of the film made by John B. Hotchkiss, but he was quite negative about the film made by the younger Mary Erd. In a letter Veditz wrote in 1915, Padden found him to be "derisive, complaining that she [Erd] did not have a 'film face' and that the film itself was a 'failure.'" He also commented that "Mrs. Erd had not used 'the sign language,' but instead used 'gyrations.'"[22] This is strong evidence that the language was changing and evolving. It was also a growing medium for artistic expression, especially in the performance of theatrical works.

through the elimination or contraction of separate semantic elements. Given these changes and the growing dominance of oralism in schools for the deaf, the NAD resolved to preserve and improve the Gallaudet sign language. They called "upon schools for the deaf not only to preserve, but improve on this sign language, and to give systematic instruction in the proper and correct use thereof."[20]

Perhaps the best known of the NAD films is "The Preservation of the Sign Language" signed by George Veditz in 1913. He had graduated from Gallaudet in 1884, making him a member of Supalla's second group, and he was president of the

Theatrical Productions

Student drama productions have a long history at Gallaudet, dating to at least 1892, with the formation of the all-male Saturday Night Club. Other groups became involved in producing plays through the years, including the women's Jollity Club (1893–1928) and the Dramatics Club (formed in 1893).[23] By the 1940s a significant student theater program had been established, and all the performances were presented in ASL.

The Dramatics Club gained national attention in 1942 with its production of *Arsenic and Old Lace*. The play was running on Broadway at the same time, and when the producers learned of the Gallaudet production, they brought the cast to New York for a one-night-only performance. This marked the first time that deaf actors appeared on Broadway. The May 18, 1942, edition of *Newsweek* magazine carried the following report:

Sunday evening May 10, Joseph Kesselring's gentle tale of murder was enacted on Broadway without a spoken word. The actors were deaf-mutes, as were most of the 800 others in the Fulton Theater. It was the first time any drama had been so produced publicly. The fourteen players were members of the Dramatics Club of Gallaudet College, Washington, D.C., the world's only college for the deaf. Skilled actors all, the creepy comedy suffered none at their dexterous hands. . . .

The Gallaudet Players were looking around this season for a good play when Crouse and Lindsay [producers of the original Broadway play] heard of their search and promptly offered them *Arsenic and Old Lace.* Crouse and Lindsay are that way when it comes to sharing their fun with the public. They also offered the students the Fulton Theater itself and the regular stage crew, and then capped their generosity by lending Bretagne Windust, the director. Windust, of course, has had to direct through an interpreter. . . .

So impressed was Boris Karloff, regular star of the play, that he sought out his counterpart, Eric Malzkuhn, and complimented him in pantomime, then led the company back to the stage for a special curtain call.[24]

Other members of the cast included Paul Baldridge, Raymond Butler, Richard Mullins,

The O.W.L.S. performed a play every year. This photograph was taken in 1894 in Chapel Hall.

▼ Frederick Hughes (*back right*) directing a student production.

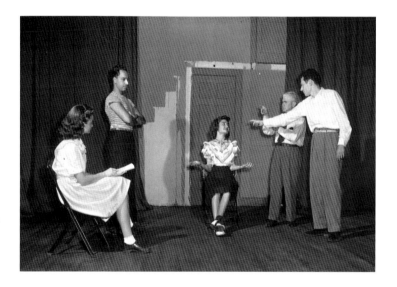

Eric Malzkuhn, Jr., was very active in the theater as an undergraduate and as a teacher. He married fellow alumna Mary Claveau (BA 1977, MA 1979).

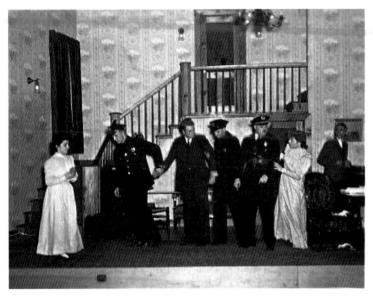

Professor Frederick Hughes directed the Dramatics Club's production of *Arsenic and Old Lace* in 1942. Eric Malzkuhn (*center*) played Jonathan Brewster, the same role that Boris Karloff played on Broadway.

HOWARD LINDSAY and RUSSEL CROUSE

present

THE UPROARIOUS COMEDY

ARSENIC and OLD LACE

By Joseph Kesselring

Played entirely in sign language by the

GALLAUDET COLLEGE DRAMATIC CLUB
of Washington, D. C.

SUNDAY EVENING, MAY 10, 1942

FULTON THEATRE
46th Street, West of Broadway
New York City

◄ The playbill from the Gallaudet Dramatics Club's performance of *Arsenic and Old Lace* at the Fulton Theater in New York City.

► Boris Karloff attended the Gallaudet students' performance at the Fulton Theatre in New York. He posed with Eric Malzkuhn (*right*) for this photo after the play.

Arnold Daulton, Frances Lupo Celano, Julia Burg Mayes, Ben Schowe, Jr., Allen Adams, and Edward Carney. The faculty director of the Gallaudet production was the multitalented and much-loved Professor Frederick Hughes. Student groups continued to mount productions, and in 1963 the college established a theater department.[25]

Life at Gallaudet during War and Depression

During the thirty-five years of Percival Hall's presidency, the United States participated in two world wars (1917–18 and 1941–45) and experienced the Great Depression that began in 1929 and lasted all through the 1930s. Although the resources of the federal government were greatly constrained during this period, funding for Gallaudet's regular operations remained unchanged. However, there was little additional funding to support growth in either academic programs or the physical plant. Campus buildings were inadequate and usually overcrowded, the salaries were too low, and the faculty was not covered by the civil service retirement system. However, Congress failed to grant the necessary funding for improvements.[26] Aside from the funding issues, World War I had little effect on the college. Though the U.S. Army set up a staging ground adjacent to the western boundary of Kendall Green in 1917, the students at Gallaudet had little interaction with the military personnel assigned to Camp Meigs.

In March of 1941, the campus began making extensive preparations in the event of air raids.

Wardens were appointed, and sand, buckets, hoses, tools, shovels, and special lights were purchased. Blackouts were prescribed, and courses given in first aid, bombs and fire fighting. President Hall spoke of the influence of the war upon the College. Four of the farm employees joined the armed forces. One instructor in the primary department enlisted in the medical corps, and one assistant professor went into chemical research in a Naval laboratory. There were many calls for deaf workers in war production plants and a number of undergraduates secured leaves of absence to go into this kind of work. By December

The U.S. Army's Camp Meigs occupied the northwest corner of Florida Avenue and Sixth Street, NE, during World War I. This panoramic view of the camp was taken from the top of House One. House Two (now Ballard House) can be seen in the right-hand corner.

attendance was down even further, but a large percentage of last year's graduates had taken positions in schools for the deaf, filling the places of hearing teachers who had left for war work. On March 1, 1943, President Hall told the board of directors of his difficulty in getting employees, mechanics, waitresses, laundresses and janitors.[27]

Of course, difficulties for the college administration were offset by expansion in job opportunities for deaf people as well as for the hearing population. The college staff, however, continued to be relatively small and provided only limited numbers of jobs for deaf people.

Gallaudet students and faculty participated in many war-related activities during the two world wars. These included the formation of an auxiliary Red Cross unit that prepared bandages during World War I and general participation in blackout and other preparations for possible attack during World War II.

Sports

Despite the hardships of the period, the college developed a rich athletic tradition. Gallaudet began competing in intercollegiate football during the 1880s. The 1930 team, coached by Frederick Hughes, had the most successful season, with a record of 6-1-1. Gallaudet began participating in intercollegiate baseball in the 1890s, and men's basketball dates back to 1904. The 1943 men's team, dubbed the

During World War II, Gallaudet faculty interpreted radio broadcasts for groups of students. Here, Edward L. Scouten (MA 1941) interprets the announcement of the attack on Pearl Harbor on December 7, 1941. Photograph by Gaylord Stiarwalt (BS 1942).

Five Iron Men, won the Mason-Dixon conference tournament, playing with just five men: Hal Weingold, Earl Roberts, Paul Baldridge, Roy Holcomb, and Don Padden. Gallaudet runners were Mason-Dixon champions in cross country in 1942. Women formed a basketball team in 1896, though they had only one opponent, and they began playing at the intercollegiate level around 1920. Intercollegiate wrestling dates to about 1907, but Gallaudet teams had particular success during the 1950s. Frank Turk excelled in both football and wrestling in the late 1940s and early 1950s.

The General Principles of Order regulating student behavior were still in effect, but over time,

Arthur "Art" A. Kruger, (BA 1933) was a pioneer in the field of deaf sports. He organized deaf sports clubs into regions across the country and generated interest in deaf sports through his writing. Kruger created the first national deaf basketball tournament, held on April 14, 1945, in Akron, Ohio. The same year, he and other Gallaudet alumni and deaf sports enthusiasts founded the American Athletic Association of the Deaf (AAAD), the predecessor of the U.S. Deaf Sports Federation (USDSF), and he served as its first president. In 1961, Kruger was instrumental in establishing a formal committee to send a U.S. team to the World Games for the Deaf, known today as the Deaflympics. He also recruited U.S. athletes and raised money to send them to the Games.

▲ Members of the Gallaudet College auxiliary chapter of the Red Cross actively contributed to relief efforts during World War I. They participated in parades (*top*) and made and rolled bandages.

▼ As World War II escalated, the U.S. government distributed civil defense equipment to cities within 300 miles of coastline. Here, Gallaudet students model their gas masks on campus.

Jerald Jordan (BA 1948) was a lifetime sports enthusiast and organizer. He joined the Gallaudet faculty as a science teacher in the Prep Department in 1959, and later served as Gallaudet's first deaf director of admissions and records. In 1961, Jordan became treasurer of the American Athletic Association of the Deaf, and in 1965, he headed the organizing committee for the World Games for the Deaf in Washington, DC. Two years later, he was appointed to the executive committee of the Comité International des Sports des Sourds (CISS, International Committee of Sports for the Deaf). He became president of CISS in 1971 and held that position until 1995. He also worked closely with the International Olympic Committee on behalf of deaf athletes.

the code relaxed somewhat. For example, even though wrestling matches began in 1907, coeds could not attend them until 1934. The policy changed because of "a strenuous publicity campaign in 1933–34 under which the Faculty relented and permitted the sexes to mix at all matches thereafter."[28] The fact that such a rule even existed would strike most of today's students as ludicrous at best, but such regulation of student behavior was common at most American colleges and universities at the time. The college also gave students "demerits for smoking, cutting class, having liquor in their room, and for making out with the girls, even for holding hands. A student who received thirty-five demerits was automatically expelled from Gallaudet."[29] The demerit system ended in 1947.

◄ The 1916–1917 women's basketball team on the front steps of Ole Jim. Their coach, Frederick Hughes, is seated in the back row.

▼ The 1932 women's basketball team with their coach, Elizabeth Benson. *Front row, l. to r.,* Raphaelina Martino De Rose, May Koehn Curtis, Marie Coretti, and Catherine Bronson Higgins. *Back row, l. to r.,* Elizabeth Benson (coach), Lucy Mabel Sigman, Willa Mae Savidge, Rose Stepan Neusahr, and Mary Ross (manager).

The 1923 women's basketball team in front of Chapel Hall. Standing in the center of the group is their coach, Leonard Elstad.

Gallaudet's men's basketball team won the 1943 Mason-Dixon conference championship. The Five Iron Men were (*left* to *right*) Donald A. Padden, Earl E. Roberts, Paul F. Baldridge, Roy K. Holcomb, and Harold S. Weingold.

The 1951 undefeated Gallaudet wrestling team. *Front row, l. to r.,* Donald M. Bullock, William D. Swaim, Sanford Diamond, and Camille L. Desmarais. *Back row, l. to r.,* Thompson B. Clayton (coach), David N. Carlson, Clyde R. Ketchum, Frank R. Turk, Jr., and Harry J. Schaffner (manager).

▲ The women's literary society, the O.W.L.S., was established in 1893. Its student and alumni members kept the organization strong into the 20th century. The 1915 club members are pictured here.

▼ The Kappa Gamma fraternity in 1906. Percival Hall is in the second row from the back, fourth from the left.

In 1953, Delta Epsilon became the second sorority founded at Gallaudet. The four founding members—Verna Eloise Bolen, Joan Macaluso, Ann Lister, and Gloria Wojick—are seated in this picture.

Alpha Sigma Pi, founded in 1947, was the third fraternity to be established at Gallaudet College. Photograph 1953.

Sororities and Fraternities

Greek organizations also continued to flourish during Hall's presidency. The Kappa Gamma fraternity, the oldest and most influential Gallaudet student organization, traces its roots to the early years of the Institution but adopted its current name in 1901. Many of its "Grand Rajahs" and rank-and-file members had careers at Gallaudet and leadership roles in the Deaf community.

The O.W.L.S. organization, which also had its origins in the nineteenth century, served a similar function for women students. In 1954, the National O.W.L.S., an alumnae organization, voted to modernize by changing the name of the sorority to Phi Kappa Zeta and changing their colors from brown and gold to navy blue and white.[30]

Kappa Gamma and Phi Kappa Zeta were the only Greek organizations continually active on campus until Taras B. Denis, Archie G. Stack, and

Andrew J. Vasnick established Alpha Sigma Pi fraternity on October 25, 1947. Eloise Bolen, Gloria Wojick, Ann Lister, and Joan Macaluso founded Gallaudet's second sorority, Delta Epsilon, on April 24, 1953.[31] Student participation in sports and student-run organizations of this sort was instrumental in the development of an effective alumni leadership group.

GALLAUDET TRADITIONS: THE RAT FUNERAL

The rat funeral is a time-honored ceremony that began in the early 1900s as an annual rite of passage for the students of the preparatory program to mark the end of their first year. In the decades preceding the rat funeral, Gallaudet's preparatory students were called "Ducks," and they were often photographed with paper cut-outs of ducks or a stuffed bird. At the start of the twentieth century, their nickname changed to "Preparats," and then "Preps" or "Rats." It is perhaps this change that helped trigger the emergence of the rat funeral tradition.

To begin the funeral, a member of the student body would obtain a dead mouse or rat. Then a group of preps made a small coffin, and a procession of pallbearers and mourners would journey with the coffin through campus. Wearing their prep beanies (striped, or later with "RAT" embroidered across the front), both male and female students participated in the procession, while undergraduate students watched from the sidelines. The procession would arrive at a predetermined location on Kendall Green, and the funeral ceremony would commence. A "reverend" read last rites before the coffin was buried. All the while, students would "cry," shedding mock tears into their handkerchiefs and at the same time try to suppress laughter. Each prep class placed a memorial slab over the grave.

The oldest photographs of the funerals in the university Archives date from the 1920s, and a color film from 1949 is stored in the University's film collection. Older issues of the *Buff and Blue* also provide commentary on the proceedings, including references to the acting Reverends Leo Latz (BA 1940) and Frances Lupo (BS 1944). After the preparatory program closed in 1995, the freshmen adopted the tradition, and it continues to this day. Although students no longer wear beanies and real rats have long since been replaced with fake ones, the rat funerals of the twenty-first century look very much like those of 100 years ago.[32]

▶ Female students line up in front of Fowler Hall for a rat funeral. Photograph circa 1920.

Both male and female preps participated in rat funerals, happily watching as the "reverend" performed the last rites. Photograph circa 1945–1949.

The rat funeral procession would attract undergraduate students, who would watch the preps walk past in their striped beanies. Photograph circa 1945–1949.

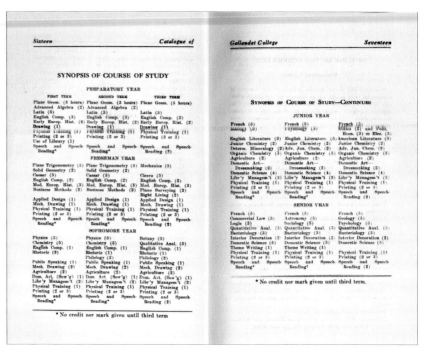

The curriculum in the 1910s paralleled that of other American colleges. In the course synopsis from 1912 (*above*), the core requirements for a bachelor of arts degree included English, mathematics, history, Latin, chemistry, French, German, public speaking, and biology. President Hall changed the course offerings to provide a more diverse selection of electives. By 1929–1930, the requirements had added physical training for every term. Other additions included classes for agriculture, domestic art, printing, and library management.

Hall's Legacy

In 1910, when Percival Hall took office, Congress appropriated $75,500 for the Columbia Institution. By May 1945, when he retired, the appropriation had more than doubled to $204,000, and income from tuition and other sources had increased from $6,000 to $48,000. During the same period, enrollment grew only modestly—from 104 in the college to 146; enrollment in Kendall School actually dropped from 66 to 62.[33] Even given some inflation in the economy during this period (1913–1945), when the consumer price index increased by about 82 percent, it is clear that federal support for Gallaudet did not diminish.[34] Nevertheless, it also did not increase fast enough to support growth in enrollment, facilities, and programs.

Because of limited increases in federal support, the physical appearance of the college did not change much during Hall's tenure. Only two new buildings—Fowler Hall and the dairy barn—were constructed, but Hall oversaw the creation of several new facilities, including a biology laboratory, a print

shop, and a research department. Hall also expanded the curriculum over the years, adding new courses in English, history, mathematics, business, and science.[35] After Hall retired, he and his wife Ethel moved into the farmhouse on campus, and they lived there until Hall died in 1953.

The Hall family (*left* to *right*: Percival, Ethel, Percival, Jr., Marion, and Jonathan). Marion worked at Gallaudet as a registrar and then left to become secretary to the commissioner of Indian Affairs. Percival, Jr., taught mathematics and Jonathan taught biology at the college. Jonathan married Aileen M. Boutilier (MA 1947).

The Administration of Leonard M. Elstad

Leonard M. Elstad succeeded Percival Hall as president of Gallaudet. Elstad was born on February 8, 1899, in Osseo, Wisconsin. He received his bachelor's degree from St. Olaf College in Minnesota. Like Percival Hall, Elstad was a hearing man who had graduated from Gallaudet's Normal Department (in 1923); prior to his appointment as Gallaudet's third president, he was the superintendent of the Minnesota School for the Deaf. During his years as president, Gallaudet went through a period of rapid change and expansion.

In the period during and immediately following World War II, the federal government grew in both size and scope. The city of Washington also experienced extensive physical development. One of

---

GALLAUDET TRADITIONS: DIAMOND AND THE LITTLE IRON DOG

The little Iron Dog is a well-known fixture at Gallaudet University, and it is a beloved mascot to many alumni. The small black iron statue has appeared in many student and alumni group portraits dating as far back as 1889 and as recently as Homecoming 2013. The statue resembles a dog named Diamond that belonged to John B. Wight and his wife Anna. Mr. Wight, who served as Gallaudet's secretary, supervisor, and business manager from 1877 to 1897, lived on Kendall Green. He brought Diamond to the college in 1878, and the dog became a devoted protector of the college grounds, keeping the dining room and kitchen free of rats and barking at unknown intruders. Diamond was well-loved by both faculty and students.

After Diamond's death in 1888, Wight found the iron dog statue in a shop. It looked so much like Diamond that he bought it and brought it back to campus. When Wight resigned from Gallaudet, he gave the statue to the college, and its care passed from EMG to President Hall and the succeeding presidents. Diamond now lives in President Hurwitz's office, but he comes out on special occasions for photographs.[36]

The little Iron Dog.

The 1947 GCAA reunion photograph in front of Chapel Hall. Percival Hall is in the center of the first row, and the Iron Dog is at his feet.

Leonard M. Elstad in his office circa late 1950s.

President Elstad's first actions in office exemplifies the change that was occurring both at the college and in the District of Columbia:

President Elstad suggested to the directors late in 1945 that it might be necessary to sell the dairy herd because it was not possible to get farm help. The herd of thirty cattle had long supplied the students with fresh milk, and when the students were away in the summer the milk was sold at the Eighth Street gate to all who were interested. But as far back as 1920, President Hall, in addressing a conference of educators of the deaf, said in regard to the college farm that young men were attracted to the big cities and it had become increasingly evident that the students were not interested in agriculture.[37]

The post-war period was a time of increasing inclusiveness in American higher education—more and more students enrolled in college, due in large part to the GI bill. Gallaudet's leaders also were looking to increase the enrollment at the college, and Elstad took an active role in the efforts to expand and improve the college's facilities and educational programs, increase enrollment, and gain institutional accreditation. The impetus for many of these changes came from two reports prepared for the Federal Security Agency, Gallaudet's federal

oversight agency, during the mid- to late-1940s. The first report, written by Harry Best, noted that the Gallaudet faculty was "too small, that it lacked specialists, and that too many teachers had to teach too many different subjects." Though Best made many recommendations, FSA officials did not think they were substantive enough to justify asking the Congress for more financial support. In the second report, Buell G. Gallagher found "a shocking discrepancy between the numbers (210) of the deaf who now go to college and the numbers (5586) who would be in college if deaf persons were enrolled in the same proportions as hearing persons." He outlined the educational needs of deaf students and then made recommendations for how to meet those needs. Gallagher also reported that the federal government had a responsibility to provide higher education for deaf students because it was not economically feasible for individual states to establish such colleges.[38]

The Push toward Accreditation

In 1946, Elstad approached officials of the Middle States Association of Colleges and Schools concerning the accreditation of Gallaudet College.[39] The accreditation movement in American higher education began in the late-nineteenth century and had become increasingly important by the mid-twentieth century, such that attendance at an unaccredited institution could severely limit a bachelor-degree recipient's ability to get into a graduate school. Unlike many other countries, the United States does not have a central governmental authority that regulates colleges and universities, and the accrediting movement developed as a way of ensuring the quality of programs within such a diverse community of institutions, both public and private. The Middle States Association (MSA), a voluntary membership organization, was (and is) the regional accrediting body for the District of Columbia. The initial response from MSA to Elstad was not encouraging. Although the college and its faculty were seen as providing significant leadership in advancing the welfare of the Deaf community, the facilities and programs were judged inadequate and outdated. Elstad, however, was not discouraged; he began a systematic effort to make the improvements necessary for the college to gain accreditation. This turned out to be a ten-year process.

The first step involved revising and expanding the curriculum. In May 1948, Dean Irving Fusfeld, a 1916 graduate of the Normal School, reported to the board that the curriculum had been revamped and that major fields of study now included education, home economics, language and literature, science and mathematics, social studies, library science, and printing. In June of that year, the board decided that the Kendall Green site was not appropriate for further development because of the commercial and industrial development of the surrounding neighborhood. Following this vote, the board began to investigate possible new locations for the college in the Washington area. By 1952, however, the board had determined that the Institution should remain at Kendall Green and that attempts to improve the physical plant should focus on redevelopment and expansion of the existing facilities.[40]

In 1952, the college received word that its formal application for accreditation had failed, at least partly because it lacked an adequate library. The MSA report noted that professors had too many varied responsibilities, including teaching more than one subject. MSA criticized these practices because they called into question the qualifications of faculty members to teach in more than one specific area of expertise, and the assignment of a variety of duties suggested that teachers were less than fully committed to their instructional duties. Other MSA criticisms focused on the poor condition of equipment and facilities; admissions policies; the need for more and varied courses, better organizational structure, and a larger board of directors.[41]

The alumni finally succeeded in gaining a board seat for a deaf Gallaudet graduate in 1951. The first member of the alumni to hold this position was Boyce R. Williams (BA 1932). However, the board remained predominantly hearing until 1988.

Coincidentally, around the same time the MSA sent its report, President Elstad received a letter from

President Elstad hired George E. Detmold (*left*) in 1953 to institute the changes necessary for the college to earn accreditation. Irving S. Fusfeld (*right*) was the first dean of Academic Affairs (1939–1953) and, later, the vice president (1953–1956). Photograph circa 1955.

an alumnus requesting the return of his $50 donation to the EMG Memorial Fund, on the grounds that the college had not proceeded with plans to use the funds for construction of a new building to house the library.[42] The memorial fund, which by then amounted to more than $100,000, in combination with other private funds and a federal appropriation, led to the eventual construction of the Edward Miner Gallaudet Memorial Library in 1956.

Also, following receipt of the MSA report, Elstad concluded that he would have to make significant changes in the administrative structure in order to secure accreditation. In 1953, he named Irving Fusfeld as vice president and George E. Detmold dean of instruction. Detmold, a hearing man, held a PhD from Cornell University and a certificate in administration from Columbia University Teachers College; however, he had no prior experience in the education of the deaf. The hiring of Detmold broke a practice, in effect during the first part of the twentieth century, of choosing Gallaudet administrators from the ranks of its normal school graduates and the directors of residential schools for the deaf. When Detmold arrived on campus, Elstad gave him explicit instructions to obtain accreditation within five years.

Detmold quickly discovered that he had a large task ahead of him, including the need to change prevailing attitudes at the college. He found that the Department of Education was still being called the Normal Department. People there thought that "normal" meant not deaf. Deaf people were not admitted. It was customary to say of a superintendent [of a school for the deaf] who had the Gallaudet MA that "he was Normal in '38."

Elstad beefed up the faculty by hiring its second PhD, but Fusfeld, then and later, advised against trying for accreditation because the college was too "special." Many agreed with him, both faculty and alumni, arguing that standards applied to other colleges should not apply to Gallaudet.[43]

The year 1954 brought the first significant change in the Institution's authorizing legislation in almost a century. Congress passed and President Dwight D. Eisenhower signed Public Law 83-420, "to amend the charter of the Columbia Institution for the Deaf, change its name, define its corporate powers, and provide for its organization and administration, and for other purposes."[44] In particular, the law changed the corporate name to Gallaudet College and reaffirmed the federal commitment to fund the Institution. The report on the legislation by the House of Representatives made it clear that the Congress expected the college to gain accreditation. The Department of Health, Education and Welfare, which now had oversight of the college, also recommended expansion and improvements to the campus.

Congressman Homer Thornberry of Texas, a strong supporter of the college and a board member, advocated for changing the corporate name because

among all the graduates of this school throughout the United States it is known as Gallaudet College. Let me put a personal experience if I may. Before I came to Congress I was vitally interested in the problems of the deaf. My mother and father were both deaf from infancy. I grew up among deaf people and among all of them the school is known as Gallaudet College.

I came to Washington and tried to find out in the phone book about Gallaudet College. I phoned downtown to the Department and of course they know of it as the Columbia Institution. But it is a misleading name.[45]

The immediate consequence of Public Law 83-420 was the appropriation of funds for substantial expansion of the Kendall Green campus. The United States experienced growing prosperity in the post–World War II period, and federal funds became more readily available for a variety of public purposes. President Elstad had great success in obtaining a share of these funds for the college. By the end of the 1950s, Gallaudet had seven new buildings—the Edward Miner Gallaudet Memorial Library, Hall Memorial Building, Hughes Memorial Gymnasium, a student union building, Ely Residence Hall, Elizabeth Peet Residence Hall, and Mary Thornberry Building. These buildings formed a quad with College Hall and Chapel Hall around a green area that came to be known as the Mall. The Government Services Administration (GSA), the federal agency responsible for most federal facilities, designed and constructed the new buildings in the style typical of the times. The plain brick boxes stood in sharp contrast to the visually graceful Victorian structures of the historic campus. Yet despite their external appearance, their internal designs reflected the needs of the deaf people who would occupy them. The Student Union Building in particular made excellent use of open sight lines and natural lighting.

The very best example of Deaf architecture on campus was the Student Union Building . . . . The building served as the social heart of the campus. The fond memories of belonging that alumni from this era share in interviews most frequently took place in this building. Here students would meet for meals, socialize in the Rathskellar lounge or the bowling alley located in the basement, or gather for a lecture or group study session in the student lounge. The facility rounded out its offerings with a chapel for worship, a bookstore, and office space for student groups. All of these spaces were organized around a two-story courtyard allowing diffused natural light to pass through the building both at ground level and the basement level. Large expanses of glass in the student lounge area faced the mall, allowing a generous visual connection between the indoor and outdoor activities.[46]

▲ The Student Union Building, built in 1959, housed the campus bookstore and a snack bar.

◄ Construction of the Edward Miner Gallaudet Memorial Library was completed in 1956.

► The interior of the Student Union Building was spacious, with large window-lined rooms for students to gather and study.

▼ From *left* to *right*: Elizabeth Peet Hall (dormitory), Mary Thornberry Building, Hall Memorial Building, and Hughes Memorial Gym formed the perimeter of the Gallaudet Mall, and were the face of a newly accredited college.

William C. Stokoe, Jr., in 1957.

Robert F. Panara in 1953.

Gallaudet's administrators assumed that the new construction would satisfy MSA's criticism of the college facilities. In the meantime, Dean Detmold launched reforms of the curriculum to make it more rigorous, and he set about upgrading the credentials of the faculty, another concern of the MSA. One of his first new hires was his friend and former Cornell student William C. Stokoe, Jr. Like Detmold, Stokoe was hearing, had a PhD, and had no prior experience teaching deaf students or knowledge of sign language. Detmold appointed him chair of the English Department. This signaled a change in the hiring of new Gallaudet faculty, and it also started a process of change in the culture of the Institution itself. A sense of how disturbing this process was to become can be gained by contrasting Stokoe's experience during this period with that of the person he replaced as chair of the English Department—Robert F. Panara (BA 1945).

Robert Panara became deaf at the age of ten, and he attended New York City public schools during the 1930s without any of the support that is now provided to a mainstreamed deaf student. His family apparently was unaware of the availability of public education for deaf students, and he had no knowledge of sign language. After graduating from high school in 1938, he moved to Massachusetts to be with his family. There, he learned of the existence of Gallaudet College and applied for admission. President Hall advised him to first spend a year at

the American School for the Deaf in order to learn sign language. He then enrolled at Gallaudet, graduated in 1945, and earned a master's degree in English from New York University in 1948. In 1949, Leonard Elstad offered him a faculty position at Gallaudet, and he began part-time work on a PhD at Catholic University. When Stokoe arrived in 1955, Panara had not completed the doctoral degree.

Panara was widely respected as a teacher by the students and other faculty members, including Stokoe. When Stokoe first sat in on one of Panara's classes, he was extremely impressed both by his teaching methods and his use of sign language. He commented that Panara

was the best lecturer in sign language going. During the class, he was discussing the novel *Wuthering Heights*. What was fascinating about his performance was that he used one hand to talk about Heathcliff, spelling the name at first with that hand, then just using the letter *H* on that hand. Then he used the other hand to represent the name Cathy, again fingerspelling at first … Not only could he separate the two characters in that manner rather than using "he" and "she" as one would in English discourse—he could sign interaction between them. . . .

It struck me at that time that here was an absolutely fascinating way of conducting a course in English literature, and it was something that I'd have to learn to do after some kind of fashion if I wanted to succeed in teaching my subject.[47]

LIPREADING THE QUEEN

In 1957, Queen Elizabeth made her first visit to the United States. In planning her itinerary, she asked to see an American college football game, and so arrangements were made for her to attend the game between the University of North Carolina and the University of Maryland in College Park, Maryland, on October 19, 1957. Someone at *Life* magazine thought that a deaf person stationed across the field from where she was sitting might be able to lipread her conversations during the game. The magazine contacted Gallaudet and Robert Panara was chosen to do the deed.

As Panara tells it, he did a dry run at the football stadium, which is not far from the college. He lipread two reporters from across the field with about 50 percent accuracy, and that satisfied the reporters. On the day of the game he took up his position across the field from the queen and observed her through binoculars, assisted by Gallaudet student Alton Silver. Panara repeated what he could make out to a reporter, most of which involved the queen asking for explanations of the peculiarities of the American game, and, as he puts it, maybe imagining a bit of dialogue also.

Life magazine decided to run the story, but word about Panara's exploit leaked out to the *Washington Post,* which revealed his name. For a brief period, Panara enjoyed national celebrity, much to the immediate pleasure of Gallaudet generally and President Elstad in particular. Later, however, the Gallaudet administration made it known that unauthorized lipreading of this sort might be considered an invasion of privacy and would not be repeated.[51]

▲ Queen Elizabeth II attended a football game between the Maryland Terrapins and the North Carolina Tar Heels with University of Maryland president Wilson Homer Elkins (*left*) and Maryland governor Theodore McKeldin (*right*) on October 19, 1957. Photograph by Warren K. Leffler for *U.S. News & World Report.* Courtesy of the Library of Congress.

▶ Robert Panara sat across the stadium from Queen Elizabeth II in order to lipread her conversations with Elkins and McKeldin. Photograph by Warren K. Leffler, October 19, 1957, for *U.S. News & World Report.* Courtesy of the Library of Congress.

Nevertheless, Stokoe, the hearing novice signer with the PhD replaced the deaf master teacher without one. Panara naturally felt that his demotion from chair of the English Department in favor of Stokoe was particularly unjust as he had been working on a PhD himself.[48] Many faculty members and students seemed convinced that Stokoe had been given preferential treatment by Detmold because of their close friendship, which dated from their days together at Cornell. Both Stokoe and Detmold were widely resented by the deaf students and faculty at the college.

Despite the resentment toward Detmold's actions, President Elstad and Board Chairman Atwood were convinced that future federal support for the college depended on gaining MSA's accreditation. According to Atwood, "early in 1956, [Congressman] John E. Fogarty [of Rhode Island], chairman of the sub-committee of the House Appropriations Committee, told representatives of the College, 'We want to see this school accredited. I think we made that very plain, didn't we?'"[49] However, one of Detmold's actions is very hard to justify—his decision to remove the venerable Frederick Hughes as instructor of the drama course and to take over the drama program himself. Detmold felt that the course taught by Hughes was not up to college standards and, thus, had to be upgraded. Panara believes that this broke Hughes's heart, and as a result, "he never again attended any Gallaudet plays."[50]

By 1957, with physical expansion of the campus well underway, enrollment (including at the Kendall School) had increased from just over 200 to about 350, the curriculum had been revised, the hiring of PhDs had begun, and the federal appropriation had grown from $204,000 to more than $3 million, including construction funding. The Middle States Association of Colleges and Schools responded by accrediting the college during that year.

The Re-integration of Kendall Green

Although the Kendall School officially excluded African American students beginning in 1905, the college never had such a policy. Nevertheless, it appears there was at least a tacit policy of exclusion. Only two African American students enrolled in the college in the nineteenth century—James Gilbert, Jr., in 1880, and Ennals Jerome Adams, Jr., in 1890. Both men withdrew before graduating.[52] Andrew Foster (BA 1954, honorary doctorate 1970) was the first black student to enroll and graduate from the college (1951–1954), and Hylda Purce was the first African American to receive a master's degree. A year after Foster entered Gallaudet, Ida Gray Hampton became the first African American woman to enroll as an undergraduate, and she received her bachelor's degree in 1957.

Coincidentally, in 1952, while Foster and Gray were attending Gallaudet, U.S. District Court Judge David Pine settled a lawsuit in favor of the parents of an African American deaf student from the District of Columbia who had sought schooling for their child at the Kendall School. It is highly significant that this decision came only two years before the Supreme Court's landmark decision in *Brown v. Board of Education* that led to the desegregation of all public schools in the United States. In the case of *Miller v. Board of Education of the District of Columbia et al.*, in which the board of directors of Gallaudet College was one of the defendants, the judge found that placement of black deaf students outside of the District of Columbia failed the current standard of "separate but equal" under the Fourteenth Amendment. According to Judge Pine, "to maintain the legality of the separation of the races, it is the duty of the District to provide equal educational facilities within the District for the deaf children of both races, if it provides for any therein."

Following this ruling, Kenneth Miller, son of Louise B. Miller (who had filed the lawsuit), and several other African American children whose parents had joined the suit, began to attend Kendall School in the fall of 1952. As historian Sandra Jowers-Barber notes, "this victory proved bittersweet for the students as they joined their hearing peers in the District's segregated school system. The policy of segregation mandated that in the aftermath of the court decision the Kendall School had to set up a separate area for Black

ANDREW JACKSON FOSTER

Andrew Foster was born in Ensley, Alabama, on June 27, 1925. He became deaf at the age of eleven after a bout of spinal meningitis. His parents then sent him to the Alabama School for the Negro Deaf in Talladega for four years, but he completed his high school education through a correspondence program run by the American School in Chicago after his family moved to Detroit.

Following his graduation from Gallaudet in 1954, Foster returned to Detroit to study for a master's degree in education at Eastern Michigan University. He continued his education further, obtaining a second master's degree in Christian Missions at Seattle Pacific College. When he returned to Detroit in 1956, he founded the Christian Mission for Deaf Africans (now Christian Mission for the Deaf) and embarked on a distinguished career of international leadership in the global Deaf community. In the late 1950s Ludwig Bafo, a visiting teacher and native of Ghana, invited Foster to accompany him to West Africa to assess the educational needs of deaf children there. In 1957, Foster traveled to Monrovia, Liberia, and then to Ghana, where he helped to establish the first school for the deaf in Ghana, the Accra Mission School for

the Deaf, and a second school opened soon after.

In August of 1959 Foster attended the World Federation of the Deaf (WFD) Congress in Wiesbaden, Germany, where he met Berta Zuther, a deaf woman who was also interested in missionary work. The following year Berta joined him in Africa to help open a school in Nigeria, and in January 1961, they were married. The couple raised their five children in Africa while maintaining the established schools and opening new schools throughout the continent. Foster prepared his African students to attend Gallaudet College, and he trained former students to be teachers. In 1970, Gallaudet College awarded Foster an honorary doctorate, and in 1975 he received the Edward Miner Gallaudet Award from the Gallaudet College Alumni Association.

In December 1987 Foster was onboard a small passenger plane that crashed in Rwanda, killing everyone on board. He was sixty-five. He is credited with helping to found some thirty schools, churches, camps, and other programs for deaf people throughout Africa. In 2004, Gallaudet named an auditorium on the campus in his honor. A bronze bust of his likeness is displayed at the entrance of the building.[53]

▲ Berta and Andrew Foster with four of their five children. Front row, *left* to *right*: Jackie, Freddy, and Tim; back row, *left* to *right*: Berta, Faith, and Andrew. Photograph circa 1968.

◄ Andrew J. Foster spent much of his adult life in Africa founding and running schools for deaf children. He is pictured here with students from the Boarding School for deaf children in Mampong-Akawapim, Ghana. Photograph circa 1961.

Kenneth Miller (*fourth from the left*) was among the first African American students in the Division II school. In 2007 he and his siblings posed with Gallaudet President Robert Davila in front of the plaque commemorating the location of the Primary Department for Negroes. From *left* to *right*: Gerald Miller, President Davila, Carol Miller Hill, Kenneth Miller, Justin Miller, Beverly Miller (Justin's wife), and Lavonda Miller (Gerald's wife).

students. The result was Kendall's creation of Division I for the white students and Division II for the Black students."[54]

The "separate area" was a complex of three adjoining small brick buildings called the Primary Department for Negroes. Prior to completion of the new buildings, the African American students had their classes in the Ole Jim. Following *Brown v. Board of Education* in 1954, the Kendall School facilities were fully integrated and this set of

buildings was converted to offices and generally known thereafter as the West Office Building. This complex was demolished in the early 1990s to clear space for the Kellogg Conference Hotel, and a wall outside the hotel contains a plaque to commemorate the history of the site.

Some Well-Known Gallaudet Classes and Alumni

Every Gallaudet class includes individuals who go on to careers of exceptional service. To illustrate the struggles and triumphs of all the classes from this general period of the Institution's history, we will examine three graduating classes—one from the 1930s, one from the 1940s, and one from the 1950s. Each had notable deaf leaders among its graduates and examination of their careers sheds light on the outcomes of a Gallaudet education during the time leading up to the college's accreditation. Many of these individuals also played key roles in Gallaudet's transition from a tiny nineteenth-century college to a modern university.

Class of 1932

The undergraduate class of 1932 entered with forty-six prep students. Twenty of these students received bachelor's degrees, a graduation rate of 43 percent. The Normal Department awarded eight master's degrees that year. This was an unusually large number of graduate degrees for this period—the annual average at this time was about five. The following brief portraits highlight three of the year's graduates—Boyce R. Williams, Alan B. Crammatte (BA 1932, MA 1935, honorary doctorate 1977), and Elizabeth Benson.

Boyce R. Williams, a bachelor's degree recipient, taught at the Indiana School for the Deaf from 1933 to 1945. He left the school to become a consultant to the Deaf and Hard of Hearing Branch within the Vocational Rehabilitation Administration (VRA), a division of the Department of Health, Education, and Welfare (HEW). In 1950, he was elected president of the Gallaudet College Alumni Association, and in 1951 he became the first deaf alumnus on the Gallaudet Board of Trustees. Williams had a successful career in the federal government promoting rehabilitation services at both the state and federal levels. In 1970 he became chief of the Deafness and Communicative Disorders Branch in the VRA (later, the Rehabilitation Services Administration in the Department of Education). He was also instrumental in founding the National Theatre of the Deaf, Captioned Films for the Deaf, the American Deafness and Rehabilitation Association, and the Registry of Interpreters for the Deaf.[55]

Alan B. Crammatte (aka ABC), received a bachelor's degree and a master's degree (1935) from Gallaudet. He worked at the New York and Louisiana schools for the deaf between 1934 and 1943. In 1943 he and his wife Florence (BA 1935) moved to Washington, DC, where ABC worked as a statistician for the Army Air Forces. In 1955 he joined the faculty of the college, where he founded and taught in the Department of Business Administration until 1977. He was active in the GCAA, serving on the board and as comptroller of the Centennial Fund and co-chair with his wife of the Alumni House Fund, among other positions. In 1968, he made a major contribution to scholarship concerning the socioeconomic status of the Deaf community with the publication of his book, *Deaf Persons in Professional Employment*. His follow-up

Boyce R. Williams.

Alan B. Crammatte.

study, *Meeting the Challenge: Hearing-Impaired Professionals in the Workplace,* was published in 1987. Crammatte believed that the "expansion of Gallaudet College from a tiny liberal arts institution was a considerable impetus toward professional growth by persons with hearing impairments. The expansion began about 1944. Accreditation in 1957 put the seal of approval on the new Gallaudet."[56]

Elizabeth Benson received an MA from the Normal Department. She was a hearing CODA (child of deaf adults) who devoted her life to working with and for deaf people. She had been teaching at the college for many years when the United States entered World War II. Benson took a leave of absence to join the American Women's Voluntary Services in 1942, where she was an ambulance driver. In 1943, she enlisted in the Women's Army Corp (WAC) and while stationed at Borden General Hospital in Chickasha, Oklahoma, she taught lipreading to deafened soldiers. In 1945 she became the first WAC in the U.S. to receive a commission and promotion to Second Lieutenant. Benson came back to the Gallaudet faculty in 1946, and in 1950 she replaced Elizabeth Peet as Dean of Women, a position she held until her retirement in 1970. She spent many summers at Hampton Institute in Virginia teaching African American students in the deaf education program. She also was a skilled signer, and she interpreted for many visitors to the campus, including Boyce Williams during board meetings, President Lyndon Baines Johnson, Senator Edward Kennedy, and other politicians and distinguished visitors.[57]

Leon Auerbach.

Harold Domich.

Elizabeth E. Benson in 1944.

Elizabeth E. Benson in 1953.

Rex Lowman.

Richard M. Phillips.

Class of 1940

The undergraduate class of 1940 entered with fifty-four preps. At graduation, twenty-six students received bachelor's degrees, a graduation rate of 48 percent. Six master's degrees were awarded in that year. Among those receiving bachelor's degrees were four future faculty members—Leon Auerbach, Harold Domich, Rex Lowman, and Richard M. Phillips.

Leon Auerbach taught printing at the Arizona School for the Deaf immediately after graduating. During World War II, he worked as a researcher at the MIT Radiation Laboratory in Cambridge, Massachusetts. Auerbach came back to Gallaudet in 1944 as a mathematics professor, and he remained on the faculty until 1984.

Harold Domich worked as a printer and then taught printing at several schools for the deaf. He joined the Gallaudet faculty in September 1956 as a social studies instructor in the Preparatory Department. Rex Lowman worked as a statistician in the Department of Health, Education and Welfare, the Census Bureau, and the Brookings Institution after

Gertrude Galloway (BA 1951, PhD 1993) had a long and distinguished career in deaf education and the Deaf community. She taught at the Maryland School for the Deaf and was active in the Maryland Association of the Deaf. She became the first female president of the National Association of the Deaf (1980–1982), the first deaf female superintendent of a school for the deaf (the Marie Katzenbach School in New Jersey, in 1990), and the first female president of the Conference of the Educational Administrators of Schools and Programs for the Deaf (1996–1998).

World War II. He returned to Gallaudet as a professor of economics in 1956 and continued teaching until 1989. Lowman also wrote and published poetry; three of his poems are included in *Deaf American Poetry: An Anthology* (Gallaudet University Press, 2009).

Richard M. Phillips was a teacher at the Indiana School for the Deaf from 1940 to 1943. During the last two years of World War II he worked as a machinist in a defense plant, and after the war he became a vocational rehabilitation counselor for the deaf in Indiana. In 1952 he accepted a position as a guidance counselor at Gallaudet, and in 1954 he became Dean of Students. He held that position until 1980 when he took over as chair of the Counseling Department.

Class of 1953

The undergraduate class of 1953 started with sixty-seven preps. Of these, thirty-six received bachelor's degrees, a graduation rate of 54 percent. Ten graduate students earned master's degrees that year. The number of degrees awarded and the size of the entering class are indicative of a trend toward increasing enrollment that was already well underway. Two of the students came from Canada. The successful careers of the following graduates illustrate Gallaudet's role in preparing students for employment in a variety of fields.

Terrence J. (TJ) O'Rourke joined the Gallaudet faculty in 1962 as an English professor after teaching at the North Dakota and North Carolina Schools for the Deaf and at Kendall School. He left in 1967 to become the director of the Communication Skills Program (CSP) at the NAD. In 1970, the CSP published the first edition of *A Basic Course in Manual Communication*, a groundbreaking text for teaching American Sign Language. O'Rourke left the NAD in 1978 to establish TJ Publishers, which specializes in sign language instructional materials.[58]

Robert R. Davila began his career as a teacher at the New York School for the Deaf in White Plains. While teaching there he earned a master's degree at Hunter College and a PhD at Syracuse University. He later served as vice president of Pre-College Programs (now the Laurent Clerc National Deaf Education Center) at Gallaudet University, assistant secretary of the Office of Special Education and Rehabilitative Services in the U.S. Department of Education, headmaster of the New York School for the Deaf at White Plains, director of the National Technical Institute for the Deaf and vice president of the Rochester Institute of Technology, and the ninth president of Gallaudet University.[59]

Donald O. Peterson became the first deaf student to receive a master's degree at Gallaudet.

▲ Terrence J. O'Rourke.

Robert R. Davila in 1953.

▶ Donald O. Peterson.

After graduating from the University of Buffalo he enrolled in the graduate department (formally the Normal Department) in 1951. The department still had a policy of excluding deaf students, so rather than give Peterson a Master of Science in Education, like the hearing students, he was given a Master of Arts in Education. He joined the faculty in the fall of 1953 as a professor in the Chemistry Department, and he taught until 1996. In 1965, he was a member of the U.S. team at the International Games for the Deaf (now the Deaflympics).[60] Peterson and his wife Ruth (BA 1972) have been active members of the GUAA.

Years Leading to Transformation

The events that took place at the college in the period from 1910 to 1957 laid the groundwork for profound transformation. For most of its first hundred years, the college was a small, traditional institution with modest aspirations to change. The reforms that Atwood, Elstad, and Detmold, all hearing men, instituted undoubtedly resulted in increased influence and enrollment for the college and to the professionalization of its administration, faculty, and deaf graduates.

During this same period a strong and tightly knit group of student and alumni leaders began to

In 1956, Kendall Green looked much like it had during EMG's and Hall's presidencies. The exception is the brand new Edward Miner Gallaudet Memorial Library, which can be seen on the left side of the photo, next to College Hall.

emerge. These leaders acquired many useful skills, including knowledge of the political process and techniques of effective fund-raising that would enable them to help empower the American Deaf community and increase the academic potential of the college. Ronald Sutcliffe (BS 1959) asserts that since that time, Gallaudet

has become a university and has produced many graduates who have gone on to graduate school, a rare accomplishment before the arrival of Detmold. Many Gallaudet graduates have earned their doctorates, and a sizeable number have gone into a wide range of professions, including in the medical, legal, political, and business worlds. Even more importantly, most of those

schools whose superintendents were so vocal in criticizing Detmold's reforms in the college are now headed by deaf individuals, many of them Gallaudet graduates.[61]

Structurally, the college came to resemble a modern American university, albeit a small one. Earning accreditation from the Middle States Association was a sign of acknowledgement from the general American academic community that the college had arrived as a respected academic institution. However, as the ties with the residential schools and the traditional Deaf culture were loosened, more and more of the faculty and staff were hearing people with no previous exposure to the Deaf world, and not all of them became fluent

In the period before and after accreditation the campus underwent substantial changes. The Laboratory and Carriage House were both demolished and replaced by a large central quadrangle or "Mall." Surrounding the Mall (*clockwise from College Hall*) stood the new EMG Library, Elizabeth Peet Hall (dormitory), Mary Thornberry Building, Hall Memorial Building (HMB), Frederick Hughes Memorial Gym, Student Union Building (SUB), and Ely Building. The Kendall School's West Office Building, originally built to house Division II classes, stood between the Ole Jim and House 7/8 (formerly known as Drake House). Photograph circa 1959.

signers during their years at the college. Nevertheless, Gallaudet continued to function as the cultural home of the American, if not the world, signing Deaf community. This essential bifurcation of the Institution, which was later characterized in an accreditation report as "Harvard vs. Mecca,"[62] created internal tensions that have yet to be fully resolved. At the end of 1957, much work remained to be done, especially in the installation of Deaf leaders in the top positions.

CHAPTER 3

From College to University, 1957–1988

In 1955, prior to Gallaudet's accreditation, the college enrollment totaled 294, including 61 preps, 219 undergraduates, and 14 graduate students. Undergraduates could major in biology, chemistry, mathematics, economics, history, political science, psychology, sociology, art, English, philosophy, business administration, education, home economics, library science, or physical education. In 1966–67, ten years after receiving accreditation, Gallaudet had 823 students—205 preps, 576 undergrads, and 42 graduate students. Total enrollment continued to grow through the 1960s, reaching more than 1,000 by 1970, and the size of the faculty also continued to increase, rising to just over 200 in that year.

As the student body and faculty grew, so did the potential for the college to have an impact on the public perception of deaf people and their abilities. By 1969, the last year of President Elstad's tenure, the federal appropriation for the college had increased to $6.5 million and total revenues stood at almost $9 million.[1] During the 1960s and 1970s the range of programs and services that Gallaudet offered increased dramatically, and these programs fueled the aspirations of deaf people throughout the nation. In 1960, almost seventy years after the founding of the Normal Department (renamed the Graduate Department), Gallaudet finally admitted deaf students to the master's degree program. Clearly, things were changing rapidly.

Greek life flourished on campus during this period, with the addition of the Theta Nu Tau Fraternity in 1969 and the Chi Omega Psi Sorority in 1970, and Gallaudet athletes found success in a number of sports, especially track and field under the leadership of Coach Thomas O. Berg (BS 1944). The number of buildings on the campus also continued to grow. With increasingly abundant federal funding, the college added several new buildings during the early 1960s, including the Washburn Arts Building (named in honor of Cadwallader Washburn), The Mary Thornberry Building (which housed the hearing and speech

Alice Lougee Hagemeyer graduated from Gallaudet in 1957 with a degree in library science. She worked at the DC Public Library from 1957 until 1991, and in that time she established programs to provide and encourage access for deaf patrons and to promote public awareness of Deaf culture. She is the founder of Friends of Libraries for Deaf Action (FOLDA), and since her retirement she has continued to be an advocate for the deaf community, pursuing full library services to American deaf people.

◀ Stained glass windows in Ole Jim. Photograph by Carla D. Morris.

Aerial view of the Gallaudet campus in 1962.

▲ The Gallaudet College Auditorium, now Elstad Auditorium, is a 762-seat theater that is used for theatrical productions and lectures. Photograph 1963.

◄ The Mary Thornberry Building, built in 1958, was home to the Department of Hearing, Speech, and Language Sciences. An extension of the building was completed in 1964. Photograph 1959.

◄ The 1973 Chi Omega Psi sorority pledges. *Top row, l .to r .,* Barbara Bernstein (BS 1975), Fern Sklar (BA 1974), Marie Greenstone (BA 1974), Jacqueline Seaburg (BS 1974), Katherine Carlsen (BS 1974). *Bottom row, l. to r.,* Melanie Skripnek (BA 1974), Mary Hall (BS 1974), Nyla Brenden (BS 1974), Violet Barnes (BA 1974), Reba Poole (BA 1973).

center), the Walter Krug and Alice Cogswell Residence Halls, and the Gallaudet College Auditorium (later renamed in honor of Leonard M. Elstad). The new auditorium provided a home for the performing arts program that eventually had an impact outside of the campus. All of this growth also brought profound changes to the way deaf people viewed their role in the governance of the Institution. These changes in attitude would be accelerated by research conducted at Gallaudet on the nature of the language and culture of the signing Deaf community.

▲ The 1973 Theta Nu Tau fraternity pledges in front of the EMG statue. *Front row, l. to r.,* Michael Norman (BA 1975), Raymond Rotella (class of 1976), Wade Terry (BA 1975). *Back row, l. to r.,* Jeffrey Bartholomew (BS 1976), Michael Harvester (BA 1975), David Killiam (BS 1975), Lannie Godfrey (BA 1974).

◄ Thomas O. Berg (BS 1944, Honorary doctorate 1997), an outstanding track and field athlete, coached the college track and field teams for thirty years. He also served as head track coach for the USA team at the World Games for the Deaf in 1957, '61, '69, '73, '77, and '89. Photograph 1961.

Research at Gallaudet

The responsibilities of American universities are often said to be threefold: teaching, research, and public service. Research on deaf education and on the Deaf community was a feature of scholarly activity at Gallaudet almost from its founding. Edward Allen Fay conducted important research on marriage patterns among deaf people in the latter part of the nineteenth century, work that has since been used in research on the nature of genetic deafness. However, truly organized and sustained research efforts did not begin until the 1950s. At that time, the college faculty included few individu-

als with doctorates. For example, in the 1955–56 academic year, just prior to accreditation, the college faculty numbered fifty-eight, including six individuals with PhDs, three with EdDs, thirty-one with MAs, and eighteen with no advanced degree.[2] The push to increase the number of faculty with doctorates continued after 1957, and eventually included significant numbers of deaf people.

The drive to gain accreditation led to an increased emphasis on research, and the new authorizing legislation in 1954 explicitly indicated that Gallaudet College had a responsibility to conduct research. The idea that research might become a focus of the college at the expense of instruction caused some concern among the faculty. In an attempt to allay their anxiety, Dean Detmold told them in 1962.

Considering the times in which we live, it [research] is a good thing, and should be encouraged. Not for a moment do we intend to neglect the high educational purpose of the College. Once, a professor was thought to live in an ivory tower far from the practical affairs of life. Those days are gone, if not forever, at least for our lifetime. The college teacher is now courted, by government and by industry, by private foundations, by political organizations, by the entire world outside the campus that previously ignored him. It is not surprising that the best brains of the country and the true repository of her ideals and culture, should be found in colleges and universities.

We can expect that members of the Gallaudet faculty will be asked from time to time to perform research in areas where only Gallaudet can claim any real familiarity and competence. These opportunities should be welcomed because we and our students and all deaf people stand to benefit from any advance of scientific knowledge in fields where we practice and profess to teach.[3]

By 1964, the college's centennial year, five research units had been established: the Office of Institutional Research, the Office of Psychological Research, the Hearing and Speech Center, the Sensory Communication Research Laboratory, and the Linguistics Research Laboratory. The Office of Institutional Research, directed by Harry Bornstein, worked primarily on the development and evaluation of instructional materials, including filmed material for teaching sign language and fingerspelling. The Office of Psychological Research, led by Jerome Schein, focused on test development and began the demographic study of the deaf population that later led to its being renamed the Office of Demographic Studies (ODS) in 1966. These studies eventually included an annual survey of deaf and hard of hearing students enrolled in schools and programs in the United States. The Hearing and

Speech Center, directed by Robert Frisina, conducted studies of the effects of hearing loss and proficiency in speech and speechreading. The Sensory Communication Research Lab under James M. Pickett conducted basic research on the perception of sound by deaf people. William C. Stokoe, a professor in the English Department, directed the Linguistic Research Laboratory (LRL), which conducted research on the structure of what was then called the Sign Language but later came to be known as American Sign Language (ASL). In 1971 Stokoe left the English Department to become the full-time director of the LRL. There was also an International Center for Research on Deafness, organized by Jerome Schein and Powrie V. Doctor.

All of the research unit directors were hearing men, and all became familiar names in the various fields of deafness-related research. Only Powrie Doctor and Robert Frisina had any previous experience working with deaf people in a signing environment. Doctor, who had grown up with a deaf brother, graduated from the Normal School in 1931 and was a long-time member of the faculty. Frisina received an MA from the normal school in 1950 and went on to earn a PhD in audiology from Northwestern University. The other directors all had PhDs in fields relevant to the areas in which they taught or did their research. Stokoe came to Gallaudet in 1955, Frisina in 1956 (although he had taught briefly at the Kendall School in 1950–51), Schein in 1960, Bornstein in 1962, and Pickett in 1964.

Although the work of the ODS and the other research centers had a great deal of influence on the practice of deaf education, it was Stokoe's research in the LRL on the structure of ASL that became most closely associated with Gallaudet in the world outside the college.

William C. Stokoe and the Linguistic Status of American Sign Language

When William Stokoe came to teach English at Gallaudet, he was a scholar of Middle English, the period of English literature that stretched from about 1100 to 1400 AD, and he had no prior knowl-

Powrie Vaux Doctor (MA 1931) began teaching at the college in 1928 when he was 25. During his forty-year career, he taught English and History and served as chair of the Government Department. The Powrie V. Doctor Chair of Deaf Studies is named in his honor. The portrait above is from 1942 and the photograph on the left is circa 1960.

James "Mac" Pickett served as director of the Center for Auditory and Speech Sciences at the college from 1964 until 1987. Photograph circa 1973.

Jerome D. Schein joined the Gallaudet faculty as a professor of psychology in 1960. During his tenure he also served as director of the Office of Psychological Research. He left his position at the college in 1968 and became director of the Deafness Research and Training Center at New York University. Photograph 1986.

D. Robert Frisina (MA 1950), served as director of the College's Speech and Hearing Department from the mid-1950s until 1966, when he helped establish NTID in Rochester, New York. Portrait circa 1959

Harry Bornstein served as director of the Office of Institutional Research and later as director of the Gallaudet Signed English Project. Photograph 1971.

edge of sign language. He quickly developed a scholarly interest in the signing of his students, which he believed differed fundamentally from the English-based signing and fingerspelling that he had been taught to use in his classes. Before arriving at Gallaudet, Stokoe had become interested in an anthropological approach to the study of language that assumes all languages are fundamentally equal with respect to their grammatical complexity and ability to serve the needs of their users. According to this view, there are no "primitive" or "inferior" languages, there are simply differences among them, and these differences are based on structural features that share fundamental similarities.

Stokoe's study of the Sign Language, which soon came to be known as American Sign Language (to distinguish it from other sign languages, such as British Sign Language), is widely credited with establishing the legitimacy of ASL as a language. The details of his work and the work of others who joined him will not be pursued in this book as they have been widely recounted elsewhere,[4] but we will explore its impact on both Gallaudet and deaf education generally.

The truly revolutionary aspect of Stokoe's approach was its assumption that the language of deaf people was worthy of study in its own right. Stokoe believed that research on the linguistic abilities of deaf people should be based on more than simply a desire to correct their use of English. The political offshoot of this view is that Deaf people are essentially an ethnic group with their own language, ASL, which they have a fundamental right to use in their daily lives and their classrooms. It does not take a large leap of imagination to link this perspective to the growing civil rights movement for African Americans and other minority groups that was emerging in the United States at this time. As applied to the Deaf community, this view went against a century of "progressive" scholarship and research that sought cures to improve the human race, including deafness, and touted oralism as the way to achieve this goal. Stokoe began observing the way his students signed and found their use of language differed markedly

from what he had been learning from other teachers at Gallaudet.

These personal discoveries fitted well with the cultural and linguistic anthropology I had been reading before coming to Gallaudet. These studies suggested that people deserved to be recognized on their own terms, not someone else's. Thus, in this interpretation, deaf people were not defective hearing people, as the old guard in deaf education had believed, but simply people to be respected for their unique characteristics. . . .

The signing I saw deaf people using was . . . foreign to the manual activity mixed with speech that we new hearing teachers were taught. The official medium of instruction at the college, hearing teachers' signing was a more or less—usually less—complete manual translation of the English sentences we were speaking. Deaf students, by contrast, put signs together fluently and fast, but the resulting constructions did not resemble English sentences.[5]

While Stokoe's research was a revolutionary advance, it also signaled a return to an older view of sign language that accorded it respect and assumed that it had educational value for deaf people. Deaf people had long seen themselves as a social group—a "people," the "people of the eye" as George Veditz put it in 1910,[6] and they generally understood that the "sign language," as the name suggests, was really a language. What Stokoe and his colleagues at the LRL accomplished was to gain acceptance of this idea by the public at large.

George Detmold encouraged Stokoe to continue his endeavors even though many on campus at first opposed or ridiculed the research. Gil Eastman (BA 1957), who joined the faculty in 1957, recalled that "my colleagues and I laughed at Dr. Stokoe and his crazy project. It was impossible to analyze our sign language." In 1960, Stokoe published his first two major works, *Sign Language Structure* and *The Calculus of Structure*. Many faculty members reacted negatively, a reaction that Jerome Schein attributed to the fact that "Bill's [Stokoe's] closeness to Detmold made many jealous. . . . As for Bill's research, it promoted ASL as a true language,

Following her graduation, Dorothy Sueoka Casterline (BA 1958) worked as a linguistics research assistant. She collaborated with Bill Stokoe and Carl Croneberg to create *A Dictionary of American Sign Language on Linguistic Principles* (1965). Photograph circa 1966.

▶ Carl Gustaf Croneberg (BA 1955) (*left*) became an instructor at Gallaudet in 1960 and worked with William Stokoe (*right*) and Dorothy Casterline to write *A Dictionary of American Sign Language on Linguistic Principles* (1965). His appendices to the dictionary provided groundbreaking insights into the Deaf community's language and culture and on sociolinguistic variation within ASL. Photograph circa 1960s.

something that, in the eyes of many in the [English] department, demoted English."[7]

Stokoe wrote *The Calculus of Structure* as a textbook for teaching English sentence structure to deaf students by taking advantage of the students' mathematical abilities. However, many of his colleagues in the English Department found it unusable, including his friend and colleague Carl Croneberg, who said, "I used it only one day a week in a three-day schedule, and I am pretty sure it was the day disliked most by both me and my students. *The Calculus* was a very rational analysis of the elements of an English sentence, but at the end of the course I had absolutely no desire ever to use it again."[8]

Stokoe's most influential publication was most likely the 1965 *Dictionary of American Sign Language on Linguistic Principles*, written with two of his deaf Gallaudet colleagues, Croneberg (BA 1955) and Dorothy C. Sueoka Casterline (BA 1958). They compiled the dictionary employing an abstract script devised by Stokoe that attempted to write ASL much like a spoken language. Croneberg's appendix to the dictionary is considered by many to

be the first work on the sociology of the signing American Deaf community. Oliver Sacks, the well-known physician and writer, has summed up Stokoe's contribution in these terms: "Sign language, at this time [the 1950s], was not seen as a proper language, but as a sort of pantomime or gestural code, or perhaps a sort of broken English on the hands. It was Stokoe's genius to see, and prove, that it was nothing of the sort; that it satisfied every linguistic criterion of a genuine language, in its lexicon and syntax, its capacity to generate an infinite number of propositions."[9]

During the 1960s, '70s, and early '80s, a long list of young scholars gained experience in the world of academic research by working with Stokoe at the LRL, including James Woodward and Harry Markowicz, both of whom taught at Gallaudet for many years; Laura Ann Petitto, who returned to Gallaudet to direct the Visual Language/Visual Learning (VL2) project in 2011 after a long and distinguished career at McGill University and Dartmouth College; Carol Padden, daughter of alumni Don and Agnes Padden, who served for many

Granville Redmond (*left*), an accomplished deaf painter and actor, appeared in a number of silent films with Charlie Chaplin (*right*). Photograph taken in 1917 on the set of *A Dog's Life*.

years on the Gallaudet board and who, in 2010, became the first deaf person to receive a prestigious MacArthur Foundation Fellowship; Ben Bahan (BS 1978) and MJ Bienvenu (BA 1974), both of whom are professors in the Deaf Studies Department at Gallaudet; and I. King Jordan (BA 1970), who became the first deaf president of Gallaudet.

Although Stokoe had his detractors, there is no doubt that his work had a lasting influence on the way Deaf people think about their language and their culture. A hearing colleague of Stokoe's recalls walking with him on the campus in the early 1990s, long after he retired. They ran into one of the elders of Gallaudet's Deaf community, Robert "Sandie" Sanderson (BA 1941), who was then a Gallaudet board member. They had been discussing what the appropriate sign might be for a particular concept and asked Sanderson for his opinion. He responded by signing to Stokoe, "Why are you asking me? You wrote the dictionary."[10]

The Performing Arts at Gallaudet and Beyond

The United States has had a rich tradition of ethnic theaters. New York City has long been home to professional theater companies performing in German, Yiddish, Italian, and other languages.[11] Similarly, Deaf storytellers and actors had been performing in Deaf clubs and social organizations all over the country for many decades, and several deaf actors (most notably Granville Redmond and Albert Ballin) had appeared in silent films.[12] The drama club at Gallaudet College had been staging ASL theatrical productions for almost a century. By the 1960s, a time of cultural change and experimentation in America, American Sign Language began to be accepted as a legitimate language, and there was a growing perception of the Deaf community as a separate cultural group, much like an ethnic minority. The time seemed right for the establishment of a professional theater company performing in ASL for national audiences, hearing and deaf people. While this may have been a radical idea because it would be in sign language, it was not completely outside the American experience.

The impetus for a national theater company of deaf actors stems from a meeting between the actress Anne Bancroft and Edna S. Levine, a well-known psychologist who worked at the Lexington School for the Deaf and as a professor at New York University. Bancroft had been visiting schools for the deaf to prepare for her role as Annie Sullivan in *The Miracle Worker* and Levine suggested that she learn more about sign language and the Deaf community.[13] Levine was an avid theatergoer, and "she was convinced that a theatre of the deaf would appeal to all people."[14] She arranged for Bancroft and director Arthur Penn to see the spring 1959 production of *Othello* at Gallaudet, and they were "so taken with the beauty of the performance that they joined Levine in seeking a grant from the Vocational Rehabilitation Administration." Though they were turned down, Levine persisted, joined by set designer David Hays and Mary Switzer in the U.S. Department of Health, Education and Welfare (HEW), and their efforts resulted in the formation of The National Theatre of the Deaf (NTD), under the auspices of the Eugene O'Neill Theater Center in Connecticut. The company made its first appearance in an NBC television special, *Experiment in Television*, in March 1967, and later that year they began their first tour.[15]

Gallaudet alumni formed the core of NTD's early troupe. Bernard Bragg (BA 1952) had studied

The cast of the National Theatre of the Deaf's production of *My Third Eye* (1971–1972) included many Gallaudet alumni. Pictured *l.* to *r.*: Freda Norman, Patrick Graybill, Richard Kendall, Tim Scanlon, Mary Beth Miller, Dave Berman, Dorothy Miles, Linda Bove, Carol Fleming, Ed Waterstreet, Joe Sarpy, and Bernard Bragg.

Members of the National Theatre of the Deaf ensemble receiving a Tony award in 1977. Pictured *l.* to *r.*: Betty Bonni, Joe Sarpy, Ed Waterstreet, Linda Bove, Freda Norman, Bernard Bragg, and interpreter Bob Blumenfeld. Photograph by David Hays; reprinted by permission of the National Theatre of the Deaf.

with Marcel Marceau and performed professionally as a mime in nightclubs and on television. He became involved early on in helping to found NTD, assisting Levine in the grant process, and he was instrumental in recruiting other deaf actors for the company.[16] The other Gallaudet company members included Violet Armstrong, Linda Bove (BS 1968), Gil Eastman (BA 1957), Phyllis Frelich (BS 1967), Patrick Graybill (BA 1963, MSE 1964), Mary Beth Miller, Dorothy Miles (BA 1961), Shanny Mow (BS 1961), Audree Norton (BS 1952), Howard Palmer (BA 1959), June Russi (AAS, 1959), Tim Scanlon, Andrew J. Vasnick (BA 1951), Joe Velez (AAS 1956), Ralph White (BA 1946), and Ed Waterstreet (BA 1968).[17] One of NTD's best-known productions from this era is the play *My Third Eye*, which was written by the cast members. Some of the play's scenes were autobiographical, including Bragg's recollections of leaving his home in Brooklyn to enroll in the New York School for the Deaf.

When I was four and a half years old, I was awakened one morning, bathed, dressed in fresh, new clothes, and given my breakfast. My mother and I left the apartment together, and I never went back there again.

As we walked to the subway, I asked, "Where are we going?" but my mother didn't reply. I felt a peculiar panic I'd never felt before. "Mother, where are you taking me," I asked again.

"Don't worry, I am with you. Everything is all right," she replied. For the first time in my life, this reassurance wasn't enough. I was frightened.

When the subway ride was over, we walked several blocks to an ominous building on Riverside Drive. Once inside, I smelled, for the first time, the institutional odor of cleanliness and disinfectant, I felt confined by the high ceilings, and dwarfed by the emptiness of the glistening corridors.[18]

Following their time with the National Theatre of the Deaf, a number of the actors secured roles in motion pictures and television productions. Bernard Bragg appeared in the 1979 television movie . . . *And Your Name Is Jonah*. Phyllis Frelich won the 1980 Tony award for best actress for her performance in *Children of a Lesser God* on Broadway and received an Emmy nomination in 1986 for Outstanding Supporting Actress in a Miniseries or a Special for her portrayal of Janice Ryder in *Love Is Never Silent*; she has appeared in numerous other movies and television shows. Linda Bove appeared on the PBS children's program *Sesame Street* for more than thirty years, and, with her husband Ed Waterstreet, founded Deaf West Theatre in 1991. Julianna Fjeld (BA 1970) was the co-executive producer of *Love Is Never Silent*, which won the 1986 Emmy for Outstanding Miniseries or Special. Many other Gallaudet/NTD alumni have appeared on stage, in

As an undergraduate student, Phyllis Frelich (BS 1967, honorary doctorate 1992) was an active member of the drama club and had starring roles in several theatrical productions. She is a founding member of the National Theatre of the Deaf and has appeared in many plays, including creating the role of Sarah in *Children of a Lesser God*, movies, and television shows.

Shanny Mow (BS 1961) has had a long and distinguished career in the theater. He was a member of the NTD ensemble from 1978 to 1980 and 1985 to 1987, and was the NTD's playwright in residence for many years. He has written and directed plays all over the U.S. and internationally, including at NTD, the Fairmount Theatre of the Deaf of Cleveland, the Kennedy Center, and in Stockholm.

Terrylene Sacchetti (MSSD, 1984) began her acting career right out of high school. She has appeared on television and in films and is the founder of Clerc's Children, a bilingual language intervention program for deaf infants and toddlers and their parents.

Peter R. Wisher came to Gallaudet in 1955 as a professor of physical education and as head basketball coach. He founded the Gallaudet Dance Company that same year and served as director and choreographer until his retirement in 1981. Photo circa 1972.

movies, and on television. The entire NTD troupe received a special Tony Award for theatrical excellence in 1977.

The tradition of Gallaudet involvement in theater at the national level has continued, notably by Terrylene Sacchetti (Model Secondary School for the Deaf 1984) who is best known for her recurring role as Laura Williams in the television program *Beauty and the Beast*, which aired from 1987 to 1990. Marlee Matlin, who won an Oscar for her performance in the movie version of *Children of a Lesser God* and had an extensive career in television roles, received an honorary degree from Gallaudet in 1987 and later served on the board of trustees.

Dance performances also became an important part of public events at the college, with the founding of the Gallaudet Dance Company. Peter Wisher, a professor in the Physical Education Department, established the company in 1955, with Gilbert Eastman as one of the founding members. The company has become well-known for performances outside the Gallaudet campus. Over the years, they have performed at the White House and on stages in Egypt, Israel, Canada, Costa Rica, Denmark, Peru, Barbados, St. Lucia, Brazil, Guatemala, South Korea, the Bahamas, and France.

▶ Members of the dance company performing "The Impossible Dream" at their graduation in 1977. The dancers, pictured *l.* to *r.*: Martha Sheridan, Debra Wood, Kathy Jones Weldon, and Hershella Hearns Ashford. Pictured in the background on the far left (*l.* to *r.*): Alan B. Crammatte, Thomas Mayes, Gilbert Delgado (MS 1954), and John Schuchman. Courtesy of the Gallaudet Dance Company.

Gilbert (Gil) C. Eastman (BA 1957) founded the Theatre Arts Department (then called the Department of Drama) at Gallaudet and taught there from 1957 to 1992. He was involved in all aspects of theater, including directing, stage managing, playwriting, and translating. He was the co-host of the award-winning television program "Deaf Mosaic," for which he received an Emmy Award from the National Academy of Television Arts and Sciences. The Gilbert C. Eastman Studio Theatre, a black box theatre on campus, is named in his memory. Photograph on left circa 1957.

The Arrival of Edward C. Merrill, Jr.

Leonard Elstad retired in 1969, after twenty-four years as the third president of Gallaudet. Elstad's length of service contributed to a curious bit of Gallaudet lore—numerology surrounding the tenure of Gallaudet presidents. Gallaudet number theorists noticed that EMG served as president of the college for forty-six years (1864–1910), Percival Hall, thirty-five (1910–1945), and Elstad, twenty-four (1945–1969), thus each president served eleven years less than his predecessor. We will see how this numerology was to apply to those who came after President Elstad, but we can tip our hand here by revealing that his successor, Edward C. Merrill, Jr., stayed until 1983, a fact that did not bode well for his successor. The selection of Edward C. Merrill, Jr., marked a departure from the board's pattern of the previous half-century. Merrill was an educational administrator who had many years of experience in higher education, but he had no previous experience in the education of the deaf or at Gallaudet College and no knowledge of ASL. He held a bachelor's degree in English from the University of North Carolina and a PhD in Educational Administration from George Peabody College for Teachers. At the time of his appointment, he was dean of the College of Education at the University of Tennessee.

Soon after taking office on July 1, 1969, President Merrill assessed how the college functioned, and he put in motion a program of changes. He realized that

although he [President Elstad] had done remarkable things for the College, he had not been a strong administrator during the last three or four years of his tenure. He had turned the management of the College over to the dean, Dr. Detmold. Persons in the Department of HEW (Health, Education, and Welfare) at the assistant secretary level, told me that Gallaudet was standing still and that support would wane unless more of the needs of the deaf population were met by the College. They also indicated that if I proposed new and stronger programs they would help me get the funding.

During my first year, I initiated reviews of programs and had in several consultants. This resulted in publishing 26 goals for the college in the *New Era* report which was accepted by the Board. This provided the basis for change and growth at Gallaudet over the next few years.

President Edward C. Merrill in sign language class in 1969 (*left*), and at his desk in 1971 (*right*).

In 1971, Merrill appointed John S. Schuchman, a member of the History Department who held a PhD from Indiana University, to succeed Detmold as chief academic officer. Dean Schuchman, a hearing child of deaf adults (CODA) and a fluent signer, oversaw rapid growth in enrollment and fundamental changes in the structure and governance of the academic program, especially in the complexity of the organization itself. His title later changed to vice president for the Division of Academic Affairs, and the unit was subdivided into several colleges and schools, each with a dean or director. George Detmold continued to serve on the faculty until his retirement in 1976.

The Great Society, MSSD, KDES, and Physical Growth of the Campus

Even before Merrill arrived at Gallaudet, the college had begun to benefit from an expansion of government programs and services frequently referred to as the "Great Society," a term that U.S. President Lyndon Baines Johnson used to characterize his administration. Much of the growth was directed at improving educational outcomes in the United States, including the education of deaf children.

In the early 1960s, the Gallaudet College Alumni Association (GCAA) learned that the college had developed plans to increase enrollment to 1,600 students by 1970. The alumni felt they had

not been adequately informed of these plans, and they expressed concern that the admission standards would be lowered. GCAA board members participated in hearings before the House Subcommittee on Appropriations, and in 1964 HEW Secretary Anthony Celebrezze appointed the Advisory Committee on the Education of the Deaf. The committee's report, issued in 1965 and generally known as the Babbidge Report after its chairman, Homer Babbidge, was highly critical of the state of deaf education and called for a major effort by the federal government to improve educational outcomes for deaf children.[20]

As a direct consequence of the Babbidge Report, Congress authorized and funded two major new programs at Gallaudet, the Model Secondary School for the Deaf (MSSD) and the Kendall

Dean John S. Schuchman presenting at an alumni workshop on April 1, 1977.

Demonstration Elementary School (KDES). These programs had a two-fold mission: first, to provide exemplary educational programs to the students enrolled in the schools; second, to develop new "model" programs that had the potential to improve educational outcomes for all deaf students and to disseminate information about these programs to the field of deaf education.

The Model Secondary School for the Deaf Act (P.L. 89-694), signed by President Johnson on October 15, 1966, required that Gallaudet and the executive branch of the federal government negotiate an agreement governing the operation of the school. In May 1969, HEW Secretary Robert Finch and Gallaudet President Elstad (as one of his last acts in office) signed an agreement authorizing the establishment and operation of MSSD as a residential secondary school for deaf students. Congress appropriated funding in 1972 for construction of a complex of buildings, including a main classroom building, a gymnasium, dormitories for students, and housing for faculty and administrators, and the main facilities were ready for occupancy in 1976. The MSSD complex is located at the northern end of the Gallaudet University campus. The original design of the main classroom building incorporated several innovative design features, especially with respect to open classrooms without permanent walls. Over time, this design proved unworkable to classroom instructors, and interior walls were gradually added.

President Johnson made two visits to Gallaudet—the first to participate in the college's centennial celebration in 1964 and the second to make a surprise visit to the Gallaudet commencement in 1966. At the centennial ceremonies, Johnson presented the college with the President's Committee on Employment of the Handicapped Award, and he made a speech in which he commended the college and its mission.

The great battle, the great adventure for Americans living tonight is not only to preserve our freedom and to preserve our peace but to defend, preserve and strengthen those pillars of our society: education,

Elizabeth Benson interpreted for President Lyndon B. Johnson when he addressed the guests at the Centennial Banquet on June 6, 1964.

compassion, and morality. To you here who are devoting your lives as committed, concerned and compassionate citizens, I am proud and honored to present tonight to Gallaudet College the 1964 Award from the President's Committee on Employment of the Handicapped.[21]

In 1970, Congress passed, and U.S. President Richard Nixon signed, the Kendall Demonstration Elementary School (KDES) Act (P.L. 91-587), changing the historic Kendall School into a demonstration elementary day school (the federal charters for MSSD and KDES allow for residential students only at the secondary level) and expanding its role to include research, development, and dissemination. Construction of a new facility for KDES began in 1977 and was completed in 1980—the site was next to that of the new MSSD facilities. The MSSD and KDES complexes completely

Exterior of the Kendall School, located on the northern end of campus. This building was eventually demolished to make way for the current facility. The students and staff ate together in the school cafeteria. Photographs 1962.

Interior of MSSD in the late 1970s.

Aerial view of campus taken on September 29, 1982. The "Mall," located on the southern end of campus, is in the foreground. The library/learning center (later named for President Merrill), completed in 1981, is in the center of the photograph.

changed the character of the northern end of the campus, and new college dormitory construction had a similar effect on its central section, an area that had contained open fields and woods. The General Services Administration (GSA) no longer controlled construction on the campus, leaving the college free to obtain the services of architects who could provide innovative designs. College dormitory construction came in response to the dramatic increase in enrollment following accreditation, and other major projects began during the 1970s and early '80s, including a new library/learning center (later renamed in Edward Merrill's honor) and gymnasium (the Field House).

Major construction ended in 1983, with completion of the Field House—the last building built with 100 percent federal funding, and this event also signaled the beginning of serious private fundraising to support construction of new facilities. It is highly significant that Gallaudet received federal appropriations for construction every year for a period of thirty years, from 1953 to 1982, spread over the administrations of Presidents Elstad and Merrill.[22] All totaled, Congress appropriated more than $125 million for building projects (at least $300 million in today's dollars), an indication of the strength of federal support for the college and for its modernization and the expansion of its programs and levels of service. Since 1983, however, while the government has participated in some cost-sharing projects at Gallaudet, all of the buildings constructed on the campus have been built primarily with private funds.

The community around Kendall Green underwent substantial change during the 1950s and 1960s as well, and this led to an increasing sense of isolation on the campus, both cultural and physical. For most of its history, the population of the District of Columbia had been mostly white—in 1940, for example, more than 70 percent of Washington's residents were white, while fewer than 30 percent were African American. By 1970, those percentages had almost exactly reversed.[23] During this period, Gallaudet remained a mostly white enclave within an increasingly African American neighborhood. The riots following the assassination of Dr. Martin Luther King, Jr., in April 1968 caused substantial destruction of the commercial centers near the campus, especially along H Street, NE, and National Guard and other federal troops were deployed to restore order. Gallaudet's leaders responded by maintaining the fence around the campus and controlling access at a small number of gates, a practice that was to have significant strategic consequences during protests by members of the Gallaudet community in 1988 and 2006.

Dr. Edward C. Merrill in regalia in 1969, at the beginning of his tenure as president of the college.

Portrait of Dr. Leonard M. Elstad by Bjorn Egeli, presented to the college by the alumni association in 1968.

Commercial activity in the neighborhood remained depressed into the decade of the 2000s.

Advocacy, Public Service, and Expanded Research Activities

Service to the public is the third major responsibility of American higher education institutions. As Gallaudet's role and influence expanded and its enrollment increased, the board and the administration recognized a need for more comprehensive

Left: U.S. Army soldiers set up camp on the field behind the Gallaudet College Auditorium (now Elstad Auditorium; *left*), and Dawes House (*right*) during the 1968 riots in DC. *Right*: The soldiers took up residence inside Hughes Gym.

planning to guide future growth. The expansion of public service, outreach, and advocacy began at the initiative of President Merrill, and it is closely associated with three deaf administrators—Thomas Mayes, Albert Pimentel (BA 1957), and Roslyn Rosen (BA 1962, MA 1964). According to Mike Kaika (BA 1972), a longtime member of the Gallaudet alumni office staff,

◀ Dr. Thomas Mayes in 1974

▼ Dr. Roslyn Rosen, the newly appointed dean of the College for Continuing Education, in 1981.

Mayes was often called the "Father of Continuing Education" for deaf and hard of hearing people in this country. . . . In 1972, Dr. Mayes became Gallaudet's first Dean of Continuing Education and later, Vice President of Public Services until his retirement. After he received his Ph.D. from Michigan State University, Mayes became a faculty member at California State University at Northridge in 1965, where he was responsible for instituting the Leadership Training Program that has produced numerous deaf leaders around the world. In 1969, recognizing his leadership skills, the Gallaudet University Board elected him a Trustee and he remained on the Board until 1972, when he joined the administration of the College.[24]

During Mayes's tenure as an administrator at Gallaudet, the college conducted a strategic planning study and published its results in 1978 in a report entitled *New Challenges, New Responses*. Goal number 11 of the report specifically addressed public service and advocacy, and it charged Gallaudet to "respond more fully to its obligation to be a leader in championing the rights of deaf people everywhere."[25] As a result, Mayes established a wide array of outreach initiatives, including the National Academy, Adult Basic Education, Continuing Education and Extension Programs, Summer Programs, Gallaudet College Press, and the National Information Center on Deafness.

In 1971, Albert Pimentel left his position as executive director of the Registry of Interpreters for the Deaf to become the director of public service programs for the college. These programs laid the groundwork for many of the units that later developed within the new division of public services that Mayes organized. Pimentel later served as

executive director of the National Association of the Deaf and as headmaster of the New York School for the Deaf in White Plains.

Roslyn Rosen became the dean of the College for Continuing Education under Vice President Mayes in 1981. Pre-College National Mission Programs, although operated separately, were an essential part of this general outreach and advocacy program. Don Pettingill, a deaf man who resumed his education at age fifty-two and received his bachelor's degree from Gallaudet in 1976, was instrumental in developing outreach activities for pre-college and continuing education programs during this era. The outreach activities of the college and pre-college programs eventually reached hundreds of thousands of deaf people and professionals who work with deaf people. Mayes retired in 1986.

Goal number 16 of *New Challenges, New Responses* called for Gallaudet to expand its commitment to basic and applied research of benefit to deaf people by establishing the Gallaudet Research Institute (GRI).[26] Raymond Trybus, who had been the director of the Office of Demographic Studies, became the dean of GRI. One of GRI's signature projects is the Annual Survey of Deaf and Hard of Hearing Children and Youth. The survey collects

R. Orin Cornett came to Gallaudet in 1965 to serve as vice president of Long-range Planning. He developed the Cued Speech system in 1966, and in 1975, he became a research professor and director of Cued Speech Programs. Dr. Cornett also invented the *diplacusimeter* (pictured here), an instrument that measures diplacusis (a type of tinnitus). Photograph 1967.

▲ Albert T. Pimentel speaking in support of the Rehabilitation Act Amendments at a demonstration in front of the White House on November 6, 1978.

▶ Don G. Pettingill circa 1978.

demographic, audiological, and other educationally relevant information, which is used by federal and state education agencies for budgeting and planning purposes. GRI also administers new versions of the Stanford Achievement Test to a representative sampling of deaf and hard of hearing students and uses the results to create age-based norming tables for the test. Another GRI initiative is the Small Research Grants Program that encourages research by Gallaudet faculty and staff.[27]

Gallaudet researchers traditionally have focused their studies on issues of importance to deaf education and deaf people. Institutionally based research has since expanded to include genetics and brain sciences, but the core focus on language and education has remained mainly the same. Despite this emphasis on language, Gallaudet administrators closed the Linguistics Research Laboratory (LRL) following William Stokoe's retirement in 1984. They cited rising costs associated with operating the laboratory and rising expectations for basic

research on ASL to be conducted by faculty in the Linguistics Department, but some on campus and in the Deaf community interpreted the closing as a repudiation of Stokoe's work and influence. This is certainly how Stokoe himself interpreted the event, and he did not return to the campus until 1988, when he was awarded an honorary doctorate. It may not be entirely coincidental that there was increasing support for research on signed surrogates for speech, including the Cued Speech method developed by Orin Cornett, Gallaudet's vice president for Planning, during the late 1960s and early 1970s. The method of speaking and signing known as Simultaneous Communication (Sim-Com) had also become dominant in Gallaudet's classrooms as new faculty arrived who had no knowledge of ASL.

Other research initiatives also developed outside of the areas of traditional focus, especially within the discipline of history. During the 1970s, Jack R. Gannon (BA 1959), the director of Alumni Relations, was at work on a monumental history of the Deaf community—*Deaf Heritage: A Narrative History of Deaf America.* The National Association of the Deaf published the book in 1981. During the early 1980s, John Schuchman, vice president for Academic Affairs and professor of history conducted videotaped interviews as part of an extensive Deaf community oral history project, and John V. Van Cleve, professor of history, compiled the *Gallaudet Encyclopedia of Deaf People and Deafness,* published in 1987 by McGraw-Hill.

Goal 16 of *New Challenges, New Responses* also called for the formal establishment of Gallaudet College Press to seek, encourage, and publish scholarship on all topics relating to deaf people. Although the college had long published work under that name, the Press did not exist as a formal organization until its official inauguration in 1980. By the time of its thirtieth anniversary in 2010, the Press had successfully released more than 400 titles; disseminated more than one million books, videotapes, CDs, and DVDs; and generated revenues from sales in excess of $13 million as a scholarly publishing house.[28]

Left to *right:* David Peikoff, Georgie E. Holden (Director of Public Relations), and Jack R. Gannon at an informal get-together on September 4, 1968.

Partygoers at the faculty/staff dinner in honor of Dr. Elstad on April 30, 1969. Pictured *l.* to *r.*: Hortense Henson Auerbach (BA 1940), Dr. Elstad, Agnes Dunn Sutcliffe (BA 1959), Ronald E. Sutcliffe (BS 1959), and Leon Auerbach (BS 1940).

The Alumni Grow in Numbers, Influence, and Accomplishments

As enrollment in the college increased, so did membership in the alumni association, which continued to expand its reach throughout the country and abroad. The GCAA also continued to work toward long-standing political goals at both the institutional and national levels. These goals included the development of leadership opportunities for deaf students and alumni, improvements in Gallaudet's educational programs, and increased representation of alumni on the board of trustees. This period also saw formal representation of the alumni within the organizational structure of the college and the establishment of new chapters throughout the country (see chart on p. 89).

The first Alumni Office opened on Kendall Green in 1960, and in that same year the GCAA published *The Silent Muse,* an anthology of prose and poetry by deaf writers. In 1961, the GCAA launched its Centennial Fund drive, with a goal of raising $100,000. David Peikoff, then president of GCAA, chaired and organized the efforts with energetic zeal. He put together a committee that included his wife Polly, Alan and Florence Crammatte, Leon and Hortense Auerbach, Boyce Williams, and others who worked tirelessly to convince alumni and other deaf people to contribute to the fund.[29] In 1962 the Alumni Office moved from the Student Union Building to Dawes House.

In 1964, the GCAA voted on a number of issues pertaining to its relationship with Gallaudet.[30] It passed a resolution calling for the joint maintenance of an alumni program on the campus, and it urged the college to provide a program in leadership training. It also endorsed the establishment of

ESTABLISHMENT OF GALLAUDET UNIVERSITY
ALUMNI ASSOCIATION CHAPTERS

1895	Minnesota	1969	Down East (Maine)
1901	Pittsburgh (Pennsylvania)		Alabama
1905	District of Columbia		Arkansas
1906	Metropolitan (New York)	1971	Free State (Maryland)
1907	Michigan		Montana
1913	Connecticut	1972	Jessamine (South Carolina)
1919	Akron (Ohio)		Beehive (Utah)
1927	Northern California (NorCal)	1974	Georgia
1928	Pacific Northwest (Washington)	1976	Alberta (Canada)
1930	Chicago (Illinois)		Bay State (Massachusetts)
1944	Greater Los Angeles (California)		Mount Rushmore (South Dakota)
1946	Indiana	1977	San Diego (California)
	Kentucky	1978	Aloha State (Hawaii)
1947	Santa Fe (New Mexico)	1979	Valley of the Sun (Arizona)
	Jacksonville (Illinois)	1981	Metro Detroit (Michigan)
	Kaw Valley (Kansas)		Central North Carolina
	Knoxville (Tennessee)	1982	Puget Sound (Washington)
1948	Mohawk Valley (Rome, New York)	1983	Greater New Orleans Area (Louisiana)
	Robert E. Lee (Virginia)		Big Spring (Texas)
1949	Tucson (Arizona)	1984	Mississippi
1950	Carolinas (North Carolina),	1985	Aurora (Alaska)
	St. Augustine (Florida)	1986	Metro Atlanta (Georgia)
	Austin (Texas)	1987	Dallas/Fort Worth (Texas)
1952	Mile High (Colorado)	1988	PenJerDel (Pennsylvania, New Jersey, Delaware)
1956	Wisconsin		
	West Virginia	1989	Greater Sacramento Valley (California)
1960	Nebowa (Nebraska-Iowa)	1990	Ocean State (Rhode Island)
	Riverside (California)	1991	First-in-Flight (North Carolina)
1962	Spud (Idaho)		San Antonio (Texas)
1968	Genessee Valley (New York)	1993	Nippon (Japan) (first overseas chapter)
	Louisiana	1994	New Jersey

regional technical or vocational schools to prepare or retrain deaf people for the workplace. The members urged the college to give credit for manual communication courses and suggested that a full-time in-service director be hired to provide new faculty members with training in both oral and manual communication skills. They asked that the Gallaudet board of directors be increased from thirteen to twenty-five members, with six of the new positions filled by deaf alumni selected by the GCAA. Lastly, the members voted to take full control of the Edward Miner Gallaudet Statue Fund Drive that had originated with the DC chapter in 1962.

John Lopez (BA 1966) was a political activist and advocate for the Deaf and Hispanic Deaf communities. He was actively involved with the District of Columbia Association of Deaf Citizens (DCADC), the National Hispanic Council of the Deaf and Hard of Hearing (now called National Council of Hispano Deaf and Hard of Hearing), and Telecommunications for the Deaf Inc., (TDI), among other organizations. As a member of the 9-1-1 Access Committee, he was instrumental in adding language requiring TTY and relay access to public-safety call centers in Title II of the Americans with Disabilities Act. He also served in the Clinton White House Policy Office and as a member of the Deaf and Hard of Hearing Consumer Advocacy Network.

Glenn Anderson (BA 1968) has had a long and distinguished career in vocational rehabilitation and training. He was the first deaf person to work as a vocational rehabilitation counselor in Michigan and the first deaf African American in the U.S. to earn a doctorate degree. From 1982 to 2008 he was a professor and director of training at the Rehabilitation Research and Training Center for Persons Who Are Deaf or Hard of Hearing at the University of Arkansas in Little Rock. In 1989, Anderson was appointed to the Gallaudet Board of Trustees, and in 1994 he became the first deaf African American chair of the board.

On June 24, 1967, GCAA officially presented the Centennial Fund, totaling $520,000 in cash and pledges, to the college, and the two organizations signed an agreement to establish three funds: the Graduate Fellowship Fund to assist deaf scholars studying for doctorates, the Laurent Clerc Cultural Fund to encourage and promote cultural activities among deaf people, and the Alumni House Fund for the purpose of constructing a permanent home for the GCAA. Also in 1967, GCAA issued a statement applauding the establishment of the National Technical Institute for the Deaf (NTID) at the Rochester Institute of Technology with approval and high hopes. The alumni considered NTID to be a significant addition to educational and employment opportunities for deaf people. In addition, GCAA endorsed the establishment of MSSD, and it urged the college to establish a permanent office to conduct research on American Sign Language.

In 1968, the college budgeted for and opened the Office of Alumni Relations on the campus and hired Jack R. Gannon (BA 1959) as its first full-time director. That same year, GCAA awarded the first Graduate Fellowship Fund grants. In 1969, Gannon became a member of the President's Cabinet, and the alumni association formally presented the Edward Miner Gallaudet statue to the college It also presented an oil portrait of retiring President

Elstad, $2,000 donated by individual alumni and friends to Dr. Elstad's International Deaf Educational Assistance Fund (IDEAF), and the first Laurent Clerc Cultural Fund awards. By June 1970, GCAA had 1,480 life members. Once again, they requested that the Gallaudet University Board of Directors increase the number of deaf persons serving on the board. GCAA committed itself to promoting Total Communication in schools and programs for deaf children throughout the country and abroad and went on record favoring a program of leadership training for deaf adults. It also asked Gallaudet to place more stress on excellence in teaching as well as on the ability of faculty to communicate with the students, and, per the agreement for disbursement of the Centennial Fund, it asked the board to initiate the financing and construction of an alumni house.

Through the 1970s and '80s GCAA continued to grow in numbers and in national and international prominence. It published *The Gallaudet Almanac*, a comprehensive fact book covering all aspects of the college's history, in 1974. Then, in 1975, it published *Notable Deaf Persons*, a collection of nearly one hundred biographies of deaf people written by Guilbert C. Braddock (BA 1918). Gil Eastman (BA 1957) traveled to France in 1980 as GCAA's representative to honor Laurent Clerc, America's first deaf teacher of deaf students, at his birthplace in La

Gil Eastman in 1984.

Left to *right*: Gerald "Bummy" Burstein, David Peikoff, and Jack R. Gannon on April 8, 1989.

"Ole Jim" in March 1980 (*left*) during the renovations. Workmen removed the stucco exterior that had hidden the original ornamental wood and leaded glass windows. The building reopened in 1982 (*right*) and was renamed the Peikoff Alumni House in 1995 to honor David and Polly Peikoff.

Balme. In 1982, the alumni association moved into its long-awaited home in the renovated original gymnasium, or "Ole Jim." It also worked with the U.S. Postal Service to issue a stamp in honor of the Rev. Thomas Hopkins Gallaudet. GCAA became one of the first American organizations to join the World Federation of the Deaf in 1983, and it cosponsored Yerker Andersson's (BA 1960) campaign for president of the federation. In that year, membership in the GCAA increased to 4,000. In 1985, the GCAA sent its president, Gerald "Bummy" Burstein (BA 1950), to France to participate in the two hundredth anniversary of Clerc's birth, and it dedicated a garden at the Cosmos Club in Washing-

PHOTO 51 This postmarked envelope commemorates the completion of the Alumni House (Ole Jim) restoration project. The official opening took place on June 25, 1982, during the 31st Triennial Reunion of the Gallaudet University Alumni Association. The 20-cent stamp honoring Thomas H. Gallaudet (*lower right*) was issued in 1983 as part of the *Great Americans* series. Courtesy of the author.

Daisy Slagle Cartwright (BA 1974) in 1976 with students in the Philippines.

Pauline Spanbauer (BA 1974) in 1976 with students in the Philippines.

Guy Vollmar (BA 1974) in 1977, instructing students in the Philippines.

ton, DC, in honor of Edward Miner Gallaudet, one of the founders (along with Alexander Graham Bell) and the fifth president of the club.

In 1980, President Merrill instituted a survey of all former undergraduate students who had left

MAJOR FINDINGS OF THE 1980 GALLAUDET ALUMNI SURVEY

1. The unemployment rate for graduates is very low, at only 3 percent.
2. Among those graduates who are working, 85 percent are employed in professional occupations, especially in education.
3. Family incomes of graduates are well above the national average.
4. A significant number of graduates have earned advanced degrees—39 percent have master's degrees and 3 percent have doctorates.[32]

Gallaudet prior to the fall of that year and who could be identified on the Alumni Office mailing list, including graduates and nongraduates. In early 1981, questionnaires went out to 5,299 former undergraduates, and about half of them (2,637) returned responses. Overall, the study suggested that deaf Gallaudet graduates had good opportunities to obtain well-paying professional employment and that they were pursuing successful careers. The percentage of bachelor's degree recipients who went on to earn graduate degrees was particularly impressive (see box). These results have been replicated consistently in later studies of alumni, and the rate at which Gallaudet bachelor's degree recipients earn advanced degrees has been shown to be well above the national average.[31]

Gallaudet graduates also developed a tradition of service as Peace Corps volunteers during this period. Since 1967, more than fifty-five deaf people, most of them Gallaudet graduates, have served in the organization that President Kennedy created in 1961. They have worked in many different countries, including Benin, Ecuador, Ghana, Guyana, Kenya, Malaysia, Nepal, Philippines, Sierra Leone, St. Lucia, St. Vincent, and Zambia. These Deaf volunteers have served as teachers and role models in countries that questioned the value of educating deaf children. Their presence in leadership positions has challenged accepted ideas of what deaf children can become and the ability of deaf adults to assume

▲ Frances "Peggie" Parsons (1943–1945, BA 1967) in 1977, visiting the Plateau Deaf School in Nigeria. Parsons was instrumental in establishing a deaf presence in the Peace Corps beginning in 1969 with a trip to the Philippines.

▼ Allen Neece in 2009 with the girls' handball team from the Tumu Tumu School for the Deaf in Kenya.

authority.[33] In 2011, the Gallaudet University Museum opened an exhibit to celebrate the fiftieth anniversary of the founding of the Peace Corps and the service of Gallaudet alumni.

The "Rubella Bulge" and the Northwest Campus

Perhaps the greatest challenge facing President Merrill and the college during the early 1980s was the need to prepare for a large increase in the number of deaf students seeking higher education. This need came from two factors: first, a general increase in the number of deaf high school students who wanted a college education; second, a much larger population of deaf students graduating from high school due to the effects of a rubella epidemic in the mid-1960s. Rubella, more commonly known as German measles, is a relatively common, infectious, childhood disease that has few, if any, lasting effects. However, when a woman contracts German measles during her first trimester of pregnancy, the fetus may develop sensory impairments, especially deafness and/or blindness.

Historically, rubella epidemics occurred in six to nine year cycles, and the 1963–65 epidemic was particularly severe. In the United States, an additional 8,000 individuals were born deaf and 3,600 born deaf-blind as a result of maternal rubella. Enrollment at Gallaudet had been increasing steadily for the previous quarter century, following accreditation, and by the late 1970s the undergraduate enrollment stood at about 1,200. Because of the rubella epidemic, the Gallaudet Planning Office estimated that, if the proportion of deaf students enrolling in the college remained steady, the number of undergraduates would almost double to more than 2,000 by 1984. Enrollment in the graduate school was expected to remain stable at about 300 until the late '80s when it would start to increase gradually as the rubella students began to complete their undergraduate degrees.[34] The college responded by seeking more funding from Congress to support an increase in staff, and it also began to plan for new facilities to house the influx of students and to provide more classroom space.

Ultimately, the administration and the board decided that it would be better to try to acquire existing facilities, rather than construct new buildings for what would probably be a temporary increase in enrollment. College officials discovered that the campus of the former Marjorie Webster Junior College in northwest Washington, DC, was sitting empty. The federal government owned the property, which had been used for a brief period as a training facility by the Federal Emergency Management Agency (FEMA). Gallaudet officials persuaded Congress to transfer the property to Gallaudet in 1981. Public Law 97-80 (November 20, 1981) directed FEMA to "convey [the Marjorie Webster campus] by

The Northwest campus occupied eight acres in northwest Washington (*above*). The buildings date from 1928 when Marjorie Webster Junior College first opened. The main building (*below*) could be seen from the campus entrance. Photographs circa 1982.

quit-claim deed, without consideration, to Gallaudet College." Congress also provided the funds to renovate the campus, and it reopened in 1983 as the home of Gallaudet's Preparatory Program.

According to the planning office forecasts, the undergraduate enrollment would peak in 1984 at 2,000 and then gradually return to the pre-"bulge" total of 1,200–1,300 by about 1990. As it turned out, the rubella enrollment did not reach its ultimate peak of 1,900 until 1991, and took longer to complete its passage through the college. As a final historical footnote to the "rubella bulge" era at Gallaudet, it is important to note that the 1963–65 epidemic in the United States led to a massive immunization program. This program was so

successful that in 2005 the Centers for Disease Control and Prevention announced that the rubella virus no longer existed in the country.[35] This has had the effect of eliminating a major cause of deafness and reducing the number of deaf children being born in the United States.

Appointment of W. Lloyd Johns

When Edward C. Merrill, Jr., retired in 1983, some people on campus speculated that he might be replaced by a deaf person, and Merrill himself urged the board to consider appointing a deaf person as his successor.[36] By this time there was no shortage of deaf people with appropriate credentials—*Deaf Heritage*, published in 1981, included a lengthy list, compiled by Rosalyn Gannon, of deaf people who held earned doctorates, many of them Gallaudet graduates, faculty members, and administrators.[37] Merrill had promoted several deaf individuals to upper-level administrative positions, including Robert Davila as vice president for Pre-College Programs, Thomas Mayes as vice president of the Division of Public Services, Roslyn Rosen as dean of the College for Continuing Education, and Merv Garretson (BA 1947) as special assistant to the president for Advocacy. Garretson had come to the college as a professor in the graduate school in the early 1960s and subsequently had been involved in the establishment of MSSD, as its first principal. One of his initiatives as special assistant to the president after his promotion in 1978 was to organize a Deafness Related Concerns Council (DRCC) to address questions of equal employment opportunity for deaf people at Gallaudet.[38]

Despite the educational and administrative gains that had been made by deaf people, it seems that the board did not give any serious consideration to the selection of a deaf person to succeed Merrill. After conducting a national search, the board appointed W. Lloyd Johns, a hearing man who had been head of the California State University's Sacramento campus. He had no previous experience working with deaf people and did not know any sign language. The Gallaudet "minus 11"

Edward C. Merrill, Jr., (*left*) and W. Lloyd Johns (*right*) during the transition between their presidencies in 1983.

W. Lloyd Johns in 1983.

numerology for projecting the tenure of presidents set the length of his service at no more than two or three years, and his administration was indeed a short-lived phenomenon, as he failed to complete even one year. He resigned for personal reasons that were never officially disclosed. This came as quite a shock to the Gallaudet community, which was used to long years of service by its chief executive officers. For all of its first hundred years, the college had had only four presidents. The board of trustees appointed Jerry C. Lee, the vice president for Administration and Business, as interim president and then offered him the position on a permanent basis without a search, the lack of which caused some discontent on the campus as another opportunity for appointing a deaf president had been lost.[39] Jerry C. Lee began his tenure as president in 1984.

The Administration of Jerry C. Lee

Jerry C. Lee came to Gallaudet in 1971 from the corporate world. He held a bachelor's degree from West Virginia Wesleyan College and MA and EdD degrees from Virginia Tech, the latter earned while he was an administrator at Gallaudet. President Lee's tenure was also relatively brief, at least by the standards of previous Gallaudet presidents; he served for only three years. These were highly significant years, however, in that the first groups of rubella bulge students arrived, and the college gained university status. Early in Lee's administration, John Schuchman, now the vice president for

Jerry C. Lee during his 1984 inauguration speech.

Academic Affairs, resigned and was replaced by Catherine Ingold, the dean of Arts and Sciences. Schuchman, who had served as chief academic officer since 1971, returned to the History Department faculty and continued his scholarly work on the Deaf community.

One of Lee's chief concerns was the financial situation of the college. The federal government had entered a period of growing budget deficits, and Gallaudet anticipated having to find more support from private sources as the availability of federal funds decreased. College administrators saw an opportunity to increase revenue by increasing the tuition rates. These charges historically had been quite low, about the same as the average rates at U.S. public universities. Aware that deaf students had a variety of financial aid sources available to them, the administration began a multi-year plan to increase tuition to the top of the range for public institu-

The 1987 Gallaudet football team ended their season with a 9-1 record. The star players included Todd Silvestri, #52, (*middle of the second row*) Jimmy Segala, #15 (*third row, third from the left*) and Shannon Simon (*fourth row, eighth from the left*).

Gallaudet quarterback James A. "Jimmy" Segala in action during the 1988 football season.

tions. As a consequence, the proportion of the institution's total revenues that came from private sources increased rapidly. When Lee became president, Gallaudet received $56 million in appropriated income and $68 million in total funds. By fiscal year 1987—88, the year in which he resigned, the appropriation had increased to $62 million and total income stood at $83 million. The appropriation as a percentage of total support for the Institution had, thus, decreased from 82 percent to 75 percent.

President Lee also took steps to revive Gallaudet's athletic tradition, especially its football program. He believed this would have two benefits—it would improve Gallaudet's public visibility, and it would help to revitalize the student body. In 1985, Bob Westermann, who had been the coach at MSSD, was hired to coach the college football team and was able to improve the team's record to 9–1 by 1987. The team also received recognition in national rankings that year. They continued to play well following Lee's departure from Gallaudet in 1987. The most celebrated players from this era were Shannon D. Simon (BS 1992), Todd Silvestri (BS 1992), and James Segala (BS 1993). All three have been inducted into the Gallaudet Athletics Hall of Fame.

Lee could be very persuasive in pursuit of his goals, and this determination paid off in his attempt to obtain a statue for the front of the Field House. Lee had passed the statue several times on his way to Dulles Airport in Virginia, and he wanted it on campus as a physical representation of Gallaudet's mascot, the bison. Ben Williams, a sculptor in Montana created the bison and sold it to the founder and president of J. W. Kaempfer Company, a Washington-area real estate developer. Kaempfer placed it in front of an office building near the Theodore Roosevelt Bridge in Rosslyn, Virginia, which is where Lee had seen it. Lee put his persua-

Former coaches Bob Westermann (*left*) and Richard Pelletier (*right*) with Shannon D. Simon during the 2009 Gallaudet Athletics Hall of Fame induction ceremony.

Former Gallaudet football coach Bob Westermann congratulates Todd Silvestri at his 2009 induction into the Gallaudet Athletics Hall of Fame.

JAMES SEGALA

James Segala was inducted into the Gallaudet Athletics Hall of Fame in 2010. In his speech, he said, "I was about to quit my first year because it was such a culture shock. . . . I was never taught sign language before I came to Gallaudet. It was hard for me to come to Gallaudet." But, he added, "I wanted to come here to be the best quarterback in Gallaudet history and also help the program win games." As quarterback of the football team, Segala "led the Gallaudet football program to back-to-back Atlantic Collegiate Football Conference (ACFC) championships in 1988 and 1989. His sophomore year (1987) he ranked seventh in NCAA Division III football for passing and was eleventh in '88 as he was named ACFC Offensive Player of the Year. The four-year starter at quarterback finished his senior year in 1989 with 1,770 passing yards to go with seventeen touchdowns. He was also a star on the diamond where he played four years for the Bison baseball program."[40]

Bob Westermann (*left*) and Gallaudet Director of Athletics Michael Weinstock (*right*) congratulate Jimmy Segala on his 2010 induction into the Gallaudet Athletics Hall of Fame. All Hall of Fame photographs by Matthew Kohashi, courtesy of Gallaudet Athletics.

The Bison statue acquired by President Jerry C. Lee stands in front of the Field House complex. Photograph circa 1986.

sive powers to work and convinced Kaempfer to lend the bison to Gallaudet. Several years later, the college bought the statue outright.[41]

Lee's most important accomplishment as president was to gain university status for the college. He worked with Republican Senator Lowell Weicker of Connecticut, who introduced the original bill in November 1985. Gallaudet provided information concerning the college's size, complexity, and national mission that would justify renaming it Gallaudet University. The law that eventually emerged from the House and Senate committees, the Education of the Deaf Act (EDA), integrated MSSD and KDES into the corporate structure of Gallaudet University, so that all parts of the Institution would henceforth be authorized by a single piece of legislation. The law also reauthorized

Senator Lowell Weicker, Jr. (*left*), pictured here with Jerry Lee in 1986, was instrumental in securing passage of the legislation that granted university status to Gallaudet.

the NTID and established an endowment plan for both institutions that provided for federal matching of privately raised funds. Finally, the EDA authorized the creation of a National Commission on Education of the Deaf (COED) that was to report to the Congress in two years.

Upon signing the EDA on August 4, 1986, President Ronald Reagan made the following statement:

I have today signed S. 1874, the Education of the Deaf Act. S. 1874 reestablishes Gallaudet College as Gallaudet University and authorizes both the university and the National Technical Institute for the Deaf through fiscal year 1991. Gallaudet, the National Technical Institute for the Deaf, and their related institutions are important components in the educational service system for the deaf in this country. The contributions of both institutions are well known and are a source of great pride for all of us.[42]

In 1987, only three years after his appointment as president, Lee announced that he was leaving the university to become a vice president of Bassett Industries.[43] At the time of his departure at the end of 1987, the board of trustees established a four-person Central Administration Management Team (CAMT) to manage the university until a new president could be selected. The CAMT consisted of Catherine Ingold, provost; James Barnes, vice president for Administration and Business; Robert Davila, vice president for Pre-College Programs; and Merv Garretson, special assistant to the president.

The Commission on Education of the Deaf

The EDA established the Commission on Education of the Deaf (COED) in 1986 to conduct a major national study of the condition of deaf education. No similar study had been done since the Babbidge Report of 1965. Frank Bowe (MA 1971), a deaf and disability rights activist, teacher, and author, chaired the commission. The COED held hearings and collected information on many different educational programs for deaf students, including Gallaudet, NTID, and the Regional Postsecondary Education Programs for the Deaf. The commission issued requests for reactions to their preliminary findings in the *Federal Register*, and this prompted extensive interest and comments by the general public. Gallaudet prepared detailed responses to a variety of questions and Gallaudet representatives attended all of the hearings held in Washington, DC.[44] Many of the commission's questions focused on the role of Gallaudet in deaf education, especially the contributions made by MSSD and KDES, which had been established to improve the deficiencies identified two decades earlier by the Babbidge Committee. COED asked Gallaudet officials to review drafts of its report, and it became clear that the final report would contain several recommendations with which of the college did not agree.

The COED's final report in February 1988 began with the claim that "the present status of education for persons who are deaf in the United States, is unsatisfactory. Unacceptably so. This is the primary and inescapable conclusion of the Commission on Education of the Deaf."[45] Of the commission's fifty-two recommendations, nine specifically referred to Gallaudet, MSSD, or KDES, and included the following:

1. The Department of Education should have greater oversight of Gallaudet's activities, including research and effectiveness of programs at MSSD and KDES.
2. The Department of Education should evaluate Gallaudet's programs every five years.
3. Gallaudet should limit the enrollment of international students to 10 percent of the total student body, and should charge them higher tuition.
4. Gallaudet should not be permitted to enroll hearing students in baccalaureate programs, a practice begun in 1985.
5. Gallaudet should strengthen its already positive efforts to hire and promote deaf employees to increase the percentage from the current 25 percent.

Dr. Frank Bowe (*third from right*) at a 1988 meeting of the Commission on Education of the Deaf (COED). Eight of the twelve commission members were deaf or hard of hearing. Pat Johanson (*second from right*), the COED staff director, and Robert Mather (*far right*), the staff counsel also are deaf. Johanson later joined the faculty at Gallaudet.

6. Congress should amend the Education of the Deaf Act to require that a majority of Gallaudet's board of trustees members be deaf. [46]

Congressional hearings on the COED report were scheduled for March 21, 1988, and several Gallaudet staff members began to prepare background materials for the new president, who would be expected to testify on the university's behalf.

Choosing a New President

Any consideration of what happened next must include at least a cursory examination of where the Institution stood in 1988. In the three decades since Gallaudet had earned accreditation, it had grown from a small liberal arts college into a modern American university. Enrollment had increased four-fold, and hundreds of additional students attended Gallaudet's demonstration elementary and secondary schools. Thousands more participated in the university's outreach and advocacy programs. The campus had grown from a small collection of Victorian buildings into a major complex of modern structures. As the recipient of more than $50 million in federal funds annually, Gallaudet enjoyed a close relationship with Congress, but congressional expectations about Gallaudet's role in the larger Deaf community were increasing, as was scrutiny by the federal government. Given the prominence Gallaudet had achieved and its location in the nation's capital, its board could no longer take unpopular actions and assume that no one would notice.

Because of the civil rights struggle of the past three decades, the nation as a whole had undergone a transformation as well. African Americans, women, and other minority groups now asserted their rights to equal participation in the country. During the same period, the general public began to recognize that signing Deaf people had a distinct language and culture deserving of the status of an emerging minority group. Gallaudet graduates proved that they could earn advanced degrees and succeed in the professional world, and they also demonstrated their ability to influence governmental bodies. Yet their university had always had hearing male presidents, and deaf people had been confined to mostly nonacademic administrative positions. Under Presidents Merrill and Lee, deaf people began to fill more positions, partly because of the growth in size and complexity of the organization, the creation of more high-level administrative positions, and a larger pool of deaf people with doctorates. In January 1988, Robert Davila was the vice president for Pre-College Programs, I. King Jordan was dean of the College of Liberal Arts, Roslyn Rosen was dean of the College for Continuing Education, and they were not alone. The list included in *Deaf Heritage* contained the names of many deaf persons who had earned doctorates, and a good number of them were Gallaudet alumni and/or faculty and administrators (see box on p. 101).

The list also included the names of twenty-nine additional deaf people who had earned doctorates since 1969 but who had no affiliation with Gallaudet, including the university's current president, T. Alan Hurwitz. Even more deaf people had earned doctorates during the years since 1981.

By 1988, therefore, there was no shortage of deaf people with appropriate credentials and levels of experience, and expectations were high that a deaf person would finally be appointed to the Gallaudet presidency. Moreover, the pool of potential deaf

leaders had broadened at least partly because of the influence of Gallaudet University. In a 1976 study of deaf leaders, William Stokoe, Russ Bernard, and Carol Padden found a demographic shift underway among the leaders of the American Deaf community, such that the younger members of that group increasingly tended to be born deaf, while the older members had been deafened in late childhood or during their teenage years.

If it was once the case, say thirty or forty years ago, that the leaders in the Deaf community were deafened, not deaf, it is quite clear from this study that those who lead tend to be those born deaf or becoming deaf in infancy. And if hard of hearing persons once had roles of importance in the affairs of Deaf Americans, it is not true now. Only one of the 33 [subjects of the study] considers "hard of hearing" a more appropriate description than "deaf" (but this goes with other indications of non-membership in the group considered above). Decibel ratings of loss of hearing, where available, bear out this self-judgment. The . . . [statistics] presented here confirm recent evidence that there is an emerging awareness of and pride in the community and its control of power.[48]

The glue that held the whole group together was American Sign Language and attendance at Gallaudet. According to Alan Crammatte, who was deafened in his teens, "in those days we [late deafened students] were accepted if we were willing to learn sign language and integrate ourselves into the Deaf community. Because we could speak or write fluently in English we could act as go-betweens with the hearing world."[49] By 1988, the increased number of Gallaudet graduates who had been born deaf or early deafened and who had gone on to advanced study had reduced the importance of this symbiotic relationship and broadened the pool of potential leaders.

It was within this context that Gallaudet's board began to search for a new president to replace Jerry C. Lee. We should recall again that the board consisted of three public members, two from the House of Representatives and one from the Senate (all hearing), twelve private members who were

DEAF GALLAUDET ALUMNI, FACULTY, AND ADMINISTRATORS
WITH EARNED DOCTORATES, 1969–1981

Richard Babb
Eugene Bergman
Barbara Brauer
Suleiman Bushnaq
Steven Chough
Edward Corbett
Harvey Corson
Robert Davila
Lawrence Fleischer
Jerome Freeman
Victor Galloway
Emanuel Golden
Harvey Goodstein
Gerilee Gustason
Tom Humphries
Carl Jensema
Richard Johnson
Judith Johnson
I. King Jordan
Barbara Kannapell
Nancy Kensicki
Herbert Mapes
William Marshall
Peter Mba
Betty Miller
Michael Moore
Ronald Nomeland
Malcolm Norwood
Chuzo Okuda

Edwin Parks
Richard Phillips
Curt Robbins
Roslyn Rosen
Robert Sanderson
Ben Schowe
John Schroedel
Larry Stewart
Allen Sussman
Ronald Sutcliffe
Seth Teeteh-Ocloo
Geno Vescovi
Douglas Watson [47]

Robert Davila (*left*), Harvey Jay Corson (*right*), and I. King Jordan (*below*) were among the semifinalists in Gallaudet's search for a new president.

hearing, and four private members who were deaf. The board appointed a search committee of eleven, chaired by alumnus Philip Bravin (BS 1966), a deaf board member and IBM executive. The committee comprised five other board members and five members of the Gallaudet community, representing alumni, students, faculty, and administration. Five out of the total eleven were deaf. The search officially began in October 1987 with an announcement of the position. The qualifications included an earned doctorate and successful administrative experience but not extensive knowledge of deafness or sign language skill; however, those qualifications were considered highly desirable.[50]

Sixty-seven people applied for the position, including nine who were deaf. In January, the search committee interviewed a short list of a dozen candidates and subsequently identified a group of six semifinalists, including three who were deaf: I. King Jordan, Robert Davila (both administrators at Gallaudet), and Harvey Jay Corson (BA 1964), who was the superintendent of the Louisiana School for the Deaf. All three held earned doctorates. The other three semifinalists were Elisabeth Zinser, vice chancellor of the University of North Carolina, Greensboro, and two university presidents. During the selection process, members of the Deaf community, including alumni, made repeated attempts to

Mervin D. Garretson, special assistant to the president, urged the search committee to consider appointing a deaf president to succeed Jerry Lee. Photograph circa 1977.

persuade the board to select a deaf president.[51] The search committee eventually submitted a list of three finalists—Elisabeth Zinser, Harvey Corson, and I. King Jordan.

Some members of the Deaf community suspected that the board, led by Chairwoman Jane Bassett Spilman, had already made up its mind. Merv Garretson, who interacted regularly with Spilman as a member of the CAMT, wrote that

"Spilman pretty much had her mind on the candidate from North Carolina, Elisabeth Zinser, . . . Zinser was highly rated by most of her interviewers, although she could not sign and had no background in deaf education. Spilman demonstrated disgusting insensitivity and I would say, even effrontery, in continually singing the praises of Dr. Zinser, in the presence of Bob Davila,

Students, faculty, staff, and alumni attended a rally on the football field on March 1, 1988, in support of a deaf president.

himself one of the candidates. It was as if he didn't even exist. I had written to both Dr. Lee and Ms. Spilman, urging them to give every consideration to the eventual deaf finalists, Harvey Corson and King Jordan, both with doctorates and years of experience in education."[52]

Nevertheless, hope remained alive that the board would finally do the right thing and select one of the deaf candidates.

The board of trustees notified the Gallaudet community that it would announce its choice for president at its regular meeting scheduled for the first week of March. In the days leading up to the announcement, there was growing excitement on campus and rallies in support of the appointment of a deaf president. The most significant of these events took place at the university's football field on March 1. The idea for the rally had been put forward by a group of recent Gallaudet graduates who came

to be known as the Gallaudet Ducks.[53] Approximately 1,500 people attended the rally, and a number of Deaf leaders from Gallaudet and around the country, including Jack Levesque, B. J. Wood, Jeff Rosen, Gary Olsen, Yerker Andersson, and Roslyn Rosen, addressed the crowd. According to Jack Gannon, "the rally succeeded and it failed. It made believers out of many and made many students realize, perhaps for the first time, that there were qualified deaf leaders ready and eager to take the helm of their university. It failed, however, to make a dent in the thinking of many of the decision makers."[54]

As the board meeting approached, members of the Deaf community from around the country came to Washington in anticipation of either a celebration or something quite different. On the evening of Sunday, March 6, the board announced it had selected Elisabeth Zinser as Gallaudet's seventh president.

CHAPTER 1

DEAF PRESIDENT NOW, MARCH 6–13, 1988

The Gallaudet Board of Trustees met on Sunday, March 6, 1988, at the Mayflower Hotel in downtown Washington, DC, for its final deliberations on the choice of a new president. Suspicions arose on campus because of the off-campus location, which ran contrary to the board's usual practice of meeting in the Edward Miner Gallaudet Building. Students, faculty, staff, alumni, and other concerned individuals began gathering on campus in anticipation of the board's announcement, which was scheduled for eight o'clock P.M. However, around six o'clock, an alumnus and a student stopped by the Public Relations Office to see if there was any news, and there they saw a press release declaring

Gallaudet University Appoints First Woman President. The Board of Trustees is confident that Dr. Elisabeth Ann Zinser will prove to be an effective and innovative leader who will represent Gallaudet University with distinction.[1]

A shocked and angry crowd gathered on Florida Avenue, where speakers began urging them not to give up. At one point, Gary Olsen, executive director of the NAD, suggested that they march to the Mayflower Hotel, a distance of about three miles, to demand an explanation.[2]

When they arrived at the hotel, the hotel manager refused to let them in the lobby. After a while, board chair Jane Bassett Spilman agreed to meet with a few representatives, along with board members Phil Bravin and Judge Thomas Penfield Jackson, on the third floor of the hotel. What happened at this meeting has become the stuff of DPN legend. In particular, some of the deaf participants claim that Spilman made a remark to the effect that deaf people are not able to function in a hearing world. Some of those present claimed that she said it, others that she did not.[3] Because Spilman could not sign, the question hinged to some extent on whether or not her interpreter had presented her comments correctly. But that in itself created an issue in the minds of many deaf people— how was it that the chair of the Gallaudet board did not possess even rudimentary sign language skills? To some, this would appear tantamount to the board chair at Harvard not knowing English.

Whether Spilman actually made this comment or not, the board's action in appointing Zinser was widely interpreted as implying that they believed it. The usual excuse for not installing a deaf president was that deaf people could not communicate effectively with the outside world, especially government officials and potential donors (the

◄ House One, home of the Gallaudet presidents.

The campus as it looked in the late 1980s. The early half of that decade had seen many changes with the renovation and construction of many buildings, including Kendall Demonstration Elementary School, Model Secondary School for the Deaf, the Field House, and the Merrill Learning Center.

inability of a nonsigning hearing person to communicate with deaf people at Gallaudet never seemed to be an issue). Another excuse stated that perhaps deaf people lacked adequate management and organizational skills. The eventual actions of the Deaf community during the DPN protest effectively refuted this prejudice. All that was ever offered in support of Zinser's appointment was that she appeared to be a rising star in American higher education and that the two deaf finalists needed more experience.

Following the small meeting inside the hotel, Spilman addressed the crowd outside, some of whom had already left to march elsewhere in Washington rather than wait any longer for her. This larger meeting did nothing to dispel the anger of the protesters or help to convince them that Zinser was a good choice for president. During the course of the meeting, Spilman was asked if she could sign (answer: no), how long she had been a board member (answer: eight years), and why Zinser was judged more qualified than the two deaf

◀ On March 7, 1988, after a lengthy meeting between DPN representatives and the board of trustees, a large crowd gathered in the Field House. Jane Spilman planned to publicly announce that the board was rejecting the protesters' four demands and the selection of Zinser would stand.

▶ Elisabeth A. Zinser was assistant chancellor at the University of North Carolina Greensboro campus when she applied for the position of president of Gallaudet.

Board of trustees member Philip W. Bravin (*right*) served as an intermediary between student leaders and the trustees. His son Jeffrey (BA 1991, *left*) actively participated in the protests.

finalists to serve as president even though she had no background in deafness and an advanced degree in nursing, a subject not taught at the liberal-arts-oriented Gallaudet University. Spilman did not respond to this last question but indicated her willingness to attend a forum on campus on Monday to discuss this and other questions with the campus community. This forum was then scheduled for 1:30 P.M. in the Field House.

After Spilman spoke, Phil Bravin addressed the group and disclosed that the vote had been ten to four in Zinser's favor. Three deaf members (Bravin, Robert Sanderson, and Frank Sullivan, all alumni) and one hearing member (Laurel Glass) had voted for a deaf candidate.[4] The fourth deaf member, Harvey Corson, was himself a finalist for president and, thus, did not vote. It later became public knowledge that the four votes against Zinser had been for I. King Jordan. None of the three congressional board members, Representatives David Bonior (D-MI), Steve Gunderson (R-WI), and Senator Daniel Inouye (D-HI) were present for the vote.

In the initial press release, the board framed its decision as a win for women's rights, which suggests that the members were fully aware of how the Deaf community would feel about their choice. Presenting it this way, perhaps disingenuously, as support for a different cause and as a way to attract support from women, was also a source of irritation. The hearing board members appear to have had no idea

of the depth of those feelings and the level of opposition that existed to the selection of yet another hearing president.

The protest that evolved during the next week marked a watershed event in the history of Gallaudet, the American, and even the global, Deaf community. It is universally known in the Deaf World as DPN—Deaf President Now. Although much of what transpired during the protest had the feel of spontaneity, there is abundant evidence that the course of the protest was carefully planned and organized to achieve maximum effect, and that its planners, organizers, and leaders were virtually all deaf and either students or alumni of the university.[5]

Closing the Campus

By the morning of Monday, March 7, the protesters had effectively closed the campus. Because Gallaudet's campus is fenced in and has relatively few entry points, the task of closing it is less challenging than would be the case at many other urban campuses.[6] In March of 1988, there were six gates that provided vehicular access; a seventh gate next to the vehicle gate at Seventh Street and Florida Avenue was for pedestrian use only. It takes only a small number of determined people with padlocks and vehicles with flat tires to barricade the campus and severely limit access. If the Gallaudet campus had been similar to that of George Washington University (GWU; also in Washington, DC), the protest might have taken quite a different course. The GWU campus is crossed by several city streets, some of which function as major commuter routes, and their closure would lead to major disruptions of business in the city. At Gallaudet, the campus closing caused relatively little disruption in the surrounding community, and this resulted in little outside pressure being put on metropolitan police to intervene and reopen the campus.

The campus remained closed for business, if not completely closed physically, for the next week, although the barriers were only partly impermeable. One hearing administrator recalls approaching the main gate on Florida Avenue on the first day of the closure and finding it manned by a student he had taught during the previous semester. Suffice it to say that the student had not done well, and the administrator was not allowed through the gate. However, he fell in with a deaf colleague, Herb Rosen (BA 1959), whose wife Roz and son Jeff were heavily involved in the protest, and the two walked around to the gate on Sixth Street, where they entered the campus unimpeded.[7]

Merv Garretson, who had retired officially on March 1, returned to the campus as the protest began. He describes entering the campus with Robert Davila, the other deaf member of the Central Administration Management Team, while the two hearing members, Provost Catherine Ingold and Vice President James Barnes were denied admittance.

Although the campus was closed, Bob and I were permitted access by the students, but not Jim Barnes

and Cathy Ingold who kept trying to get security officers to open the gates, to no avail! They alternatively threatened and cajoled the determined students, who refused to budge. One morning Carol [Garretson] and I stood by and simply stared at Jim and Cathy as they struggled to show their power and authority, now nonexistent and completely squashed by the angry students and their supporters.[8]

In any event, the students manning the barricaded gates, especially the main gate at Eighth Street and Florida Avenue, were not interested in keeping that many people out; instead, they were screening out mostly hearing administrators and especially Elisabeth Zinser. The protesters were particularly intent on keeping Vice President Barnes out of the campus. His support for Zinser was widely believed to be personal as much as it was an indication of devotion to duty. In fact, he had expressed such support in meetings with his staff prior to Zinser's appointment.[9] But, given his responsibility for safety and security and general campus operations, as well as carrying out the directives of the board, he was in effect duty bound to try to keep the campus open and secure Zinser's access to it.

As the week went on, many deaf and hearing people who were sympathetic to the strike began flocking to the campus, including union activist Moe Biller, head of the American Postal Workers Union. Biller attended a rally on Thursday, March 11, to encourage the crowd and to deliver a check for $5,000 from the union as a contribution to the Deaf President Now Fund. In addition, representatives of the news media, including all major television networks, were frequently present and were also readily admitted. In all of this interchange, hearing ASL interpreters played a very important role—they were constantly present with the protesters and are generally credited with helping them to clarify the causes and goals of the protest to representatives of the news media.

The Ducks Wade In

What allowed the protest to gather momentum so quickly and effectively? Gallaudet faculty members

On Monday, March 7, Gallaudet personnel found all of the campus entrances blocked by the students and their cars. Photograph by Yoon K. Lee (BA 1990).

The use of steel bicycle locks on the doors of the academic and administrative buildings barred faculty from holding classes and staff from entering offices, and ensured a full closure of campus. Photograph by Johnston Grindstaff (BA 1987, MS 1991).

▼ John Maucere (class of 1987, *right*) explains to Provost Catherine Ingold (*center*) that all personnel are being denied entrance to campus.

John Christiansen and Sharon Barnartt conducted extensive research on the forces at work during the protest, and they assign a central role in its planning to a group of young alumni known as the "Ducks." The group began with only two deaf people in late 1987 who began to consider what actions would be needed to ensure the selection of a deaf president.

In October the loosely defined fringe group [the Ducks] consisted of only two deeply committed activists. Within a few months, however, six young deaf men had come together to form a close-knit circle. The beginnings of this group were inauspicious enough. From time to time three young deaf couples (including one of the activists) had been getting together for dinner. At one of these dinners, in December, one of the husbands suggested establishing a "men's club" to discuss a variety of "intellectual and political issues and the need for a deaf president." The others agreed this was a good idea, and they invited three other young deaf men to join them early in the new year at a bowling alley in Riverdale, Maryland, for an evening of discussion, bowling, and drinking to see how the men got along together. In the words of one of them, the five men who made it to this gathering (one man could not attend) "hit it off really well." All five of them agreed that the next president of Gallaudet needed to be deaf, but no

concrete plans for future action were developed at this time. They did, however, agree with Mike O'Donnell's suggestion that as a way to provide themselves with an identity, they start calling themselves the "Ducks." O'Donnell said later that he suggested the name Ducks because the group reminded him of a "close-knit family of birds." Individual members of the group would be involved in various activities, but they would also emphasize working together—as a "flock"—to achieve the goals they set for themselves.

The Ducks were James Tucker, Fred Weiner, Paul Singleton, Jeff Rosen, Steve Hlibok, and Mike O'Donnell. [Author's note: Dwight Benedict also was one of the Ducks.] At the time the group was formed Tucker was a graduate student at the University of Maryland who was also teaching in the English Department at Gallaudet. In

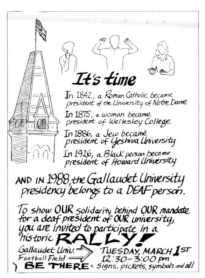

It's time

In 1842, a Roman Catholic became president of the University of Notre Dame

In 1875, a woman became president of Wellesley College

In 1886, a Jew became president of Yeshiva University

In 1926, a Black person became president of Howard University

AND IN 1988, the Gallaudet University presidency belongs to a DEAF person.

To show OUR solidarity behind OUR mandate for a deaf president of OUR university, you are invited to participate in a 'historic RALLY!

Gallaudet Univ. ➡ TUESDAY, MARCH 1ST
Football Field ➡ 12:30 – 3:00 pm
) BE THERE : signs, pickets, symbols and all

The Ducks began planning a rally in support of a deaf president in February. They wrote and distributed a flier to encourage students, faculty, and staff to attend.

Paul Singleton (BA 1981, MA 1989), one of the seven Ducks, served as the opening and closing speaker for the March 1 rally on the football field.

Fred Weiner (BS 1988), another of the Ducks, spoke to a group gathered on the mall during the rally on March 1.

addition, he was working part-time as an academic advisor in the Academic Advising Office. Singleton was a graduate student at Gallaudet and also working part-time in the Student Life Office. O'Donnell, a recent Gallaudet graduate, was the director of the Special Services Office at the U.S. Capitol. Rosen was an Equal Employment Opportunity Commission (EEOC) attorney in Washington, Weiner was a special assistant to the executive director of the NAD, and Hlibok was beginning his career as a stockbroker with Merrill Lynch.[10]

The Ducks organized the March 1 rally on campus that is generally credited with greatly increasing sentiment among students, and in the Deaf community generally, that a deaf president could be appointed in 1988; and they had been working behind the scenes to that purpose for several months. They also organized a candlelight vigil on March 5 outside the campus apartments where the board members were staying. By the beginning of March, the Ducks and other alumni had begun letter writing campaigns to members of Congress, hoping to influence the outcome of the board's presidential selection process.

Prior to the March 1 rally, the Ducks created a flier that introduced one of the "hooks" that drew outsiders to the cause. The flier explicitly stated a connection to a more general civil rights aspect of the deaf president movement and highlighted that it was long past time for Gallaudet to have a deaf person at its head. Jeff Rosen, one of the Ducks, is credited with introducing the phrase "Deaf President Now," which became the rallying cry for the protesters and, ultimately, the name for the entire affair. This phrase, which appeared in signs on the flier, is particularly apt because, in addition to its succinctness and punch in English, it also has visual impact, especially at a

▲ During the rally on March 1, the attendees moved to different areas on the campus. James (Jamie) E. Tucker (BA 1981), another of the Ducks, addressed the crowd in front of Kendall Demonstration Elementary School.

Ducks member Jeff Rosen (BA 1982, *right: center*) and student leader Jerry Covell (BA 1989, *right*) were interviewed by a news reporter after the rally on March 1.

▶ Every night during DPN, a crowd gathered in Hughes Memorial Gymnasium. Ducks member Dwight Benedict (BA 1980) was one of the speakers to address the group.

distance, when signed large in ASL. In particular, completion of the sign for "president" leaves the hands in perfect position for making the downward motion of "now" with great emphasis. The phrase also proved particularly easy for deaf people to teach to nonsigning hearing people.

Members of the Ducks maintained a supportive presence on campus throughout the entire week of the protest. However, the Ducks as well as other alumni leaders wisely stayed in the background during the protest itself and let the student leaders shine through, reinforcing the belief that Gallaudet was continually providing leaders of the highest quality to the American Deaf community. Nothing could have illustrated more clearly to the general public that Gallaudet students possessed well-developed leadership skills and that they were honing them while they were students at the university.

Student Leaders Emerge with Four Demands

During the first few days of the protest, four Gallaudet students emerged as the public faces and "voices" of the protest: Greg Hlibok (Steve Hlibok's brother), Tim Rarus, Bridgetta Bourne, and Jerry Covell. All of them had been involved in the initial marches and rallies that launched the eventual protest, and all had significant experience in Gallaudet's student government. Rarus was the outgoing student body government (SBG) president and Hlibok was his successor. Covell involved himself in raising student interest in the Deaf President Now cause, and Bourne was a convert to it after first supporting the idea of a woman president.[11]

All four of the student leaders had been born deaf, and they all had deaf parents, as did six of the seven Ducks, something that is true of less than 10 percent of deaf people generally.[12] According to Christiansen and Barnartt, "it is primarily within deaf families that American Sign Language and other features of the culture of deaf people are passed on from one generation to the next. Included among the norms and values of this culture are those that emphasize the positive aspects of deafness and the deaf community, do not see deaf people as disabled, and suggest that it is important for deaf people to be actively involved in pursuing their rights and privileges in American society."[13] One thing that these students were certainly not lacking was self-confidence.

On Monday, as the protest began to gather steam, Paul Singleton, one of the Ducks, urged the students to develop a set of written demands for the protest. They initially agreed on three demands directed at the board, and then later added a fourth. Tim Rarus announced the first three demands at a rally on Monday morning. The four demands were as follows:

1. The immediate appointment of a deaf president.
2. The removal of Mrs. Spilman as chair of the board.
3. A 51 percent majority of deaf members on the board.
4. A guarantee of no reprisals against the protesters.[14]

The demand for a deaf majority on the board was not new—both the GUAA and the Commission on Education of the Deaf in its February 1988 report to Congress had made the same recommendation.[15]

At noon, a group of student, faculty, and staff representatives met with the board of trustees to discuss resolving the protest. After several hours, Spilman declared that the board would not change its decision to hire Zinser. When she and other board members eventually met with the campus community in the Field House late in the afternoon, protesters were aware of this decision. Harvey Goodstein, a deaf faculty member, went on stage and asked the audience to walk out. Many walked

out before the meeting had even begun. In another demonstration of "tone-deafness," Spilman complained about the noise when someone pulled a fire alarm in the Field House. The students' obvious response was "What noise?" Once again, Spilman was not able to make a convincing case for appointing Zinser rather than one of the deaf candidates. After the meeting ended, Spilman and the other board members left the campus. It became clear that there would be no immediate settlement of the protest or reopening of the campus.

By now, the protagonists who were to shape the events of the coming week were becoming identifiable. On the side of the protest, these included the four student leaders; alumni, led by GUAA President Gerald "Bummy" Burstein; Deaf community activists, led especially by NAD Executive Director Gary Olsen; other hearing activists, including disability activists; deaf (and some hearing) Gallaudet administrators, faculty, and staff, many of them also alumni. On the side of the board and in support of its decision were Gallaudet administrators, especially Provost Catherine Ingold and Vice President James Barnes; and Gallaudet public relations staff assisted by consultants from the Washington firm of Peabody Fitzpatrick, a firm the board had hired to help "sell" the appointment of Elisabeth Zinser.

Faculty members with tenure could feel relatively free to support the protest without fear of potential consequences, but administrators were duty bound to support the directives of the board. Nevertheless, some deaf administrators decided to side openly with the protesters, risking potential firing if the protest did not succeed. Some hearing administrators chose to remain as neutral as possible, but, as we have seen, administrators with general responsibility for operating the university's programs and maintaining safety and security had little choice other than attempt to keep the campus open and help install Zinser as president as long as she remained the board's choice. One thing is clear—whatever the personal feelings of faculty members may have been, the board received essentially no expressions of support for Zinser

◄ Michael O'Donnell (BA 1984), one of the Ducks, worked at the U.S. Capitol during DPN and was instrumental in obtaining the permit for the Friday, March 11 rally at the Capitol.

▶ On Tuesday, March 8, the student leaders took the stage to address the crowd at Hotchkiss Field. Three of the four leaders are pictured here: Tim Rarus (BA 1988, *left*), Bridgetta Bourne (BA 1989, *signing*), and Jerry Covell (*right, in white shirt*).

from either deaf or hearing faculty.[16] Given that a large part of the job of a university president is to lead the faculty, this lack of support made her eventual installation much more difficult to accomplish.

Interpreters played an important role throughout the protest, and they received a great deal of credit for its eventual success. Many were hearing children of deaf adults (CODAs) and some of their parents were Gallaudet alumni. Brenda Marshall who, along with Susan Newburger (now Karchmer) was co-coordinator of interpreting services during DPN, was the daughter of an alumnus. Given their background, it would be safe to assume that many of the interpreters supported the goals of the protest.

Some hearing staff, including security personnel, demonstrated a certain amount of "tone-deafness" themselves by using walkie-talkies to communicate with each other as the protest wore on. Few physical objects could be more obviously symbolic of hearing oppression to deaf people. Protesters responded to the provocation by assigning deaf people with interpreters to the hearing people with walkie-talkies, so that the radio-transmitted spoken messages could be "overheard" by the protesters.

Tuesday, March 8, was a particularly spectacular early spring day in the nation's capital. It dawned bright and sunny and warmed to a very comfortable temperature during the day—in short, a perfect day

for a demonstration. The protest leaders planned a major rally for the afternoon and opened the campus to maximize participation, including television and newspaper reporters. Several leaders of the various Deaf community and Gallaudet constituencies gave speeches: Allen Sussman for the Gallaudet faculty, Gerald "Bummy" Burstein for the GUAA, Gary Olsen for the NAD, Frank Turk for the Gallaudet staff, and Greg Hlibok for the student leaders. Sussman identified the underlying problem as a patronizing "plantation mentality" on the part of the board and aligned the DPN cause with the civil rights movement. Another expression also appeared at this rally—"We don't want your sympathy"—with the circular action of the sign for "sympathy" exaggerated. Deaf people at Gallaudet were fighting for support and respect, not benevolence and protection.

By the end of the day on Tuesday, a Deaf President Now Council had been formed. It consisted of the four student leaders, three alumni, three members of the staff, three faculty members, and three members from the Deaf community. Its purpose was to provide overall coordination and a central channel for communication in order to present a unified message to the news media and other interested parties. Greg Hlibok became the principal spokesman of the council and the "face" of the protest to the broadcast news media. The DPN Council met regularly throughout the rest of the week.

Attracting Media Attention

Student strikes had been fairly frequent at American colleges and universities during the 1960s and '70s, especially in support of U.S. withdrawal from Viet Nam and generally in support of civil rights and, more specifically, student rights. But protests and campus closures such as what was taking place at Gallaudet were quite unusual in the late 1980s, so media attention was quickly drawn to Kendall Green. The fact that the protest involved the world's only university for deaf people, that the issue appeared to center on fundamental civil rights, and that much of what was going on was communicated in sign language only enhanced and augmented the story as far as the media were concerned. Media attention played a central role in the success of the protest, and it could be argued that it ultimately ensured that success.

An elegant media "hook" had been provided by the logic in the Ducks' rally poster—Catholic colleges have Catholic presidents, women's colleges have women presidents, historically black colleges have African American presidents, and so on. How could it be, then, that Gallaudet, with its rich history stretching back more than a century, had never had a deaf president? By mid-week, news of the protest was airing nightly on the national TV networks, and Ted Koppel of ABC's *Nightline* wanted to do a segment on it. On Wednesday evening, Greg Hlibok, Elisabeth Zinser, and Marlee Matlin, a deaf actress who won an Oscar in 1986 for her performance in *Children of a Lesser God* and received an honorary doctorate from Gallaudet in 1987, appeared on the program. The Gallaudet board evidently declined an invitation to send a representative, so Zinser was on her own. In order to succeed, Hlibok did not actually have to get the better of Zinser, instead he needed to give a coherent account of the DPN position, and he succeeded in this. It also became clear to the television audience that Matlin, who was there to represent the general Deaf community, agreed completely with Hlibok's position—no compromise leading to a Zinser presidency was possible. Deaf people were firmly committed to seeing a

Left to *right:* Gary W. Olsen (BA 1965), GUAA President Gerald "Bummy" Burstein, Dean of Student Life for Pre-College Programs Frank Turk (RA 1952), Professor Allen E. Sussman (BS 1955), and SBG president Greg Hlibok (BA 1989) addressed a large crowd on the campus on Tuesday.

deaf president at Gallaudet "now," and they made their argument clear to the American public. On Friday, March 11, Greg Hlibok was named Person of the Week on the *ABC Evening News* with Peter Jennings.

Politicians Take Notice

By mid-week, it was becoming apparent that an overall strategy was driving the protest. The campus was effectively closed, clear and coherent demands had been published, a strong rationale had been developed as justification for the demand for a deaf president, media attention had been gained, and a multipronged drive for support from a variety of influential constituencies had been launched. One of the most important of these constituencies resided just a mile from the campus at the U.S. Capitol.

Even before the protest began, the board of trustees received letters from very influential politicians, including Vice President George H. W. Bush and Senator Bob Dole. In fact, the letters from these two contestants for the Republican presidential nomination had arrived before the board had selected Zinser, and they were intended to influence the board to choose a deaf candidate.

WE   SHALL   OVERCOME.

◄ As media attention and nationwide support for the DPN movement grew, political cartoonists attempted to capture the sentiment felt by many at the time. Cartoon by Mike Keefe for the *Denver Post*, reprinted by permission.

▼ On March 1, 1988, Vice President George H. W. Bush wrote a letter to the Gallaudet Board of Trustees in which he asserted that "Gallaudet has a responsibility to set an example and thus to appoint a President who is not only highly qualified, but who is also deaf."

Dole, who had suffered a devastating and debilitating wound during World War II, was a particularly strong advocate for disability rights. These two letters were among many sent to the board by political leaders before the presidential selection was made, along with letters from numerous organizations, including the NAD. Although these letters arrived before the protest began, they contributed to the board's understanding of how isolated it had become as the protest wore on.

Given Gallaudet's proximity to the Capitol, its close historical relationship with the federal government, and its large annual appropriation from Congress, it was natural that the protesters would seek support from members of Congress and their staff. Fred Weiner, one of the Ducks, had spent a year on Capitol Hill and was knowledgeable about congressional affairs. So, the protesters quickly set about informing representatives and senators about the issues involved and the goals they sought to accomplish. All of the attention coming from the news media ensured that House and Senate members would take notice. Gallaudet's congressional board members had not voted during the selection process that led to Zinser's appointment, and they were not accustomed to taking an active

One of Gallaudet's strong advocates, Congressman David E. Bonior (honorary degree 1984) of Michigan, served as a trustee from 1979 to 2001, and was commencement speaker in 2001. During DPN, Bonior publicly announced his support of the protesters on March 9, 1988. Photograph 1984.

Congressman Steve Gunderson of Wisconsin publicly announced his support of the DPN protest on March 11, 1988, stating, "You have sensitized our nation to the hopes and dreams of not only the hearing-impaired but all handicapped."

role in the university's internal affairs, preferring to act in a supportive role. However, as the protest evolved, they could not remain outside the fray for long. And, once they became involved, Gallaudet's board had to respond to their concerns because of the university's reliance on federal funding.

Student and alumni groups began to meet with members of Congress, including Gallaudet board members David Bonior (D-MI) and Steve Gunderson (R-WI). Bonior remembers

it was mid-morning on Wednesday, March 9, 1988. There were about fourteen of us gathered in my office. Something big was happening.

The previous Monday, Gallaudet University students had staged a lock-out [Bonior was a strong union supporter] on the campus and were refusing to allow entry until there was a deaf president at Gallaudet. I had asked Jack Gannon to put together a group of people, most of whom were from the Gallaudet faculty, staff, student body, and administration, to talk with me about the Board of Trustees' Sunday decision to appoint a hearing person to be the university's next president.

The mood in my office was simultaneously electric and sober. This was not a group of immature, sensation-seeking teenagers. They were clear-eyed students and professionals. The professionals in the group included a former dean, PhDs, teachers, and alumni, all deaf, who had devoted many years to Gallaudet. They had been instrumental in creating the educational excellence we have all come to expect from the world's only accredited liberal arts university of the deaf.

As their story unfolded, I became overwhelmed by the passion with which they spoke, the depth of their

feeling, and the strength of their resolve to see a deaf president at Gallaudet.

This was a symbolic "coming of age" for deaf and hearing-impaired people the world over. It was bigger than just Gallaudet, or the Board of Trustees, or those of us gathered in my office. It was bigger than just this moment in time.

Gallaudet has long been a Mecca for deaf and hearing-impaired people. The world deaf community looks to Gallaudet for leadership for innovation, for hope, and inspiration. If there could not be a deaf president here, at Gallaudet, at this time, then where, and when? There was no turning back. As I listened and watched, I finally understood what the world would come to understand—the Gallaudet students could not lose.[17]

Events Heat Up

Elisabeth Zinser arrived in Washington early on Wednesday, March 9, and was taken straight to the offices of Peabody Fitzpatrick Communication (PFC), the public relations firm hired by the board. Spilman, Catherine Ingold, James Barnes, and representatives from PFC were waiting for her to bring her up to date on the protest and to prepare for a press conference at the National Press Club at noon. Zinser then met with I. King Jordan (one of the deaf finalists) and the four student leaders. Then, she and Jordan joined Spilman at the Press Club, where reporters were waiting. Spilman and Zinser took many questions, and then Jordan got up to speak. During his remarks, he expressed support for Zinser's presidency.[18]

Later Wednesday night, Zinser appeared on *Nightline* with Greg Hlibok and Marlee Matlin. The fact that a major news program such as *Nightline* devoted an entire segment to the DPN protest is an indication of how significant the situation had become. News media across the country carried stories about the protest and the students' demands, and these helped to shape public opinion. It is quite possible that the *Nightline* experience helped to convince Zinser that she could not serve successfully as Gallaudet's president.

Soon after the press conference, Jordan began receiving phone calls from people all over the country, and he started to have second thoughts about his remarks. He had been at Gallaudet a long time—he received his bachelor's degree in 1970, left to get a PhD in psychology at the University of Tennessee, and returned as a faculty member in the psychology department. In 1983, Jordan became chair of the Psychology Department, and in 1986, he was appointed dean of the College of Arts and Sciences.

On Thursday, March 10, Jordan attended a rally on the Gallaudet campus and announced that though he recognized the board's authority to appoint a president, he personally was angry about its choice. More specifically, he declared that he now supported all four of the student demands.[19]

WHY DID KING JORDAN CHANGE HIS MIND?

John Christiansen and Sharon Barnartt, in their analysis of the Deaf President Now! events concluded that

the two people who had the most influence on Jordan as he was agonizing over what to do were his wife [Linda] and Edward Merrill . . . Merrill called Jordan from his home in North Carolina, and the two of them had a long talk on the TDD [Telecommunication Device for the Deaf]. Jordan said Merrill told him to follow his conscience, to "listen to your heart." Merrill also advised Jordan to "come out with a statement that really reflected his convictions [and], if he felt that the president of Gallaudet should be deaf, to say so. . . . Don't ever say anything you don't really believe."

In the final analysis, Jordan, like many others on campus, seemed to misread what was happening at Gallaudet and around the country and did not perceive the depth and breadth of discontent being expressed by hundreds, even thousands, of people. When he later realized, in his words, that the protest had become a civil rights movement, he began to see things in a different light. By Thursday he also began to feel that there was a good chance the protest might succeed and that the

board of trustees would have to admit it had made a mistake.

After he made his comments in front of Chapel Hall, Jordan felt there was no chance he would become president of Gallaudet. In fact, he said later he felt his "chances were gone forever." He also thought he would probably have to step down as dean after announcing his support for the protesters.[20]

AUTHOR'S NOTE. As a Gallaudet administrator who served under Jordan during his entire presidency, I would add that King Jordan is a person who believes strongly in the rule of law, and his first instinct would generally have been to support the legally installed governance structure of the university, so his decision to support the protest was quite likely a difficult one personally. As we will see in the next chapter, this instinct may help to explain his actions in a similar situation eighteen years later, with much more problematic results.

PHOTO 21 Senator Tom Harkin from Iowa is a lifelong advocate of the deaf community. In 1988, Harkin was chair of the Subcommittee on the Handicapped, and on March 1 he sent a letter to the board urging the selection of a deaf president. Photograph 1988.

On Thursday, March 10, Dean I. King Jordan (BA 1970) announced his support of the protesters and their list of demands in front of Chapel Hall. His wife Linda held his notes for him. Photograph by Yoon K. Lee.

On Friday morning, March 11, Elisabeth Zinser (*left*) formally announced her resignation at a press conference. She was accompanied by Jane Spilman (*center*) and Kenneth Parkinson (*right*), the university's lawyer.

Later Thursday evening Elisabeth Zinser decided to decline her appointment as president, but this did not become known until early Friday, March 11. In remarks concerning her reasons for withdrawing, Zinser said that she had come to understand that "[The Gallaudet presidency] was also a symbol of the social stature of deaf individuals. I knew that this was not an ordinary situation." She went on to say that "if this had not been such a monumental event in the history of the deaf culture, I might have put the restoration of order first."[21] Elisabeth Zinser never set foot on the Gallaudet campus as the president-elect of the university. She eventually came to be much appreciated by the Deaf community because of the grace with which she withdrew and the speed with which she came to understand the historic nature of the occasion and the significance of the Gallaudet presidency to the Deaf community.

The March to the Capitol

On Friday, March 11, the protesters once again had a great day for a significant demonstration, an afternoon march to the Capitol. By now they were aware that one of their demands had been partially met—Elisabeth Zinser had resigned, clearing the way for the appointment of a deaf president, assuming the board itself had by now received and

understood the message. But the protesters were intent upon keeping the pressure firmly on the board until it agreed to the rest of the demands.

When the marchers arrived at the Capitol, Representative Steve Gunderson (one of the congressional board members) told them, "If this is your march on Selma, I want to congratulate you on your successful arrival." During the rally, Robert Silverstein read a letter from Senator Tom Harkin (D-Iowa) congratulating the students and calling them "my heroes." Senator Harkin, who had a deaf brother and knows sign language, is a longtime supporter of the university. Another speaker sent supportive remarks from Senator Lowell Weicker of Connecticut, one of the sponsors of the Education of the Deaf Act.[22]

On Saturday, March 12, the students and their supporters spent the day celebrating on the campus. Although there were picnics and cookouts, the DPN Council continued to meet during the day. The board of trustees still had not met all of the demands, and the council vowed to continue the protest until that was fully accomplished. Oliver Sacks, the well-known neurologist and nonfiction writer, visited the campus during DPN, and he described the day as follows:

Saturday has a delightful, holiday air about it—it is a day off (some of the students have been working virtually nonstop from the first demonstration on Sunday evening), and a day for cookouts on the campus. But

◀ DPN's four student leaders, (*l. to r.*) Tim Rarus, Bridgetta Bourne, Greg Hlibok, and Jerry Covell, walked at the head of the crowd during the march to the Capitol on Friday.

▼ Leaving campus from the main gate, the DPN marchers made their way south on 8th Street NE. It took them about two hours to arrive at the Capitol. Supporters came out to cheer, wave, and even join the march.

▼▼ Friday's march drew approximately 3,000 participants from all over the United States, who then gathered at the front of the Capitol building.

even here the issues are not forgotten. The very names of the foods have a satirical edge: the choice lies between "Spilman dogs" and "Board burgers." The campus is festive now that students and schoolchildren from a score of other states have come in. . . . There has also been an influx of deaf artists from all over, some coming to document and celebrate this unique event in the history of the deaf.[23]

By the time the board met on Sunday, March 13, it found the vice president of the United States, many members of Congress, virtually the entire American Deaf community, and much of the American public allied against it. Elisabeth Zinser, their first choice for president had resigned and gone home. Even the weather gods seemed to have blessed the protest, serving up day after splendid day, each of them ideal for outdoor activities, including marches and demonstrations. Most people who serve on university boards of trustees do so out of a sense of civic responsibility and to serve

the public interest. In most cases, they probably also enjoy some degree of enhancement of their personal reputations as a result of their service. Rarely do they expect to face the type of nightmare situation that had evolved at Gallaudet. Not only were the board members' reputations not being enhanced, they were being vilified in the national media. By the time they began returning to Washington, the selection of a deaf president had become pretty much a fait accompli. The remaining question concerned whom they would pick.

The Board Acts

During the day on Sunday, March 13, the board met at the Embassy Row Hotel in downtown Washington and agreed to all four of the demands. Around 7:40 that evening, Phil Bravin called the alumni office on a TDD and asked to talk to Greg Hlibok. Students ran out of the Ole Jim to find Hlibok since Bravin refused to talk to anyone else. Though the press was waiting for news in the hotel lobby, Bravin insisted on talking to the students at Gallaudet first. Once Hlibok returned to the Ole Jim, he and Bravin had a long conversation on the TDD (see box) that began with Bravin asking Hlibok to name his siblings just to be sure he was actually talking to Hlibok.

Following his conversation with Greg Hlibok, Bravin announced to the press that he was now the first deaf chair of the Gallaudet University Board of Trustees. He then introduced Jane Bassett Spilman, who said that she was resigning from the board so as to remove any obstacle that might be created by her continued service. Finally, Bravin told the world that I. King Jordan had been appointed the first deaf president of Gallaudet.

At a second press conference that evening, Bravin presented Jordan to the crowd waiting outside the hotel. In sign and speech, Jordan told them,

I am thrilled to accept the invitation of the Board of Trustees to become the president of Gallaudet University. This is a historic moment for deaf people around the

THE BOARD ANNOUNCES A NEW PRESIDENT

The conversation between Phil Bravin and Greg Hlibok is repeated in full here because it illustrates so much about the Deaf community—the importance of interpersonal relationships within the community and the significance of direct communication among its members. While Bravin and Hlibok typed back and forth to each other, people in the crowd at Ole Jim who could see the screen raised their hands and signed to the rest of the group so everyone would know what was being said.

Bravin (typing): I WISH TO ANNOUNCE THE SELECTION OF I. KING JORDAN OF GALLAUDET AS THE NEW PRESIDENT   JANE BASSETT SPILMAN RESIGNED (bedlam broke loose among the Ole Jim crowd causing static) TASK FORCE ON COMPOSITION OF DEAF PEOPLE AND NO REPRISALS   GA

Hlibok (typing): WONDERFUL   WANT TO BE SURE   JORDAN IS PERMANENT OR INTERIM   QQ   GA

Bravin: PERMANENT   GA

On learning this news the crowd in Ole Jim let out another roar causing more static on the TDD. "Quiet! Quiet!" commanded Hlibok.

Hlibok: WHO IS CHAIR OF BOARD NOW   Q   GA

Bravin: I AM   GA

More shouting! "Quiet! Quiet!" people in the crowd reminded each other.

Hlibok: SPILMAN RESIGNED AS BOARD CHAIR OR AS MEMBER Q   GA

Bravin: BOTH   GA

Another uproar from the onlookers. More static on the TDD.

Hlibok: TIME FRAME FOR TASK FORCE   Q   GA

Bravin: WORKING ON IT AND WILL APPOINT MEMBERS TOMORROW WILL ANNOUNCE IT TOMORROW   GA

Hlibok: IF YOU HAVE TIME ARE YOU WILLING TO MEET ME ASAP   Q   GA

Bravin: WILL MAKE PRESS ANNOUNCE-MENT AFTER THIS   GA (It was 7:52 p.m.)

Hlibok: THANKS APPRECIATE IT LAST QUESTION WHAT WILL BE MAKE UP OF TASK FORCE   QQ   GA

Bravin: (Static appeared on Bravin's end) REPEAT ALL NUMBERS   GA

Hlibok repeated his question.

Bravin: YET TO BE DETERMINED BUT MAJORITY WILL BE DEAF   GA

Hlibok: GREAT ANYTIME YOU WANT TO SPEAK TO ME SEND SECURITY WE ARE ELATED   GA

Bravin: CORRECT   Q   EVERY-THING WILL BE BACK TO NORMAL [on campus]   Q   GA

Hlibok: YES WE WILL GET EVERYTHING BACK TO NORMAL BUT NEED TO TALK ABOUT THIS AND COUNCIL WILL MEET AFTERWARDS   GA

Bravin: ASKING FOR A PRESS RELEASE ASSUMING ARE THINGS BACK TO NORMAL   Q   GA

Hlibok: YES WE HAVE NO DOUBT THINGS WILL BE BACK TO NORMAL BUT NEED TO TALK FIRST   GA

Bravin: CANNOT BE IN A POSITION TO WAIT FOR YOU   GA

Hlibok put Bravin on hold while he conferred with Jeff Rosen and Jerry Covell, then answered: UNIVER-SITY WILL BE OPEN ON OUR FAITH THAT YOU WILL TALK WITH US ABOUT THE TASK FORCE COMPRISED OF MAJORITY OF DEAF PEOPLE   GA

Bravin: DEAF TRUSTEES RIGHT   Q GA

Hlibok: RIGHT   GA

Bravin: CAN ASSURE YOU OF THIS   GA

Hlibok: HOLD THANK YOU SO HAVE A GOOD EVENING   GA TO SK SK

Bravin: GREG MEET ME AT THE PRESI-DENTS OFFICE AT 9 AM TOMORROW AND UNLOCK EVERYTHING   GA

Hlibok: FINE   GA OR SK

Bravin: SK SK SK[24]

AUTHOR'S NOTE. In 1988, the TDD was the only way for deaf people to have direct conversations over the phone. The machines used only capital letters, and deaf people used the following conventions: Q means that the preceding sentence was a question, GA means "go ahead" and is an indication that the person typing has finished his or her conversational turn, and SK stands for "stop keying" and indicates that the person typing is finished with the conversation. Since the advent of email, instant messaging, texting, and video chats, TDDs are now rarely used.

△ Sunday night, March 13, Phil Bravin held a press conference at the Embassy Row Hotel where he announced that he was the newly elected chair of the board of trustees and that I. King Jordan would be the next president of the university.

▽ After Bravin made his announcement, Jordan addressed the crowd and gave his acceptance speech.

High school students from MSSD also joined the march to the Capitol. MSSD students are pictured here with their Deaf President Now banner on the steps of the Capitol building.

On Sunday night, March 13, one week after the protest began, a crowd gathered in the Field House to see student leaders (l. to r.) Jerry Covell, Tim Rarus, Greg Hlibok, and Bridgetta Bourne formally announce the appointment of I. King Jordan as Gallaudet's new president.

A raucous victory celebration ensued after the crowd learned that the board had agreed to the students' four demands. I. King Jordan (center) and Tim Rarus (right) share a moment of mutual congratulations. Also pictured, Jeff Bravin (left) and Jordan's daughter Heidi.

Sunday's victory celebrations ran long into the night and the following morning. Ducks Fred Weiner and Jamie Tucker (*left*) and students Roger Kraft (BS 1990, MS 1994) and Christy Cummings (Class of 1988) (*right*) were among the celebrants.

world. In this week we can truly say that we, together and united, have overcome our own reluctance to stand for our rights and our full representation. The world has watched the deaf community come of age. We will no longer accept limits on what we can achieve.

And I must give the highest of praise to the students of Gallaudet for showing us exactly how even now one can seize an idea with such force of argument that it becomes a reality.[25]

When Jordan and Bravin arrived at Gallaudet Monday morning, the campus was fully open, cleaned up, and undamaged. Bravin announced that in addition to acceding to the four demands, the board had approved several other actions, including the awarding of honorary doctorates to Jack R. Gannon and William C. Stokoe—two individuals whose contributions to public understanding of the history, language, and culture of deaf people helped to create the climate that made DPN possible. They, along with actor Bernard Bragg, would receive their honors in May at the first Gallaudet commencement presided over by a deaf president.

DPN in Retrospect

The Deaf community at Gallaudet was well organized and well prepared to seize the initiative in March 1988 to achieve the long-cherished goal of seating a deaf person in the president's office. Alumni led the way, but currently enrolled students quickly and ably assumed leadership roles as well. Moreover, the protest was conducted in the best tradition of American civil disobedience—without violence and in accordance with one of the most cherished rights of the American people enshrined in the first amendment to the Constitution, "peaceably to assemble, and to petition the Government for a redress of grievances."

Shortly after Jordan's appointment, new board chair Phil Bravin gave a speech on campus in which he urged hearing faculty and staff not to abandon the university but to use their skills to support President Jordan and help move Gallaudet forward under the leadership of a deaf majority board. Most hearing employees did stay on, but Jordan's appointment also resulted in a shift in hiring policies at the university, particularly for the executive and administrative positions. In response to the criticism by the Commission on Education of the Deaf, the percentage of deaf employees began to rise from the 25 percent noted in COED's report.[27]

Following the success of DPN, the Deaf community at Gallaudet had to confront a very significant question: Was the Deaf community primarily a disability population or a language/cultural minority group? Several national disability groups lent their support to the protest, including the Disabled

SOME OF THE WEEK'S LIGHTER MOMENTS

In *The Week the World Heard Gallaudet*, Jack Gannon assembled some stories he characterizes as "the week's lighter moments," and a few of them are fondly repeated here.[26]

Chuck Buemi, a Gallaudet alumnus, may have earned his spot in history Sunday night, March 6, when the crowd took off for the Mayflower Hotel. Chuck, who is a printer at *The Washington Post,* which is located near the hotel, noticed that the crowd was headed in the wrong direction! He ran to the front and rerouted the group in the right direction and into history.

Students watched as DC police arrived at the Florida Avenue entrance of Gallaudet University on Monday morning, March 7. The officers embarked from their patrol cars, walked around to the trunks, pulled out their loudspeakers, and started shouting commands. After a while observers saw the police officers return to the car trunks, throw the megaphones back, and slam the trunk doors.

A thin young man volunteered his time to serve as a message runner during the height of the protest. At one point he became so tired that he collapsed in exhaustion. A group of concerned persons gathered around him to provide assistance. "Quick! Quick!" said someone in the crowd, "Get Dr. Zinser! Get Dr. Zinser! She has a degree in nursing!"

Howard Busby [an alumnus and Gallaudet administrator] was very pleased with the good turnout at the staff meeting in the Elstad Auditorium on Thursday afternoon. A very important discussion was about to take place when a young college student ran into the auditorium, interrupted him and asked for floor privileges. "Oh, sure," said Howard graciously. The student walked on stage and informed the audience that she had just heard that Dr. Zinser was on her way to the campus in a helicopter. Pandemonium broke loose. Before he fully realized what

During the DPN protest, Metropolitan Police Department (MPD) officers were stationed on Florida Avenue in front of the campus to keep protesters, bystanders, and drivers safe. Some MPD officers even found themselves caught up in the excitement and learned the sign NOW. Photograph by Yoon K. Lee.

had happened, Busby found himself staring at an auditorium full of empty seats.

A reporter asked a student: "Is it true that many board members don't know any signs?"

"Oh, no, not anymore," the student responded. "They all know three signs now—'Deaf President Now! Deaf President Now!'"

AUTHOR'S NOTE. I think I know how the helicopter rumor got started. I had managed to get on campus and was chatting with a couple of deaf colleagues (possibly Mike Moore and Herb Mapes). I joked that I had heard that the board had come up with the clever stratagem of flying Zinser in by helicopter and landing it on the football field. Shortly thereafter, the rumor had swept the campus. Apparently some students "oversaw" the conversation, picked up on the signs and fingerspelling for "helicopter," "Zinser," and "football field," and the rumor was born.

American Veterans (DAV) whose aid had been enlisted by Gallaudet alumnus David Birnbaum. While it was clear that deaf people might benefit from aligning themselves with the disability movement, deaf people in the United States generally resisted the notion that they were handicapped or disabled. Could the Deaf community claim to be both a language minority and a disability group? This question still has not been satisfactorily resolved, but there is considerable evidence that DPN was beneficial to the general American movement for disability rights, especially with respect to the passage of the Americans with Disabilities Act (ADA).[28] This landmark bill was passed overwhelmingly by Congress and signed into law by President George H. W. Bush on July 26, 1990.

Fred Weiner, who was in his late twenties in 1988, captured the feelings of many deaf people when he wrote about DPN five years later. He said that he had hoped to see a deaf person become president of Gallaudet during his lifetime. But in the months leading up to DPN, he wrote that "it was unbearable, this stifling, crushing sense of gloom that pervaded even the heartiest supporter of the deaf president dream. . . . But hope springs eternal."[29] Evidently, at least some deaf people were not certain of the outcome of DPN before events began to unfold.

The clearest symbol of the exhilaration many deaf people felt concerning the outcome of the protest is a lapel button created by Gallaudet alumnus and faculty member Clayton Valli. The button, which began to appear on campus shortly after King Jordan's appointment, comprises the printed expression "PAH!" above an illustration of a cartoon character making the sign that generally represents "success." The whole complex, including the lip movement associated with making the sound PAH, is an ASL sign that is translated as "at last!" In this regard, it is reminiscent of words spoken in Washington by Dr. Martin Luther King, Jr., in 1963: "Free at last! Free at last! Thank God, Almighty, we are free at last!"[30]

The PAH! button, designed by Clayton Valli (MA 1985), declared the success of the Deaf President Now movement.

CHAPTER 5

Deaf Leadership Begins, 1988–2006

On Monday, March 21, just two weeks after becoming president of Gallaudet University, I. King Jordan appeared before a Senate subcommittee to testify on behalf of the university concerning the report of the Commission on Education of the Deaf (COED). His presence at the hearing created a great deal of interest among the news media. Frank Bowe, the commission chairman, gave the opening testimony, which the *New York Times* reported as follows:

"The state of the art in deafness education today at all levels is unsatisfactory," Frank R. Bowe, chairman of the Commission on Education of the Deaf, said in testifying on a report by the commission that made 52 recommendations in educating the deaf. "We still have high school graduates reading below a third-grade level," Mr. Bowe told the Senate Labor and Human Resources Committee's Subcommittee on the Handicapped.[1]

The *Washington Post* also published an extended report on the hearing.

As Gallaudet University students returned to classes yesterday [following spring break], a special congressional commission said the U.S. Department of Education is not doing its job educating deaf people in the United States and called for major changes in government policy and school procedures.

The Department of Education immediately questioned several key recommendations in the 144-page report by the Commission on Education of the Deaf [having to do with the "least restrictive environment" and mainstreaming]. Congress created the commission two years ago to investigate the quality of education of the deaf in the United States and to make recommendations.

Irving King Jordan, Gallaudet's new president, who is deaf, said he had reservations about some commission proposals related to the university. Jordan was added to the witness list after Gallaudet student protests two weeks ago focused attention on the liberal arts school and on issues concerning the deaf. . . .

Jordan said that he had "serious reservations" about some of the recommendations related to Gallaudet, such as the commission's proposal to eliminate federal subsidies for foreign students. He said that would cost the school most of its foreign students.[2]

In fact, the COED report included nine recommendations directed specifically at Gallaudet and its pre-college programs. Most called for some degree of regulation of or restrictions on the university's activities, including the percentage of

◄ Paul Kelly has been the vice president for Administration and Finance since 1988. He is the chief financial officer of Gallaudet University and a senior advisor to the president and board of trustees on all matters related to the fiscal, physical, and personnel resources of the university.

► Ann Davidson-Powell, professor emerita, became interim provost soon after DPN, and she stayed in that position for two years. She then returned to the Department of Biology, where she taught until her retirement. In 2000, she received the Distinguished University Faculty Award. Photograph circa 1989.

international students and the number of deaf members on the board of trustees.[3] Jordan devoted a considerable amount of time early in his administration dealing with these recommendations and positioning himself vis-à-vis the federal government. The congressional feeling of goodwill toward Gallaudet following DPN made Jordan's task somewhat easier, as did the fact that one of the COED recommendations was now moot—the board had begun the process of achieving a deaf majority. A second recommendation to increase the number of deaf employees at the university became one of the major objectives of the Jordan administration. The university also agreed to a third recommendation to end its practice of enrolling small numbers of hearing students in the undergraduate program, with the stipulation that those students already attending Gallaudet could finish their degrees.

On Kendall Green, Jordan acted quickly to make changes in his central administration. Jim Barnes, vice president for Administration and Business, resigned within the first few days of Jordan's administration and was replaced by Paul Kelly, a CPA and attorney. Prior to DPN, Provost Catherine Ingold had accepted the position of president of the American College in Paris and had announced her intention to leave Gallaudet. Ann Davidson-Powell was appointed interim provost, becoming the first African American to hold a

cabinet-level post at Gallaudet. At the time, Davidson-Powell was the dean of Preparatory Programs at the northwest campus.

When Jordan took office, the enrollment in undergraduate programs at Gallaudet was peaking at more than 1,800, as a result of the rubella bulge. Students could choose from a full range of major programs, including those typical of the liberal arts (i.e., history, English, art, math, and psychology), but they could also pursue more technical areas such as computer science and business. Graduate enrollment too had increased during the 1980s to more than 300. Most of the graduate students were hearing and they chose fields such as education, counseling, audiology, and school psychology. Gallaudet had only one doctoral-level program, in educational administration and supervision. One of the hallmarks of the Jordan era was the expansion and diversification of graduate programs. New doctoral-level degrees were offered in clinical psychology, linguistics, education, and audiology. Master's-level programs in social work and Deaf studies also were added.

Enrollment at MSSD and KDES presented more of a problem in 1988. The number of students at MSSD peaked at just over 400 in the early 1980s and then began a steady decline, dropping to just over 300 by 1989. Enrollment at KDES had peaked at 200 during the early 1980s but the decline was less precipitous by the end of the decade. Maintaining or increasing enrollment at all levels of the Institution became an increasingly important issue as time went on.

Relations with the Federal Government

Because of the long-held prejudice that deaf people could not interact successfully with government officials, President Jordan and Chairman of the Board of Trustees Bravin made a concerted effort to develop a positive relationship with Congress and the White House. The fact that many members of Congress had expressed support for DPN and its goals helped them in their quest for continued federal funding. It did not take long for Jordan to make a favorable impression on Congress, as can be seen in the following article from the *Washington Times*:

It was an unusual scene at the congressional budget hearing yesterday: After Gallaudet University's president I. King Jordan testified he was satisfied with the federal funding proposed for the campus next year, a legislator began to grill him on why he wasn't asking for more money.

Such sights are almost unknown on Capitol Hill in an era of tight budgets and perpetual pleas for additional funding.

Mr. Jordan told the committee repeatedly he was satisfied with the budget the administration had recommended for Gallaudet. That position appeared to irk Rep. Joseph Early, Massachusetts Democrat, who said Mr. Jordan could be "twice as aggressive" in pushing for more funding for a new computer system for the campus.

But Mr. Jordan said the university officials are studying the type of system that would be the best for students and the most cost-effective. He promised to come back to the Congress with a request for money to install it. . . . [Author's note. Perhaps it was only coincidence, but a major computer manufacturer whose equipment was under consideration by Gallaudet had its headquarters near Mr. Early's congressional district. Board Chair Phil Bravin also attended the hearing and, as the Gallaudet contingent left the hearing room, he signed to me that he knew that things like this went on in Washington, but he never expected to witness it personally.]

Observers said yesterday's hearing demonstrates the degree of Congressional support for Gallaudet University and the way it is accomplishing its mission as the only liberal arts college for the deaf in the world.

"Gallaudet has terrific support on the committee and in the Congress," said Rep. Steny Hoyer, Maryland Democrat and a member of the appropriations panel that reviewed the university's budget yesterday. The budget "will remain pretty close" to the way it is now, he predicted.[4]

Five years later, things had changed in Washington. The budget deficit had continued to expand, and the Republican Party had gained control of the House of Representatives for the first time in forty years. Despite these changes, Gallaudet continued to receive favorable treatment in congressional appropriations, as the following report on the budget hearings illustrates.

Still, the outlook for the 1996 budget, which should be decided in the fall, is less optimistic, especially for Howard [University]. Gallaudet, which receives about $80 million a year, is less vulnerable because it has a reputation for solid management, congressional staff members said.

Legislators, including Rep. John Edward Porter, chairman of the House appropriations subcommittee on education, said some cuts should be expected for both schools, although how much is unclear.

"I think the subcommittee is very supportive, has been supportive and will be supportive," said Porter (R-Ill.). "On the other hand, we do have a very difficult budget allocation that we must meet, and I think that any program, department or line item under our jurisdiction has to contribute to helping bring the budget into balance."[5]

The wrangling over the budget between Democrats and Republicans eventually led to government shutdowns in late 1995 and early 1996, but Gallaudet weathered the crisis with only minimal disruption.

A major event in the history of the Gallaudet alumni community and the Deaf community occurred in 1989 when President George H. W.

Gary Malkowski was awarded an honorary degree from Gallaudet in 2011. He was a Member of the Provincial Parliament in Ontario, Canada, from 1990 to 1995. He is now a special advisor to the president of the Canadian Hearing Society.

Yerker Andersson, professor emeritus, came to the United States in 1955 to study at Gallaudet College. During his long career at Gallaudet (1964–1996) he taught in the Department of Sociology and Social Work and in the Department of Deaf Studies. He received the Distinguished University Faculty Award in 1992.

Wilma Newhoudt-Druchen was raised in Cape Town, South Africa, and came to the United States in 1988 to study at Gallaudet. She has served as a member of the South African Parliament since 1999. In 2011, Newhoudt-Druchen was elected vice president of the World Federation of the Deaf.

Bush appointed Dr. Robert R. Davila, Gallaudet's vice president for Pre-College Programs, to the position of assistant secretary for the Office of Special Education and Rehabilitative Services (OSERS) in the U.S. Department of Education. Davila grew up in Southern California, the son of Mexican farmworkers. He attended the California School for the Deaf in Berkeley and then Gallaudet College. He had risen from teacher to administrator, and his appointment gave him the highest position ever held by a deaf person in the federal government. As assistant secretary of OSERS, Davila had control of a multimillion-dollar budget in support of special education programs, and he also became the chief executive branch oversight officer for Gallaudet. However, ethics rules required that he recuse himself from matters concerning the university or its programs during his first year in office. At this point in history, Gallaudet alumni occupied what were arguably two of the three most important positions in deaf education, the third being the directorship of the National Technical Institute for the Deaf (NTID).

Assistant Secretary Davila played an important role in shaping government oversight of Gallaudet through the reauthorization of the Education of the Deaf Act (EDA) in 1992. As the chief oversight

officer for Gallaudet, Davila followed Bush administration policy by proposing amendments that would have severely restricted the university's freedom of operation. King Jordan successfully opposed several of the proposed restrictions but was unable to prevent congressional adoption of amendments that limited the number of international students at Gallaudet and NTID to 10 percent of their total enrollment. Congress also mandated a surcharge on the international students' tuition. The university pointed out that international students had never exceeded 15 percent of Gallaudet's total enrollment and that, because of marginal cost considerations, any taxpayer subsidization of their education was very small—but to no avail. In addition, the university could point to the substantial contributions Gallaudet's international students had made to the world Deaf community and to their countries of origin. One of these students, Yerker Andersson of Sweden, had a distinguished teaching career at the university and served as president of the World Federation of the Deaf from 1983 to 1995. Two other international alumni went on to win election as legislators in their national or provincial parliaments: Gary Malkowski (BA 1982, MA 1984) from Ontario, Canada, in 1990 and Wilma Newhoudt-Druchen

PHOTO 6 Robert Davila in October 1990.

opportunity, have built yourselves—and in the process, you have built for the rest of us, your fellow citizens of this country and the world—a much better world. You have regiven all of us our hope. Gallaudet is a national treasure. It is fitting, as Dr. [Glenn] Anderson said, that President Lincoln granted your charter, because he understood better than others the sacrifices required to preserve a democracy amid diversity. And ultimately Lincoln gave his life to the cause of renewing our national life. He signed your charter in the midst of the Civil War. He had the vision to see not just farmland and a tiny school, but the fact that we could use education to tear down the walls between us, to touch and improve lives, and lift the spirits of those who, for too long, had been kept down.

Over the years, pioneers have built Gallaudet, sustained by generations of students and faculty

(BA 1992, MA 2005) at the national level in South Africa in 1999. Although subsequent Gallaudet presidents have opposed these restrictions on international students and have succeeded in relaxing them to a degree, they continue in force.

As a political appointee of President Bush, Davila had to resign in 1993 when President Bill Clinton took office. He then became the first deaf headmaster of the New York School for the Deaf in White Plains and the first deaf chief executive officer of NTID. As the head of NTID, he eventually opposed the restrictions on international students imposed by the EDA.

When Iowa Senator Tom Harkin announced the end of his short-lived campaign for the Democratic presidential nomination on May 9, 1992, he chose to do it at Gallaudet as a token of his affection for the university. Another indication of Gallaudet's increasing visibility came when President Bill Clinton spoke at Gallaudet's commencement on May 13, 1994. No U.S. president had visited Gallaudet since Lyndon Baines Johnson attended the commencement in 1966. President Clinton acknowledged that

You students of Gallaudet University who have struggled so mightily, first for simple dignity and then for equal

President Bill Clinton during his address at Gallaudet's 1994 commencement exercises.

committed to the richness and possibility of the deaf community and the fullness of the American dream. This school stands for the renewal that all of America needs today. . . .

I used to say that I still believe in a place called Hope, the little town in which I was born. Today, I say, I know the future of this country will be in good hands because of a place called Gallaudet.

For 125 years young people have believed in themselves, their families, their country, and their future with the courage to dream and the willingness to work to realize those dreams.

You have inspired your President today and a generation. And I say to you, good luck and God speed.[6]

During the 1990s, congressional oversight increasingly focused on Gallaudet's graduation rate, which hovered at or just below 50 percent. Where once this had been seen as an indication of student failure, it now was viewed as indicative of institutional failure. Gallaudet reported a 40 percent undergraduate completion rate in 1990, first to Mr. Natcher, the Democratic chair of the House appropriations subcommittee, then to Mr. Porter, the Republican chair in 1995. This rate assumed that students could take unlimited time to complete a bachelor's degree, and many Gallaudet students did take many years, sometimes leaving for several years and then returning to complete their degrees.[8] In 1997, the Department of Education began to require that all colleges and universities report and publish their graduation rates using a standard formula. According to this method of calculation, only those who took six years or less to complete their degrees could be counted. As a result, Gallaudet's completion rate fell to 25 percent.[9] Gallaudet administrators argued that, given the university's mission of service to the Deaf community, it had to be inclusive in its admissions policies by accepting "at risk" students, while at the same time it had to have a rigorous degree program that some students would fail to complete. However, this argument became increasingly unacceptable to Congress and the Department of Education.

PHOTO 8 *ABC Evening News* anchor Peter Jennings (*center*) exits the commencement stage with I. K. Jordan (*right*) and Phil Bravin (*left*). Photo by Chun Louie in May 1991.

The Deaf Way

Gallaudet asserted its position as the cultural center of the Deaf world during the second year of the Jordan administration when it hosted an international festival celebrating the arts and culture of deaf people. Called "The Deaf Way," the phrase is a translation of an ASL sign emblematic of Deaf culture and reflective of its uniqueness that means "it's the Deaf way of doing things." The sign seems to have come directly from French Sign Language.[10] More than six thousand people from 81 different countries attended the conference and festival in Washington during July 1989. They attended presentations, live artistic performances, films, and art exhibitions. Every night they gathered in the International Deaf Club. Thirteen years later, in July 2002, Gallaudet hosted a similarly successful sequel, known as Deaf Way II. This time more than nine thousand people from 121 countries came to the conference and arts festival.[11]

Diversity Grows on Campus

During Jordan's presidency the percentage of deaf faculty and staff increased markedly. Harvey Jay Corson, an alumnus and finalist in the 1988 presidential search, replaced Ann Davidson-Powell as permanent provost in 1990, becoming the first deaf person to serve as chief academic officer of the university. His appointment signaled a growing trend for deaf people to occupy more and more of the positions of responsibility in the Gallaudet administration and at all levels in the Institution. When Gallaudet reported to the COED in 1987, only 25 percent of the total workforce at the university was deaf, including 18 percent in administrative positions, 34 percent in faculty positions, and 33 percent among the professional staff. By 1996, these numbers had increased to 32 percent of the total, including 31 percent in administrative positions, 36 percent of the faculty, and 41 percent of the professional staff. In 2005, the year in which King Jordan announced his retirement, deaf people held 41 percent of the jobs at Gallaudet: 40 percent of administrators, 44 percent of the faculty, and 51 percent of the professional staff.

The increases in deaf employment are significant in that they occurred at a time when the university was downsizing its entire workforce, a result of declining enrollment after the rubella bulge ended in the 1990s.

Gallaudet had been segregated until the 1950s, with no black students and few students of color in the college or Kendall School between 1905 and 1951. Although there had always been African American employees, including some who were deaf, Kendall School did not have any African American teachers until 1952 when the school became integrated. The first four black instructors hired to teach the African American students were Rubye Frye, Bessie Thornton, Mary E. Phillips, and Robert Robinson, and all were hearing.

By the mid-1990s, African Americans and other minority groups held approximately 10 percent of faculty and administrative positions. Though a significant increase, the percentage was still below the proportion of minorities in the general population. To call attention to racial and multicultural issues at Gallaudet, President Jordan set aside April 15, 1993, as Diversity Day. The university suspended normal operations that day and devoted all of its attention to exploring and discussing issues surrounding race at Gallaudet. Although celebration of racial diversity was the primary focus, there was also open discussion of the impact of differences in gender and sexual orientation. As attention was brought to bear on questions surrounding racial diversity at Gallaudet, employment of individuals from minority groups continued to increase, such that by the end of the Jordan administration, 16 percent of the faculty were members of minority groups, and almost half of these individuals were also deaf. Employment gains among the administrative group were even greater—by 2005, 24 percent were from minority groups, and a third of these were also deaf.

In 1994, Phil Bravin stepped down as chair of the board. Gallaudet alumnus, Dr. Glenn Anderson, a member of the university's board of trustees since 1989 and a professor and researcher at the University of Arkansas at Little Rock became the new chair. He thus became the second deaf person and

More than 6,000 people attended the first Deaf Way conference and festival in July 1989. Entertainers from around the world participated in the opening ceremony.

Greg Hlibok discusses DPN during a panel discussion.

Dancers from various countries delighted festival attendees with their performances.

Many theater companies and individuals performed during the festival, including the Taipei Theater of the Deaf from Taiwan (*left*) and Gyorgy Koltal from Hungary (*right*).

The International Deaf Club tent on Hoy Field served as a gathering place for attendees throughout the conference.

In July 2002, more than 9,700 people from around the world met in Washington, DC, to share their art, research, and languages at Deaf Way II.

▶ The fifteen plenary speakers, including Barbara Brauer (*pictured on the screen*), explored a variety of issues concerning global Deaf communities. Photograph by Ralph Fernandez (BA 1991).

The many performances included My Dream dance company from China (*left*, photograph by Allen Matthews) and Russia's Toys Theatre (*right*, photograph by Dick Moore [class of 1973]).

◀ Works by international deaf artists were on display in eight museums and galleries around Washington, DC. The exhibit at the Millennium Arts Center included "Palm Wine Taper," by Hilary Allumaga of Nigeria.

▶ Chuck Baird, one of four artists in residence, created "Bird of Paradise" as part of his handshape and flower series *Efflorescing*, which was exhibited in the Gallaudet Student Union Building.

"In Search of Adam" by Yuri Chernuha of Russia was part of the exhibit at the Kennedy Center.

DOUGLAS CRAIG: A CAMPUS LEGEND

On a winter night in 1870, Senator Aaron Harrison Cragin of New Hampshire found a deaf African American boy wandering the streets of Washington. The boy apparently did not know his name or where he lived, so Senator Cragin took him to the Columbia Institution. The boy became a ward of the Institution and was given the name Douglas Craig, in honor of abolitionist Frederick Douglass and Senator Cragin. He was a student in the pre-segregation Kendall School until 1879, and, from that time until just before his death in 1936, he worked at the college. He lived on campus for most of that time, except for a period of eight years when he was married.

During his years on campus, Craig held many different jobs, and he was considered a jack-of-all trades. Some of the students dubbed him "Master of Mechanics" because he could fix just about anything. His various tasks at the college included winding the Tower Clock, mowing the grass, carrying students' luggage to their dormitory rooms, passing notes between students, and picking up the mail at the U.S. Post Office near Union Station.[12] He was a much-loved figure at the college, and now, a street on the campus is named in his honor.

In one of his many roles at the college, Douglas Craig carried the campus mail on his bicycle to and from the DC General Post Office. Pictured behind Craig is Diamond, the pet dog of John B. Wight, the college's secretary, supervisor, and business manager. Photograph from the 1890s.

▶ Shortly after his death, a memorial in *The Buff and Blue* described Craig as having "a body of steel, a big heart, a jolly disposition, and a desire to make life more cheerful with those whom he came into contact." This photograph was taken in 1932, four years before his death.

Glenn B. Anderson began his professional career as a Vocational Rehabilitation (VR) counselor in Michigan. In 1989, he was appointed to Gallaudet's Board of Trustees, and he later served as board chair (1994–2006). In 1995, Anderson was inducted into Gallaudet's Athletic Hall of Fame for track and field. More recently, Anderson served on the National Council of Disability (2002–2005). Photo 1993.

first African American to occupy this position. Anderson grew up in Chicago and graduated from Gallaudet in 1968, with a BA in psychology. He earned a master's degree from the University of Arizona and a PhD in rehabilitation counseling from New York University in 1982. He joined the University of Arkansas at Little Rock in 1982.

VIP and Academic Reform

In 1993, the college divided the provost's position into two vice presidencies, one for Academic Affairs and a second for Pre-College Programs. Corson became vice president for Pre-College Programs, but left the university in 1994 to become superintendent of the Kentucky School for the Deaf. His successor was Jane K. Fernandes.

Roslyn Rosen became vice president for Academic Affairs, the university's senior vice president and chief academic officer. Rosen had received her bachelor's (1962) and master's (1964)

degrees from Gallaudet and an EdD (1980) from The Catholic University of America. At the time of her appointment, she was the university's dean of continuing education.

Rosen focused almost immediately on a comprehensive review of the university's academic programs, including some issues raised during the university's 1991 Middle States reaccreditation, process. She appointed a steering committee chaired by John V. Van Cleve, a professor of history, to implement the Vision Implementation Plan (VIP), and they began the review in 1994. The VIP committee presented its final report to the board in February 1995, and some of its findings had direct consequences for certain faculty and programs.

One of the first recommendations to be implemented was the closing of Gallaudet's venerable prep program, which had its roots in the first years of the college. The VIP based its recommendation on the decline in undergraduate enrollment, which had peaked at slightly more than 1,800 between 1988 and 1991 but had fallen to just over 1,400 in 1995. By the fall of 1995, all first-year students were designated as freshmen and they attended classes on the main campus. Gallaudet reassigned the Northwest campus faculty to Kendall Green and then sold the Northwest campus. As required by law, the proceeds from the sale went into the university's endowment.

A second recommendation resulted in the closure of the associate of applied science degree program (AAS) in office systems that had been offered at the Northwest campus. The VIP steering committee concluded that the university would be better served by focusing only on programs at the bachelor's level and above, as these better fulfilled Gallaudet's mission and vision. The Department of Linguistics and Interpreting had previously closed an associate of arts program in interpreting, which meant that there would be no hearing undergraduates enrolled at Gallaudet. In its place, the university approved a master's degree program in interpreting, and, a decade, later a bachelor's-level interpreting program. In 2002, the linguistics department began offering a PhD.

Roslyn Goodstein Rosen began her professional career as a rehabilitation counselor in the U. S. Department of Vocational Rehabilitation (1964–1966). Her tenure at Gallaudet included service as professor in the Department of Administration and Supervision (1981–2004), dean of the College for Continuing Education (1981–1993), and vice president of Academic Affairs (1993–1999). Rosen is currently the director of the National Center on Deafness at California State University, Northridge.

▼ Jane K. Fernandes was the director of the Hawaii Center for the Deaf and the Blind for five years (1990–1995). She came to Gallaudet as vice president for the Clerc Center (1995–2000), and then became provost (2000–2006). She is currently the provost and vice chancellor for Academic Affairs at the University of North Carolina, Asheville.

As a result of a third VIP recommendation, the university closed all but two of its research centers and reassigned the research faculty to appropriate academic departments. In making these changes the university aimed to provide greater integration of research activities with the instructional program and to increase student involvement in research.[13] The two remaining centers, under directors Thomas Allen and Donald Moores, focused their research on the demographics of the deaf student population and on effective educational programs. While the VIP study did result in some program closures, the university expanded its programs into new areas, such as ASL and Deaf studies.

By the late 1990s, many faculty members and students expected the president and the chief academic officer of Gallaudet to be deaf. When Rosen stepped down as vice president in 1999, Jordan re-created the position of provost to administer both the university and its pre-college programs, and he appointed Jane K. Fernandes, the vice president for Pre-College Programs, to the position without a national search. This created a good deal of resentment among the faculty, who generally considered it their prerogative to be involved in the selection of their academic leader. They also questioned her qualifications since her administrative experience at Gallaudet and elsewhere had been at the pre-college level. Fernandes thus began her term as provost with some doubts on the part of the faculty.

Deaf Girls Rule!

Gallaudet had a long history of women participating in intercollegiate sports— women's basketball, for example, dated to the 1890s. However, Title IX of the Education Amendments of 1972 led to improved levels of competition in women's intercollegiate sports generally, and the results for Gallaudet were very positive in the 1990s and 2000s.

During the 1998–1999 college basketball season, the university's women's team won the Capital Athletic Conference regular season championship, the conference tournament championship, and advanced to the "Sweet Sixteen" round of the

▲ (*l.* to *r.*) The 1998–1999 championship team included Therese Rollven (1999), Ronda Jo Miller (2000), Ronda Johnson (2001), Touria Ouahid (BA 2000), and Jenny Cooper (2000).

◄ Gallaudet enjoys a rich history of women's athletics, and another chapter was added by the women's basketball team during the 1998–1999 academic year. Pictured here is #22, Ronda Johnson (2001) with #30, Safeera Khan (1999), as they played against NYU.

NCAA Division III tournament. The team was coached by Kitty Baldridge, the daughter of Paul Baldridge, who had played on Gallaudet's Five Iron Men team in the 1940s. The team's accomplishments attracted attention from the national news media, and two books were written about it. *Deaf Girls Rule!*, edited by Wendy Tiefenbacher, was published by Gallaudet University Press in 2002. Tiefenbacher, an adjunct faculty member, had her documentary photography students record the team's season on film. *On the Green,* campus newsletter, noted that "this striking visual story celebrates the capabilities and accomplishments of two teams, the winning women scholar-athletes and the gifted visual arts students who captured them in images of timeless appeal."[14]

Sportswriter Wayne Coffey also wrote about the team in *Winning Sounds Like This.*[15] An excerpt appeared in the *New York Daily News,* in which Coffey describes "the 1998–99 women's basketball season at Gallaudet University [as] the greatest in school history. It ended with a record of 24–6, just two games shy of the NCAA Division III Final Four. It included a stirring victory over the College of New Jersey, then the No. 2 team in the nation, on its home court in Trenton."[16] In the next round, however, the Bison women lost to Salem State College.

For several years during the 1990s, the university's swimming team was coached by Michelle Poole (BA 1993, *back left*). She was inducted into Gallaudet's Athletics Hall of Fame for her student records in the 50- and 100-yard freestyle and 50-yard butterfly events. With Poole are the Bison team members of 1994–1995.

The 1997 women's volleyball team was the last to be coached by Margaret "Peg" Worthington, who was inducted into Gallaudet's Athletics Hall of Fame in 2008. Pictured here with Worthington are the Bison team members and their assistant coach Patrick O'Brien (BA 1985).

Ronda Jo Miller, the team's star player, played professional basketball in Denmark, joined the training camp of the Washington Mystics, a WNBA team, and later played in the National Women's Basketball League.[17] Touria Ouahid, another outstanding member of the team, played for the Swedish and American Deaflympics teams.[18]

Building the Campus and the Endowment

Private fundraising developed into a particular priority for President Jordan as federal funding became increasingly hard to obtain. He also worked hard to overcome the perception that a deaf president would not be able to interact productively with potential donors who were hearing. Private fundraising at Gallaudet took off during Jordan's presidency, and the university's endowment increased from $10 million to $165 million. By 2005, income from invested endowment funds exceeded $4 million annually, more than the total value of Gallaudet's endowment principal in 1985. Federal funding also continued to increase, such that by 2005 the annual appropriation for current operations stood at $103.6 million, with the total operating budget equaling $150.1 million.[19]

During Jordan's presidency, Gallaudet developed an overall strategy to obtain private donations primarily for construction and endowments and to get support for inflationary increases and limited program expansions from the federal government and from tuition and fees charged to students. This strategy enabled the university to continue to grow and expand its programs and maintain its physical facilities.

Gallaudet alumni leaders, including Alan B. Crammatte, had long advocated for the construction of a conference center on campus, and the concept of such a center had appeared in previous Gallaudet facilities master plans. In 1994, the university successfully applied to the Kellogg Foundation for a grant to fund construction of a conference center, and for the first time, Gallaudet created a building without federal money.

The design of the Gallaudet University Kellogg Conference Hotel was based on the concept of barrier-free communication, with spacious and well-lit meeting rooms. When the building opened in 1995, it included a tiered classroom, a video-conferencing auditorium, and a multimedia executive boardroom with full visual communication accessibility. The conference center also provides equipment for real-time captioning and wireless amplification. The auditorium and ballroom are equipped with translation booths, and front and rear projector HD screens, and the hotel rooms have flashing-light doorbells and Sorenson videophone.

The university launched its first capital campaign in 1997, with the goal of raising $30 million for scholarships, endowments, academic programs, and a new state-of-the-art student academic center (SAC). The campaign surpassed this goal, eventually raising $39 million, of which about one third supported a major renovation and expansion of the student union building, or SAC, which was later renamed the I. King Jordan Student Academic Center (JSAC). This building incorporated many high-tech and visually rich features, including the Harkin Computer Lab, named in honor of Senator Tom Harkin and his family. The Washburn Arts Building also was renovated to include a new gallery space. The gallery

The Gallaudet University Kellogg Conference Hotel opened its doors in April 1995. The building boasts a café, a large atrium, hotel rooms, a ballroom, an auditorium, and meeting rooms. All of the guest rooms are ADA compliant, and videophones are available throughout the building.

The auditorium in the Kellogg Conference Hotel can accommodate an audience of 300 people. The auditorium is named for benefactors Bertram and Olive Swindells. The room is equipped with front- and rear-screen projection and equipment for real-time captioning. Photograph by José Garcia, April 20, 2010.

By the late 1980s, Hall Memorial Building no longer met the needs of the campus. A fourth floor was added to the original south and west wings, and north and east wings were added to the building, enclosing the central courtyard. This photograph was taken during the construction between 1991 and 1993.

▶ The atrium of Hall Memorial Building provides natural light via a large skylight, giving students a comfortable place to socialize and study. Photograph 1994.

was later named in honor of the president's wife, Linda Jordan, who spent much of her time as first lady promoting the arts on campus.

The university launched a second capital campaign in 2004 to fund construction of a new building to be named the Sorenson Language and Communication Center (SLCC) after James Lee Sorenson. The Sorenson family of Utah, with which

the university had a partnership to provide video-relay services, made a large gift that the university matched with other privately raised funds.

The design of the SLCC incorporates a visual-centric philosophy of architecture that is called "Deaf Space." A student course on Deaf Space established during the early 2000s with the support of Provost Fernandes and Vice President Kelly, gave

◄ The I. King Jordan Student Academic Center is the hub of student activity on campus. It houses the Career Center, Harkin Digital Learning Center, Campus Activities, Office of Students with Disabilities (OSWD), Rathskellar, Marketplace, post office, and a chapel. Photograph by Ralph Fernandez, 2003.

▶ The Linda K. Jordan Gallery inside the Washburn Arts Building is named in recognition of Mrs. Jordan's long-time support and promotion of the arts on campus.

The interior of the Sorenson Language and Communication Center (SLCC) was designed following the design principles of "Deaf-Space." The central atrium reflects these principles with rounded corners, large windows, muted colors, and lack of visual barriers, all of which optimize lines of sight and natural lighting. Photograph by John T. Consoli, July 16, 2009.

undergraduate and graduate students an opportunity to participate in the development of innovative designs appropriate for Deaf people. Ben Bahan and other professors in the Deaf Studies Department, and Hansel Bauman, the campus architect, taught the course. Bahan and Bauman believe that the application of Deaf Space principles to the design of the SLCC

reflects a Gallaudet University commitment to an inclusive process that stands to significantly change the way new campus facilities are conceived. Drawing upon the wisdom and insights of Deaf people and the future Deaf inhabitants of the building, this approach aims to create an aesthetic that emerges out of the unique ways Deaf people inhabit the world.[20]

Tragedy Strikes the Campus

The new millennium opened ominously on Kendall Green. On September 28, 2000, Eric Plunkett, a Gallaudet freshman, was found murdered in his dorm room in Cogswell Hall. Plunkett was openly gay, and some people on campus at first believed that the murder might have been a hate crime. In response, the university set about trying to improve the campus climate. Metropolitan police, however, arrested another student with whom Plunkett had had an altercation that had nothing to do with anti-gay violence. The student was quickly released by the U.S. Attorney's office for lack of evidence, but he was made persona non grata on campus and returned home, still under suspicion by the police. Shockingly, on February 2, 2001, a second student, Benjamin Varner, was found murdered, in Cogswell Hall. The student who had been suspected in Plunkett's death was hundreds of miles from Kendall Green at the time of the second murder, so the police opened a new investigation. At this point the FBI intervened and soon found evidence linking a fourth student, Joseph Mesa, to the murders. His motive had apparently been robbery—he had the belongings of both murdered students. He was arrested, tried, and convicted of murder, and is currently serving a life term in prison.

Gallaudet is a small community and it was not prepared for this sort of violence or for the idea that one deaf person might become a serial killer preying on other deaf people. During the period between the first murder and the arrest of Joseph Mesa, the campus was in virtual lockdown, tension was high, and rumors were rampant. These events, of course, received a great deal of attention in the national media, including a lengthy story in *Time* magazine,[21] but this is not the kind of publicity any university wants. President Jordan and Provost Fernandes spent much of their time reassuring students and their distraught parents. Calm eventually returned to the campus and the result was more open discussion of diversity and respect at the university.

Attempts to Stabilize Enrollment

By the end of the 1990s, enrollment had dropped to 1,300, or roughly what it had been before the rubella bulge. Following the tragic events of 2000–2001, the number of undergraduates fell to 1,243 in 2002, despite efforts by President Jordan and Provost Fernandes to shore it up. Jordan and Fernandes introduced a number of initiatives including the admission of small numbers of hearing students

into the bachelor's degree program. The university announced the program in the fall of 2000, and this time it drew media attention and an article in the *Washington Post* titled "Gallaudet to Admit Hearing Freshmen; Number Limited to 2% of Class."[22] Although the plan was to admit only students who were proficient in ASL, the story reported that some deaf undergraduates were not happy with the idea. The university's oversight officers in the Department of Education also expressed reservations about the plan, citing Gallaudet's statement of purpose as set forth in the EDA—"The purpose of Gallaudet University shall be to provide education and training to individuals who are deaf and otherwise to further the education of individuals who are deaf."[23]

In opposing the program, the department pointed to the first part of the purpose statement, and in arguing in its defense, the university pointed to the second. The university pointed out that, to fulfill this purpose, it had been admitting hearing students into its graduate programs for more than a century without opposition from the government; it had previously admitted hearing students into an associate-level program in interpreting; and that it had briefly admitted very small numbers into its bachelor's program during the 1980s. President Jordan had closed this last program at the recommendation of the COED. The university and the Department of Education eventually reached an agreement limiting the enrollment of hearing students to 2 percent (this was later increased to 5 percent) of the undergraduate population and requiring that the hearing students agree to seek careers working with deaf people. The program began in 2001 without any serious problems and continues in operation.

Gallaudet considered a number of factors before deciding to admit hearing students in its bachelor's degree programs. The most significant was the decline in enrollment of deaf students due to demographic changes in the deaf population. These changes included a decline in the numbers of young adults generally; the elimination of several important causes of deafness, including maternal rubella; and a shift in educational placements from residential schools, the traditional source of Gallaudet students, to mainstream programs. Given the emphasis on mainstreaming, it made sense for Gallaudet to be, in effect, creating a "reverse mainstream" program by admitting modest numbers of hearing students into its bachelor's program. In addition, the university periodically received requests from deaf alumni to allow their hearing children to attend their alma mater, not only at the graduate level but also at the undergraduate

level. American higher education has a long tradition of admitting so-called "legacies." The one program for hearing undergraduates that has received strong support from the federal government is the BA program in interpreting established later in the 2000s.

The restrictions placed on the number of international student visas following the attacks of September 11, 2001, also affected enrollment at Gallaudet. The 1996 amendments to the EDA had allowed up to 15 percent of the university's total

GALLAUDET TRADITIONS: SLAB DAY

The stone slabs that dot Kendall Green hold fond memories for Gallaudet alumni. The placing of these small tombstones on the rat burial sites has been an honored tradition that marks a milestone in the lives of preparatory, and now freshmen, students. Months after the Rat Funeral, near the end of their first year, students gather again on Slab Day to hold a procession and a ceremony to place their slab in the ground. As part of this ceremony, a "priest" recites a prayer, and those in attendance light candles around the slab and leave flowers. Although the message carved on each stone varies, it typically contains the class year, the names of the male and female rat buried below the slab, the class motto, and the date the slab is placed.[25]

The class of 1982 engraved the names of their rats and their class motto across the headstone.

Like generations before them, the class of 1993, in their junior year, placed their class slab at their rat burial site.

◄ The slab of the class of 1923 was rediscovered in 2008 by campus staff when an old pine tree was removed from the House One lawn. The slab was reset on the lawn and now rests at the base of a pin oak facing the Gate House. Photograph by Trudy Haselhuhn (BA 1984), August 20, 2008.

enrollment to be international students, but in the fall of 2005 only 140 students (7 percent of the student body) came from other countries.[24]

While efforts to reverse the downward trend in enrollment were not successful, by 2005 the undergraduate enrollment had stabilized at a little more than 1,200. Graduate enrollment also stabilized at about 450. The total enrollment of 1,913 included a substantial number of nondegree continuing education students.

The Alumni Association Thrives

Gallaudet alumni had been particularly active and influential in the Deaf President Now movement. The GUAA became the first national organization to make a cash contribution in support of DPN and the alumni remained involved in the university's affairs during the Jordan administration, expanding their scope by adding new chapters (see chart on page 89) and new activities. In 1988, the GUAA established the Leonard M. Elstad Endowment Fund in honor of the university's third president. The following year the membership, which had reached 5,000, observed the association's centennial and the university's 125th anniversary. As their contributions to these celebrations, they presented an oil portrait of Gallaudet's sixth president, Dr. Jerry C. Lee, painted by deaf artist William B. Sparks, and photographic portraits of Gallaudet's fifth and seventh presidents, Dr. W. Lloyd Johns and Dr. Elisabeth Zinser, to the university. David Peikoff received the GUAA's Century Award, and the association buried a time capsule containing GUAA records and mementos to be opened in 2039. Jack R. Gannon resigned as executive secretary to become special assistant to the president for advocacy; the GUAA appointed Mary Anne Pugin (BA 1971) as his successor.

In 1992, the Laurent Clerc Cultural Fund Committee presented the university with an oil portrait of Gallaudet's eighth president, Dr. I. King Jordan, also painted by William B. Sparks. The GUAA presented the first Pauline "Polly" Peikoff Service to Others Award to Sarah Stiffler Val (BA

1967) and a special citation to recognize and honor Dr. George Detmold, former dean of the university. The GUAA continued to grow through the 1990s, reaching 6,000 members in 1995. In 1994, the Alumni Relations Office became a unit of the university's Division of Institutional Advancement, and the executive secretary's title changed to director of alumni relations and executive director of the GUAA. When David Peikoff, GCAA president (1954–1961), chairman of the Centennial Fund Drive (1961–1964), and one of Gallaudet's most distinguished alumni, died on January 28, 1995, at the age of ninety-four, the Gallaudet Board of Trustees named the university's alumni house the Peikoff Alumni House to honor him and his wife, Polly.

Sam Sonnenstrahl (BA 1979 and G 1984) became director of alumni relations and executive director of GUAA in 2002, and in July of that year, GUAA President Andrew Lange (BA 1983) participated in the Deaf Way II opening program by welcoming the 9,000 registrants. In observance of Gallaudet University's 140th anniversary, the Laurent Clerc Cultural Fund Committee presented replicas of the Gallaudet charters to the university in a ceremony in the Student Academic Center on April 16, 2004. Two large homecoming commemorative activities took place on October 22, 2004—the Gallaudet Alumni Emeriti Club had its inaugural induction ceremony in Chapel Hall with forty alumni from classes between 1944 and 1954. They were honored with medallions for their years of service, loyalty, and support as alumni members for fifty or more years. The second event was the renaming of Ely Auditorium in honor of Andrew J. Foster. In 2005, the Alumni House Maintenance Fund reached $1.2 million. When the university allocated $500,000, the renovation of the Peikoff Alumni House began.[26]

Since the early years of its founding, Gallaudet periodically sent surveys to the alumni to gauge the success of its educational programs. In the spring of 2006, 11,625 alumni received questionnaires and of these 3,921 (or 34 percent) responded. The respondents represented every class from 1938 to 2006; 406 (or 10 percent) had graduated since 1995.

GUAA AWARDS AND FUNDS

Leonard M. Elstad Endowment Fund

The Regina Olson Hughes Fellowship

The Waldo T. and Jean Kelsch Cordano Fellowship

The Gerald "Bummy" Burstein Endowment Fund

The Charles R. Ely and Donald A. Padden Athletic
   Endowment Fund

The David and Pauline "Polly" Peikoff Endowment
   Fund

Donald Alvin Padden (BS 1945) was born in Chicago, IL, in 1922 to deaf parents. As an undergraduate, he played on the famed Five Iron Men basketball team, for which he was later inducted into Gallaudet's Athletics Hall of Fame. Following graduation, he remained at Gallaudet as director and instructor of physical education for male students, and instructor of hygiene. He also worked as a printer for the Washington Post. Padden is married to fellow alumna Agnes Virginia Minor (BA 1947). Photo 1982.

Charles Russell Ely (MA 1892) was born in Columbus, Ohio, in 1870. His father, Charles W. Ely was superintendent of the Maryland School for the Deaf, thus Ely was raised in the deaf community and became a fluent signer. He began working at Gallaudet in 1891 and graduated from the Normal School in 1892. During his tenure he held various positions, including instructor in natural science; assistant professor and professor of chemistry and natural science; and vice president.

Regina Olson Hughes (BA 1918, MA 1920, honorary doctorate 1967) was born in Herman, Nebraska, in 1895. She married alumnus Frederick Hughes in 1923. In 1930, she got a job in the U.S. Department of Agriculture as a research clerk and later became a botanical artist. After retiring in 1969, she continued as an illustrator for the Smithsonian Institution's Department of Botany. In 1981, she received Gallaudet's Amos Kendall Award.

Margaret Jean Kelsch Cordano (BS 1951) was born in Bismarck, ND, in 1928 and attended the North Dakota School for the Deaf. Kelsch began her career as a laboratory technician at a commercial chicken farm. She later became head medical technician at Lakeland Hospital in Elkhorn, WI, and in 1984, she received Gallaudet's Amos Kendall Award. In 1996 the Waldo & Jean Cordano Fellowship was established to support deaf or hard of hearing students pursuing their doctorates.

In general, the findings paralleled the results from earlier surveys. Gallaudet alumni at both the undergraduate and graduate degree levels reported high rates of employment in professional occupations, and a very high proportion, about half, of the deaf bachelor's degree recipients reported earning advanced degrees. These are positive outcomes and suggest that a Gallaudet education carries a very high value.[27]

Through Deaf Eyes

The university expanded its position as a cultural resource and center for the study of Deaf history during the 1990s and 2000s. A central component of this expansion was the development of a traveling exhibit called "History Through Deaf Eyes," along with a PBS documentary and a companion book. The exhibit, developed under the direction of its curator, Jack R. Gannon, and Jean Lindquist

▲ The class of 1946 held their fiftieth reunion during Homecoming 1996. Photograph October 18, 1996.

▶ In 1997, Gallaudet's class of 1947 held their fiftieth reunion during homecoming weekend. Photograph October 1997.

GALLAUDET TRADITIONS: CLASS BANNERS

Dozens of class banners hang from the rafters in Ole Jim, a tradition that has continued for a century. Class banners are a source of pride and showcase each class's unique mark on the university. They often are made of felt and are designed by members of the class using minimal color and simple art and text so that they can be seen and recognized from a distance. The oldest banners in Ole Jim date from 1914 and 1918; the first belonged to Walter Durian (BA 1914) and was donated by his niece Ruby Osmola Durian (class of 1971) in 2010. [28]

Class banners, old and new, hang side-by-side along the walls of the second floor in Ole Jim. By the 1970s, the pennant-style banner had been abandoned in favor of the larger rectangular style. Nevertheless, the use of bright, bold colors and simple design has prevailed, often with a stylized icon of the Tower Clock. Photographs by Carla D. Morris (MA 2011), January 31, 2014.

In 2001, the Smithsonian Institution launched the photographic exhibition *History Through Deaf Eyes* in Hartford, CT. The exhibition pieces represented approximately 200 years of American deaf history. The curators drew extensively from sources held at the Gallaudet University Archives. The exhibit was displayed at the Smithsonian Institution's Arts and Industries Building in Washington, DC, and 12 other cities during a 5-year national tour.

▼ *Through Deaf Eyes: A Photographic History of an American Community* contained more than 200 full-color photographs, previously only viewable in the exhibition or the documentary film.

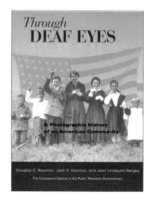

Bergey, with the support of the Smithsonian Institution, toured the United States between 2001 and 2006.

Through Deaf Eyes, the PBS documentary that aired nationwide in March 2007 is filled with stories told in ASL by deaf people, many of them Gallaudet alumni, faculty, and staff. The film tells the story of Deaf life in America while at the same time revealing American history through a Deaf perspective. The hearing filmmakers, WETA in Washington, DC, and Florentine Films/Hott Productions in association with Gallaudet, produced the film with input from six deaf filmmakers: Wayne Betts, Jr., Kimby Caplan, Arthur Luhn, Adrean Mangiardi, Tracey Salaway, and Rene Visco, who brought a Deaf cinematic lens to the documentary. The National Endowment for the Humanities, the Corporation for Public Broadcasting, PBS, the Annenberg Foundation, and the National Endowment for the Arts provided funding for the documentary film with additional funds from Sign Language Associates and Richard and Gail Elden. The companion book, *Through Deaf Eyes: A Photographic History of an American Community,* written by historian Douglas Baynton, Jack R. Gannon, and Jean Lindquist Bergey, was published in 2007 by Gallaudet University Press.

The Search for a New President

In September 2005, I. King Jordan announced that he intended to retire at the end of 2006. It had been almost eighteen years since he assumed Gallaudet's presidency, and much had transpired in the interim. When asked about his most important achievements as president of Gallaudet University, Jordan replied that while it might sound glib, his "most important achievement (singular) was that [he] succeeded."

There were many skeptics who were doubtful that I could succeed and some who were hopeful that I would fail. Had I not been successful, instead of DPN launching a new era in civil rights for deaf and disabled people, there would have been a lot of "I told you so" happening and it would have set back the movement terribly. Some people told me very openly that I wouldn't last, that I wouldn't be able to establish the kinds of relationships and have the kinds of communications with people in Congress and in corporations and foundations that are so necessary for a successful president.

I'm very proud to have been successful. I'm also very strong in reminding people that I was successful because of the tremendous support I received from many people on campus, on the Board, in Congress, in the public and in my family and friends. There were also a lot of people who understood how important it was (for me, for Gallaudet and for deaf people) that I was successful. Their support allowed me to succeed.[29]

Following Jordan's announcement, the board of trustees formed a search committee to identify candidates to succeed him. The committee had seventeen members—two professional staff, two alumni, one undergraduate student, one graduate student, one representative of the Clerc Center (MSSD and KDES), four university faculty, and six members of the board. The board expected to receive a list of finalists and name the new president at its May 2006 meeting. Glenn Anderson, a board member since 1989 and its chair since 1994, announced his resignation from the board on November 3, 2005, so that he could seek the university's presidency. In keeping with the board's bylaws, vice chair and alumna Celia May Baldwin (BA 1970) became acting chair, the first deaf woman to hold that position.

In January 2006, John Hager, the assistant secretary for special education and rehabilitative services, informed President Jordan that the university had received an unfavorable rating of "ineffective" on the Program Assessment Rating Tool (PART). The Office of Management and Budget (OMB) had established PART during the administration of George W. Bush to apply quantitative ratings to programs that received federal funding. OMB's criticism focused on the university's undergraduate persistence and graduation rates and its job placement rate for bachelor-degree recipients at the time of graduation.[30] The university was successful in having the rating changed, arguing that OMB had not taken into account a variety of factors, including the long-term career success of deaf undergraduates that had been documented in numerous alumni surveys. However, the university's reputation had been damaged, and some faculty blamed Provost Jane Fernandes, who was the person responsible for maintaining the quality of programs and reporting the results to the government.[31]

Acting chair of the board of trustees Celia May Baldwin announced the appointment of Provost Jane K. Fernandes (*left*) as Gallaudet's ninth president at an assembly on May 1, 2006, in the Kellogg Conference Hotel. Photograph by Dick Moore, on May 1, 2006.

As a student at Gallaudet, Ronald J. Stern (BA 1973) played basketball. He earned his master's degree from California State University at Northridge, after which he briefly served as Gallaudet's athletic director. Stern was director of instruction at the California School for the Deaf in Fremont for ten years, and he has been superintendent of the New Mexico School for the Deaf since 2000. Photograph by Ralph Fernandez, April 20, 2006.

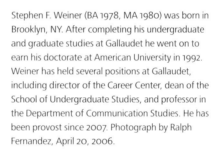

Stephen F. Weiner (BA 1978, MA 1980) was born in Brooklyn, NY. After completing his undergraduate and graduate studies at Gallaudet he went on to earn his doctorate at American University in 1992. Weiner has held several positions at Gallaudet, including director of the Career Center, dean of the School of Undergraduate Studies, and professor in the Department of Communication Studies. He has been provost since 2007. Photograph by Ralph Fernandez, April 20, 2006.

By April 2006 the presidential search committee had narrowed the pool to six individuals and had begun to interview them. Meanwhile, intensive Internet campaigns started on behalf of several candidates, some of which were quite negative. The interactive website known as Gallynet was particularly active in this regard. The search committee then narrowed the field to three finalists and submitted their names to the board in late April. The three finalists were Ronald J. Stern, Stephen Weiner, and Jane Fernandes. Stern was the superintendent of the New Mexico School for the Deaf, and significantly, he did not have a terminal degree, which was one of the requirements for the presidency. He was, however, nearing completion of a doctorate at the University of New Mexico, but he had no administrative experience at the college or university level. Weiner, who did hold a doctorate, was a Gallaudet faculty member and former dean. All three finalists were deaf.

Criticism of the search process began as soon as the list of finalists was announced. Many people on campus, especially African American members of the Gallaudet community, had assumed that Glenn Anderson would be a finalist, so his absence from the final group was particularly surprising. Given that Anderson had a PhD, while Stern did not, made the committee's decision all the more puzzling. Other groups had supported Roslyn Rosen, a former Gallaudet vice president who had a doctorate and considerable administrative experience, but she also was not among the finalists. On May 1, 2006, the board appointed Provost Jane K. Fernandes president-elect. Fernandes had a PhD in comparative literature from the University of Iowa, was deaf from birth, and had a deaf mother. She had been educated in oral environments and had begun to learn ASL when in her twenties, much like King Jordan had. Protests broke out on campus almost immediately after the board made its announcement.

Initially the protests involved primarily African American students who were upset with Glenn Anderson's exclusion from the group of finalists. Later, complaints against Jane Fernandes began to surface, including criticism of her academic leadership, particularly her leadership style, and the fact that some people found her to be aloof. Her oral background and late acquisition of ASL may also have been an issue, but the university public relations office, aided by consultants, seized upon her background as a way to frame their campaign of support for her. The phrase "not Deaf enough," began to be used, especially in the blogs, to suggest that she did not represent the Gallaudet community, but some of the protest leaders opposed framing the protest this way. Increasingly, criticism and complaints against outgoing President Jordan, who actively supported Fernandes, began to surface

as well. The press and general public do not appear to have understood the reasons for the protest, nor was there much support for it outside of the Deaf community, but as the protest wore on, a well-organized campus group identified as FSSA (faculty, students, staff, and alumni) became quite effective at neutralizing the impact of official Gallaudet PR. The group adopted the slogan "Unity for Gallaudet" and maintained that they were seeking social justice against a university that was operating under "management by intimidation."[32]

The protests died down at the end of the 2006 spring semester when students and faculty left the campus, but they picked up again in the fall. This time the protesters closed down the campus, just as had happened during DPN. On October 12, the *Washington Post* reported that

Noah Beckman, president of the student body government, said students will not negotiate. "We will not let the campus go unless Jane Fernandes resigns," he said. For the past week, the demonstrations that rattled the campus in May when Fernandes was named have flared again. What started with opposition to her and the way she was chosen has grown into a far more complicated and consuming standoff that has paralyzed the school during the midterm exam week. And a growing number of people have become annoyed by the continuous disruption of education.

Students and administrators had been in talks late Tuesday to resolve a standoff at a classroom building taken over by students Friday. But football players frustrated by the disruption of classes and by the stalemate decided to try to speed things up, said captain Jason Coleman. He said he was upset about the school's low graduation rates, which have hovered for years around 40 percent, and asked why Fernandes, who has been provost for the past six years, had not been able to change that.[33]

Things finally came to a head on October 13, when DC police tried to reopen the campus by arresting more than one hundred students, faculty, and alumni. Those arrested were soon released, but it became clear that Fernandes would not be able to

The Unity for Gallaudet movement started as a protest by students, faculty, and alumni who did not support the appointment of Jane Fernandes as university president. On the evening of May 1, 2006, students refused to move from the front gate, and the idea for "Tent City" was born. The tents came down during the summer, but by the fall the protest, and the tents, had been revived. Photograph by Ralph Fernandez, October 15, 2006.

A crowd gathered at the front gate on October 29 following the board of trustees' announcement that it would terminate Jane Fernandes's appointment as president. Photograph by Ralph Fernandez, October 29, 2006.

serve effectively as president. It took until October 29, though, for the board of trustees to terminate Fernandes's appointment and restore normal operations. On November 8, Senator John McCain, who was in the midst of launching his 2008 presidential campaign, resigned from the board. Soon after ending Fernandes's appointment, the board began the task of opening a new search for Gallaudet's next president.

Unlike DPN, the 2006 protest did not garner sympathetic news media coverage. An editorial in the *Washington Post* on October 10, 2006, typifies the criticism leveled at the university.

One only has to watch the faces and hands of the students to appreciate the depth of their anger. It is more difficult to discern what is behind that anger. The protest started with complaints that Ms. Fernandes, who attended mainstream schools as a child and learned to sign when she was 23, is not the best choice to lead a school that is a touchstone for the deaf. Then there were charges that the search process was fixed; then, grievances about a lack of racial diversity among the candidates, classes that don't prepare students, and poor graduation rates. Most absurd was the grumbling

that a student center was being named for outgoing President I. King Jordan, who, ironically, became the school's first deaf president because of student protests.

The students who have barricaded themselves behind the walls of Hall Memorial Building say they are acting in the best interests of the university. Tell that to the students who are juggling jobs and school to get a diploma, or to the parents who are sacrificing to widen their children's futures. If the protesters really care about Gallaudet, they will open up the halls to learning and work toward reaching a middle ground. University officials have been willing to make concessions; they agreed, for instance, to an outside review of the search process, only to have the students withdraw that demand. Students could get involved in the search for a new provost or push for a student vote on the board of trustees.

There is no doubt given the bitterness of the controversy that Gallaudet has deep-seated problems. Ms. Fernandes, well qualified in every way, faces an unenviable job. That she still wants to do it should be one reason to give her a chance.[34]

Christopher Krentz, a deaf former Gallaudet employee, who was in 2006 and is still a faculty member at the University of Virginia, watched the events unfold from Charlottesville. "I have to admit," he said, "that the 2006 unrest was hard for me to watch. The protestors too often seemed to have difficulty explaining the reasons for their dissent, which reflected badly on the University as a whole."[35]

Perhaps the most unfortunate aspect of the whole affair was the original search committee's failure to recommend Glenn Anderson as a finalist. He is one of a very small number of deaf African Americans with an earned doctorate and extensive relevant experience, including many years of service as chair of the board. It was, thus, entirely predictable that the black Deaf community would see this omission as an insult, just as the larger Deaf community had viewed Elisabeth Zinser's appointment in this way in 1988. Because the committee members took an oath of secrecy, we will never know how they came to recommend a person with no doctorate or higher education experience as a finalist, but the consulting firm that assisted in the search has been widely criticized for perhaps giving them faulty advice. In the final analysis, though, the protest damaged the university's reputation.

In addition to the protest, Gallaudet was in the midst of a review of its accreditation status by the Middle States Commission on Higher Education (MSCHE). Accreditation reviews are done on a ten-year cycle by a team of peer reviewers, with a midterm review in the fifth year, and Gallaudet's midterm evaluation was due in 2006. This review did not include a site visit; essentially, the university just had to submit a detailed self-study report on its current status, which it did during the summer of 2006. However, as the protest developed and press coverage intensified, MSCHE officials became concerned about a number of issues, including the closure of the campus, the termination of Jane Fernandes's appointment, the university's failure to report the negative PART rating, and the many negative comments about students, faculty, and administrators that appeared in the media and on online sites such as Gallynet. In addition, MSCHE was not satisfied with the strategic planning and student assessment processes described in the periodic report. In November, President Jordan

After completing his master's degree, William J. A. Marshall (MS 1964) began a long and successful career on Kendall Green. He left for a time to earn his doctorate at the University of Illinois, at Champaign-Urbana, after which he worked for several universities and school boards throughout the U.S. In 1976, Marshall returned as the new director and dean of MSSD. In 1979, he became a professor in the Department of Administration and Supervision and he served as department chair from 1986 to 2013. Marshall received the Distinguished University Faculty Award in 1990.

received notification that MSCHE had not accepted the periodic review report, that a new and focused report would be due early in 2007, and that the university would receive a highly unusual site visit by what was described as a "small visiting team." In short, MSCHE made it clear that the university's accreditation might be in jeopardy.

National Search Redux

To start the process of finding a new president once again, the board established the Interim President Selection Advisory Committee (IPSAC) in mid-November 2006. Their plan was to appoint someone on an interim basis before beginning the presumably more difficult task of identifying a permanent president who would be acceptable to all of the various factions that had emerged during the protests. In early December, IPSAC sent the names of three finalists to the board—Robert R. Davila, a semifinalist in 1988; Stephen Weiner, a semifinalist

Robert R. Davila served for ten years as CEO of the National Technical Institute for the Deaf in Rochester, New York (1996–2006). On December 10, 2006, he was named the president of Gallaudet. He took office at the start of 2007. Photograph by John Consoli, January 9, 2007.

from the 2006 search, and William J. A. Marshall, a professor in the Department of Administration and Supervision. On December 10, the board announced that it had selected Davila. Though the board had initially planned for him to serve only one year, it later voted to change his title to president and extend his term to three years. Because Jane Fernandes never took office, Robert R. Davila became the university's ninth president. Three weeks later, I. King Jordan retired after nearly nineteen years as Gallaudet's first deaf president. When Davila arrived in January 2007, he immediately had to prepare for the MSCHE site visit and the crafting of a lengthy report in response to its various concerns.

CHAPTER 6

Reaffirmation and Rebuilding, 2007–2014

The passions surrounding the protests of 2006 seemed to have run their course by the beginning of 2007. All was calm as Robert Davila assumed the presidency on January 2, 2007, and given his history as assistant secretary of education and director of NTID, he was ideally situated to restore confidence in the university. The two most pressing issues facing him were the concerns expressed by the federal government and the Middle States Commission on Higher Education (MSCHE). Under the federal Government Performance and Results Act (GPRA) of 1993, Gallaudet, along with all federally funded agencies, was required to establish a strategic plan with measurable goals or outcomes. Gallaudet had done this, but it had fallen short of several of its goals, which led to the ineffective rating it received in the OMB PART process in 2006. During the campus closure in the fall, a Department of Education official had contacted Gallaudet's liaison officer to ask if the campus was operating. The liaison officer answered yes because some classes were being held. Had the answer been no, the department official would have been obligated to withhold Gallaudet's federal funding.[1]

The MSCHE presented a different and more complex problem. It informed the university that it was sending a small visiting team on January 10 and that Gallaudet would have to submit a supplemental information report to the commission no later than March 1, 2007. This report had to address the following issues:

1. the effectiveness of shared governance, including the presidential search process;
2. nurturance of a climate that fosters respect among students, faculty, staff, and administration for a range of backgrounds, ideas, and perspectives;
3. mission review and implementation of a comprehensive institutional strategic plan;
4. implementation of a comprehensive enrollment management plan that addresses student recruitment, retention, graduation, and placement;
5. evidence of the academic rigor of the degrees offered; and
6. procedures for ensuring that changes and issues affecting the institution are disclosed accurately and in a timely manner to the Commission.

The commission also requested an additional report on Gallaudet's further response to the recommendations from the 2001 MSCHE evaluation team

◄ Chapel Hall windows.

Michael Moore had a long and distinguished career at Gallaudet. In addition to being a professor of chemistry, he served as chair of his department, chair of the Faculty Senate, interim provost, and interim ombuds. He was also vice president of the GUAA. He retired in 2013. Photograph John Consoli, September 20, 2006.

▼ Stephen Weiner has worked in many capacities over the years. He was director of the Career Center, dean of the School of Undergraduate Studies, and a professor in the Department of Communication Studies. He has been the provost since July 2007. Here he is speaking at the hooding ceremony on May 13, 2010. Photograph by Rhea Kennedy.

report and how the university planned to implement a documented, organized, and sustained process to assess the achievement of institutional and program-level student learning goals, including direct evidence of student learning.[2] This monitoring report was due by April 1, 2008.

The MSCHE team visited Gallaudet January 10 to 12 and met with a variety of constituencies, including the trustees, students, faculty, and administrators. During the site visit, the MSCHE team repeatedly told the Gallaudet community that the university had been out of compliance with Middle States' accreditation standards when it closed during the protest. The team's report noted several other problems, including that there was a great deal of fragmentation within Gallaudet regarding its mission and that the shared gover-

nance structure was unclear and possibly ineffective (something MSCHE had mentioned in its 2001 report). It strongly suggested that the various constituencies consider reviewing the mission and that the university should become more active in the Middle State Association and other relevant higher education organizations. Lastly, the team encouraged Gallaudet "to develop a report that [could] be a template for an operational plan for the university over the coming 18–24 months."[3]

By 2006, the factors the MSCHE considered in the accreditation process had changed quite a bit since Gallaudet had first been accredited in 1957. Rather than give weight to institutional inputs such as faculty credentials, the condition of facilities, or the number of volumes held by the library, the standards placed more emphasis on assessment of outputs or outcomes such as student achievement, English literacy, and career preparation. Strategic planning also had increased in importance—institutions were now seen as needing to change and evolve, rather than remain static. According to MSCHE, Gallaudet had weak strategic planning, and it had ignored the 2001 recommendations to improve governance. From the perspective of the Middle States Commission, the board, faculty, administration, and even students all shared the blame for the conditions at Gallaudet.

Davila's first step was to reestablish an academic leadership team. Chemistry professor Michael Moore (BA 1968) agreed to serve as interim provost following Fernandes's departure, and, in doing so, he willingly accepted what he knew would be a very difficult situation. Moore began the process of organizing a campus response to MSCHE, while Davila enlisted support from campus constituencies, including the faculty and student government. Many of these constituents contributed directly to the supplemental information report that had to be submitted to MSCHE in March.

MSCHE scheduled another visit to Gallaudet in May with two members of the January visiting team. After the second visit, the team noted that progress was being made but the university needed to move faster to implement the changes that would

Students regularly gather in the Jordan Student Academic Center (JSAC), both inside the building and on the outside terrace.

bring it into compliance with MSCHE standards. In June the Middle States Commissioners placed Gallaudet on probation and required a second monitoring report in September, with another visit to follow in October. This meant that during the summer of 2007, under the leadership of Stephen Weiner, the new provost, Gallaudet had to make substantial changes in its governance system, its undergraduate curriculum, and its mission statement. In addition, it would need to study the causes of the protest so that it could reassure MSCHE that no similar disruptions would occur when the university appointed its next president. The university fully realized the consequences of losing its accreditation—enrolled students could lose their eligibility for federal student loans, bachelor's degree recipients could lose the opportunity to attend graduate school, and graduate students in professional programs might not qualify for licensure. Several of Gallaudet's undergraduate and graduate programs, including teacher training, social work, and clinical psychology, would also be in danger of losing their accreditations from the professional organizations in their fields.

Causes of the Protest

Why did the protest occur? In response to the need to assure MSCHE that a similar protest would not occur in the future, the Gallaudet Board of Trustees, under its new chair, Ben Soukup, appointed a task force to analyze the 2006 presidential search process. It issued a report in November 2007 that identified a number of problems, including lack of clarity about required qualifications for the office, possibly too many board members on the search committee, and the use of consultants who may not have understood the special nature of Gallaudet. The task force did not find any concrete evidence that Glenn Anderson's exclusion from the group of finalists was racially motivated.[4]

In trying to explain the passion that surrounded the choice of Fernandes, Dirksen Bauman, a professor of Deaf studies at Gallaudet, points to "the near mythic role that Gallaudet University plays within the Deaf world. It is the only plot of land in the entire world where Deaf people have direct access to higher education through a signed language."[5] Many issues concerning the relative values given to English and ASL came to the surface as Gallaudet committees worked to respond to MSCHE. How extensive the English influence on ASL should be and who controls its development continue to be very serious questions, and ambivalence about the relationship between the two languages has been a cause of tension. For example, throughout the history of the university, deaf undergraduates have generally not been able to earn credits toward graduation solely by demonstrating mastery of ASL, but this has changed with the new curriculum written to satisfy the MSCHE's conditions for removing Gallaudet from probation.

John Christiansen, a deaf professor emeritus of sociology who was a member of the original 2006 presidential search committee, expressed an additional concern—the fact that

approximately eighty thousand children around the world, primarily in wealthy nations, have received cochlear implants. Many people in Deaf communities in the United States and abroad are worried about what will happen as a consequence of this technological development. Many of these children, particularly the increasing number who are receiving implants at a very young age (including a rapidly increasing number who are receiving bilateral implants), are not likely to be a part of a signing Deaf community in the future.[6]

Whether deaf children who are implanted will ever become part of a signing community remains an open question, but it is clear that Gallaudet will see increasing numbers of deaf students who have never signed. In order to address this issue, Gallaudet had, under President Jordan and Provost Fernandes, developed a strategic plan that called for Gallaudet to become an "inclusive deaf university." Bauman argues that the plan did not go far enough in explicitly calling for this inclusivity to be based upon a commitment to an ASL/English bilingualism and that this omission contributed to the tension on campus in 2006.[7]

Personal and group politics almost certainly played a role in the protest. Christiansen suggests "that part of the explanation is that Gallaudet University is more than just a university. The ninety-nine-acre, fenced-in campus is in some ways closer to Vatican City than is our counterpart in Northeast DC, the Catholic University of America. In many ways, we on the search committee were not so much in the business of selecting a new university president as choosing a new pope."[8]

Christiansen also postulates that

perhaps another part of the explanation of the mass reaction in 2006 is that many Deaf people have become quite concerned about the future of their community. This concern, which has probably increased since DPN,

may help explain why there was perhaps even more anger and emotion in 2006 than in 1988. For example, the number of students in residential schools for deaf students is much lower than it was a few decades ago. According to the Gallaudet Research Institute's Annual Survey of Deaf and Hard of Hearing Children and Youth, which monitors this on an annual basis, only about 25 percent of deaf and hard of hearing students are now educated in these traditional breeding grounds of Deaf culture (compared to approximately 55 percent who were educated either in residential schools or in day schools for deaf students in the mid-1970s). Many more deaf students today are in some type of mainstreamed educational setting. One consequence of this transformation is that Gallaudet University is now the primary agent of socialization for many people into the Deaf community.[9]

It is probably too early for a full accounting of the causes and effects of the 2006 protest, but it appears that there was not a single cause—a "perfect storm" of controversial issues seem to have come together to work against the appointment of Jane Fernandes, including, at the very least, resentment about the search process, disappointment about the board's failure to appoint particular individuals, doubts about Jane Fernandes's administrative style and accomplishments, anger about the role of President Jordan and his staff, unresolved questions about language and culture, and anxiety about the future of the university. The Gallaudet community had the substantial task of working through these issues to the fullest extent possible in order to secure a bright future for the university.

A Bilingual Mission and a New Strategic Plan

From the point of view of MSCHE, the protest raised the critical question of whether or not the Gallaudet community and its leadership understood the university's mission: Is Gallaudet primarily a university or primarily the cultural center of the Deaf community? This question had been raised in the university's 1991 accreditation self-study, "Is it Harvard *vs.* Mecca or Harvard *and* Mecca?"[10] From

MSCHE's perspective Gallaudet *could* be both, but it had to meet the standards applied to all universities. Its function as a cultural center, therefore, was in addition to its function as a university. MSCHE explicitly recognizes that universities may have specific cultural heritages; however, it requires that all of the colleges and universities it accredits set standards that their students must meet with respect to English literacy and a range of other academic skills. MSCHE required Gallaudet to have acceptable standards for English literacy, but it allowed achievement of skill in "oral" communication to be demonstrated in ASL. This suggested to members of the university community that it would be possible to craft a new mission statement that for the first time explicitly recognized ASL as one of the languages used at Gallaudet. In addition, in order to meet the expectations of the federal government, President Davila insisted that preparation for careers be recognized in the new mission statement.[11]

Davila appointed a Mission Work Group of twenty staff, faculty, students, and governance officers to develop the new mission statement.

The work group considered internal and external contexts and constituencies, including the current

GALLAUDET TRADITIONS: THE COFFIN DOOR

One of the enduring mysteries on the Gallaudet campus is why a door in Chapel Hall is shaped like a coffin. Though no one seems to know the reason, the legend is that preparatory students, and, later, freshmen who walk through the coffin door will never graduate. According to Tim Krepp, in *Capitol Hill Haunts,*

"Coffin doors" were fairly common in nineteenth-century America; they were second exterior doors to allow coffins to be brought in and out of the house. . . .

But Gallaudet's coffin door is something else. It is an exterior door on College Hall . . . . It's a quaint architectural oddity, but students (and not a few faculty) swear that any freshman who exits through it will not graduate. The legend dates back to the time of President [Garfield], who, like many presidents, visited the school. As he pulled up in his carriage, a group of rowdy freshmen exited by the door, embarrassing the school. Supposedly, they were summarily dismissed, giving birth to the legend.[12]

The coffin door in Chapel Hall, in the 1920s (*above*) and in the 1980s (*below*).

university mission statement; the Education of the Deaf Act; the MSCHE Characteristics of Excellence in Higher Education; research on the future demographics of potential Gallaudet students; mission statements of other colleges and universities, especially those with cultural and bilingual characteristics; and suggestions collected from faculty throughout the spring semester. [13]

GALLAUDET'S VISION STATEMENT AND STRATEGIC GOALS

Gallaudet University will build upon its rich history as the world's premier higher education institution serving deaf and hard of hearing people to become the university of first choice for the most qualified, diverse group of deaf and hard of hearing students in the world, as well as hearing students pursuing careers related to deaf and hard of hearing people. Gallaudet will empower its graduates with the knowledge and practical skills vital to achieving personal and professional success in the changing local and global communities in which they live and work. Gallaudet will also strive to become the leading international resource for research, innovation and outreach related to deaf and hard of hearing people.

Gallaudet will achieve these outcomes through:
- A bilingual learning environment, featuring American Sign Language and English, that provides full access for all students to learning and communication
- A commitment to excellence in learning and student service
- A world-class campus in the nation's capital
- Creation of a virtual campus that expands Gallaudet's reach to a broader audience of visual learners
- An environment in which research can grow, develop, and improve the lives and knowledge of all deaf and hard of hearing people worldwide. [15]

APPROVED BY THE BOARD IN NOVEMBER 2007 AND AMENDED IN MAY 2009

After completing the draft, the Mission Work Group met with students, faculty, staff, alumni, administrators, the president, and the board of trustees to craft the following mission statement, which the board approved in November 2007:

Gallaudet University, federally chartered in 1864, is a bilingual, diverse, multicultural institution of higher education that ensures the intellectual and professional advancement of deaf and hard of hearing individuals through American Sign Language and English. Gallaudet maintains a proud tradition of research and scholarly activity and prepares its graduates for career opportunities in a highly competitive, technological, and rapidly changing world. [14]

In order to meet the MSCHE requirements concerning curriculum reform, student assessment, and strategic planning, work groups composed of faculty, students, and staff worked intensively through the summer of 2007. The university aimed to report substantial progress in its monitoring report that was due in September. In October, another MSCHE team visited the campus, and it found that Gallaudet had "made tangible progress in a number of areas in a short period of time." It also found that the university had drafted a new, focused mission statement and a new vision statement, as well as the beginnings of a new strategic plan, an enrollment management plan with stronger admissions standards, a new general education curriculum, and a new assessment of American Sign Language as it is used in academic discourse. The team's report commended the board for conducting a thorough self-assessment, for engaging faculty and students in meaningful dialogue on communication and governance issues, and for appointing six new members. [16]

Following this visit, the MSCHE acted to remove Gallaudet's probation and placed the university on warning, pending submission of a new monitoring report in April 2008. During the winter and spring, the university community continued to work on responding to the remaining issues. Following the submission of the report in April, a fourth visiting team concluded that Gallaudet was substantially in compliance with MSCHE standards, and in June 2008, the commission voted to remove Gallaudet's warning and reaffirm its accreditation. This was, of course, a tremendous relief for the Gallaudet community.

Athletics
Deaf Girls Still Rule

The women's volleyball team has compiled an extremely impressive record since 2007. By the end of the 2010 season, Lynn Ray Boren (BA 1994) had completed his sixth season as head coach and had compiled a 145–80 career record while leading the team to three NCAA Division III tournament appearances.

In 2009, Boren coached the Bison to a 27–14 record and the Eastern College Athletic Conference (ECAC) South Region championship. The team also finished as runners-up in the Capital Area Conference (CAC) championship. Three senior players, Shana Lehmann, Justine Jeter, and Amanda Krieger, earned all-conference honors for the Bison. Two Bison women were named CAC Players of the Year—Charity Sanders in 2005, and Tamijo Foronda in 2006.

During the 2010 season, Boren guided the Bison to its first-ever North Eastern Athletic Conference (NEAC) championship in its first year in the

◄ The women's volleyball team with Coach Boren (back row, far left). Photograph by Matthew Kohashi (BA 2005), courtesy of Gallaudet Athletics.

Tamara Johanna "Tamijo" Foronda (BA 2007), the Bison outside hitter, was both 2006–2007 Gallaudet Female Athlete of the Year and the Capital Athletic Conference Female Scholar-Athlete of the Year. Photograph by Matthew Kohashi, 2006, courtesy of Gallaudet Athletics.

▼ The 2013 Women's softball team. Photograph by Matthew Kohashi, courtesy of Gallaudet Athletics.

The Gallaudet baseball team lines up prior to the start of the 2013 NEAC Tournament on Hoy Field. Head coach Curtis Pride (*far right*) stands alongside his coaching staff and players. Photograph by Matthew Kohashi, courtesy of Gallaudet Athletics.

William Bissell at bat on March 3, 2013, in a game against the University of Mary Washington. Photograph by Matthew Kohashi, courtesy of Gallaudet Athletics.

conference. Gallaudet earned an automatic bid into the NCAA Division III tournament where the Bison played fifth-ranked Christopher Newport University in the first round and lost 3–0. Four Gallaudet players earned all-conference honors—Paige Johnson, Jessica Israel, Ann Whited, and Mari Klassen. Johnson was named the 2010 NEAC

South Division Player of the Year and took home conference tournament MVP honors.

In the fall of 2013, the Gallaudet women's volleyball team claimed its fourth consecutive NEAC title. The Bison won against Penn State Berks in 2010 and 2011, Keuka College in 2012, and SUNYIT in 2013. The members of this record-setting team have received multiple awards and recognition over the past four seasons. In 2011, Kali Frowick was named NEAC Rookie of the Year. In 2012, Jessica Israel was named NEAC Defensive Player of the Year, and Ann Whited received the 2012 NEAC Player of the Year Award and became a College Sports Information Directors of America (CoSIDA) Academic All-America honoree. Whited is the first-ever female Gallaudet student-athlete to earn this prestigious award and the only student-athlete from the NEAC to earn the honor in 2012. Not only have the team's players earned recognition, but Coach Boren has as well. In 2012 he was NEAC Coach of the Year, and he has coached the USA Deaf Women's Volleyball team twice, winning a silver medal in 2009 in Taipei, Taiwan, and placing fourth in 2013 in Sofia, Bulgaria.[17]

The Resurgence of Baseball

In a move to make the Bison baseball team more competitive, Gallaudet hired Curtis Pride as head baseball coach in 2008. Pride, who was born deaf, is a native of the Washington, DC, area. He attended public schools and the College of William and Mary. An outstanding athlete, Pride had an eleven-year career in the major leagues with the Montreal Expos, Detroit Tigers, Atlanta Braves, and New York Yankees before retiring from professional baseball in 2008.[18]

The team's record has improved each year since Pride became coach. They advanced to the NEAC Tournament in 2011, 2012, and 2013. In April 2012, William Bissell was named NEAC West Division Player of the Year for the second year in a row, and Pride received Coach of the Year honors. Pride won Coach of the Year again in 2013, and Brandon Holsworth was named Pitcher of the Year. In August 2012, President Barack Obama named Pride to the presidential delegation attending the closing ceremonies of the London Olympics. Pride, who at the time was a member of the President's Council on Fitness, Sports and Nutrition, became one of six representatives traveling to London on behalf of the United States. "I am both excited and honored to be a member of the Presidential Delegation for the Closing Ceremony at the 2012 London Olympics," Pride said of his appointment. "It is a once in a lifetime experience that I will always treasure. I look forward to cheering on the USA Olympians at the weekend events."[19]

Bison Football

The Bison football team improved steadily after 2006. It completed its 2012 season with a 7–3 overall record, including a 5–2 record in the conference. This marked the first time the team had won seven games in a season since the program returned to the NCAA Division III ranks in 2007. Senior Tony Tatum won two awards that season—the Eastern Collegiate Football Conference (ECFC) Defensive Player of the Year and Special Teams Player of the Year. Freshman quarterback Todd Bonheyo was named Rookie of the Year. The ECFC singled out thirteen Bison players for their play, making this the third year in a row that head coach Chuck Goldstein's teams received double-digit all-conference honors.

For the first time in Gallaudet's history, the 2013 football team won the ECFC title. Under Coach Goldstein's leadership, the Bison had a 9–1 record and qualified to play in the NCAA Division III football championships. They faced Hobart College in the first round and lost 34–7. The 2013 record-setting team received eleven ECFC all-team honors; Goldstein was named ECFC Coach of the Year, and Adham Talaat (class of 2014) was named a finalist for the Cliff Harris Award and the Gagliardi Trophy. The Bison's performance drew national media attention, including a feature on ESPN's *SportsCenter* titled "The Gallaudet Way," and a feature story on the *CBS Evening News*.[20]

Enrollment Stabilizes

Enrollment at Gallaudet had declined steadily during the 1990s, but it stabilized by 2005 at about 1,200 undergraduates and 450 graduate students. However, the negative publicity surrounding the events of 2006

Gallaudet defensive players Adham Talaat (#90), Matt Taylor (#3), and Tyler Snider (#33) celebrate a big play during the historic 2013 season. Photograph by Matthew Kohashi, courtesy of Gallaudet Athletics.

and 2007 took a toll on recruiting and retention of students. By the fall of 2008, undergraduate enrollment had fallen to just over 1,000 and graduate enrollment had dropped to 400. After MSCHE reaffirmed Gallaudet's accreditation in June 2008, the situation began to improve, and by the fall of 2009, undergraduate enrollment moved up to 1,145 and graduate enrollment increased to 429.

By 2011, enrollment appeared once again to have stabilized at around 1,200 undergraduates (including nondegree English Language Institute students) and 430 graduate students.[21] Very significantly, by 2011 the graduation rate within six years for first time undergraduates had increased to 41 percent from its historical average of about 25 percent. The numbers of students receiving degrees had also stabilized by this time at about 150 graduate students and 180 undergraduates annually. Of the total number of undergraduates receiving degrees each year, less than five tended to be hearing.[22] During the fall semester of 2012, 1,821 students were enrolled in university programs. Of those students, 61 percent (1,117) were undergraduates, 25 percent (463) were graduate students, and 13 percent (241) were in other categories (Professional Studies and the English Language Institute).

In order to deal with the demographic factors described by Christiansen in his analysis of the 2006 protest, the university has recruited new students from educational settings other than traditional residential schools for the deaf. In addition, the university has had to ensure potential undergraduates that it welcomes nonsigning students and has had to convince graduate students that Gallaudet has overcome its difficulties with its accreditors and that it offers first-rate professional programs leading to employment in the relevant fields of study. However, with the passage of federal laws protecting disabled students, especially the Americans with Disabilities Act, the competition to enroll deaf students has increased throughout American higher education, and competition at the graduate level has increased as employment opportunities for recent college graduates have declined.

Research: VL2, Genetics, and Discipline-Based Research

In 2005, the university made an important move forward in its research program by winning a major grant from the National Science Foundation to establish a Science of Learning Center concerned with visual language and visual learning. Known by the acronym VL2 (Visual Language/Visual Learning), it is one of six Science of Learning Centers at various locations in the United States. The center brings together researchers and educators from many universities and disciplines, and it includes teams of deaf and hearing researchers to help define and carry out the center's research initiatives that focus on developing an understanding of visual language and learning by deaf children and adults. In 2011, the well-known neuroscientist Laura-Ann Petitto joined Thomas Allen, the center's director, as co-principal investigator at VL2, where she heads the brain research center. Petitto, who spent much of her academic career at McGill University and Dartmouth College, worked with William Stokoe in Gallaudet's Linguistics Research Laboratory in the late 1970s. The external researchers affiliated with VL2 are located at a variety of universities and research centers, including Rochester Institute of Technology, Georgetown University, the University of New Mexico, the University of California at Davis, and the University of California at San Diego.

In addition to helping improve the education of deaf children, one large benefit of studying visual language development in deaf people is that it opens a window for linguists and neurologists into the ways language operates. This helps scientists to identify the aspects of language that are universal to all human beings and the aspects that are dependent on the particular medium, visual or auditory, that is used for transmission.

The Hall Memorial Building (HMB) had been renovated and expanded during the mid-1990s with financial assistance from the federal government. In 2006, new laboratory space for molecular genetics and other biological research was created on the fourth floor of HMB with help from the govern-

◀ The Brain and Language Laboratory (BL2) is a Science of Learning Center, and sister to the VL2 Center. BL2 features advanced research technology, including a functional Near-infrared Spectroscopy (fNIRS), and is now host to the interdisciplinary PhD in Educational Neuroscience program. The lab opened at a ribbon-cutting ceremony on December 8, 2011.

◀ Visual Language and Visual Learning (VL2) is a Science of Learning Center, one of six funded by the National Science Foundation (NSF). The research in VL2 is multi-disciplinary, focusing on the role of visual processes, visual language, and social experience in the development of cognition, learning, and literacy.

▶ Thomas Allen is the Co-Principal Investigator and Director of the VL2 Center. He also served as dean of the Graduate School for nine years (1997–2006).

▲ Laura-Ann Petitto (*right*), Co-Principal Investigator and Science Director of VL2, describes the BL2 facilities to Soo-Siang Lim, program director for the Science of Learning Centers Program at NSF. Photograph by Matthew Vita, December 8, 2011.

▼ Research Administrator Kristine Gauna (BA 2012, *left*) and intern Kaja Jasinska (*right*) demonstrate the use of BL2's fNIRS machine. Photograph by Matthew Vita, December 8, 2011.

ment. Dr. Derek Braun, a biology professor, designed and directs the Molecular Genetics Laboratory, Gallaudet's first biological research laboratory, which competes for research grants. Three other deaf faculty members—Caroline Solomon, Raymond Merritt, and Daniel Lundberg, all PhDs—work in the lab along with a laboratory technician. The lab also gives undergraduate students and summer interns the opportunity to conduct research. In addition, the university has operated a center for genetic research and counseling for many years under the direction of Dr. Kathleen Arnos.

Gallaudet encourages faculty and staff to do research and scholarly work in the disciplines in which they were trained and within which they teach, even if the research has no direct bearing on deaf education or other issues of importance to the Deaf community. The result is more than one hundred publications and presentations annually in disciplines such as history, English, and sociology, in addition to the deafness-related areas in which Gallaudet researchers have traditionally worked.[23]

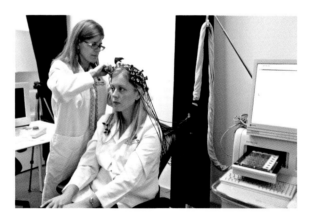

The four deaf faculty researchers that comprise Gallaudet's Molecular Genetics Laboratory are (*seated, l.* to *r.*) Derek C. Braun (BA 1995), Caroline M. Solomon, (*standing l.* to *r.*) Daniel J. Lundberg (BS 2002), and Raymond C. Merritt, Jr. (BA 1999). The foremost goal of the lab is to provide experiential learning and research opportunities for deaf and hard of hearing undergraduate students.

The Molecular Genetics lab has trained 36 students since it opened in February 2009, and 21 of these have been Gallaudet University undergraduate students; 42% have gone on to graduate school in STEM (science, technology, engineering, and mathematics) fields. The biology program's 6-year graduation rate has been 100% since 2008, and the 4-year graduation rate has been 100% since 2011. Photograph by Matthew Vita, 2010.

Gallaudet and the Lincoln Bicentennial

In 2007, Gallaudet marked the 150th anniversary of the founding of the Columbia Institution as a school for deaf and blind children with a conference and a volume of essays edited by history professors Brian Greenwald and John Vickrey Van Cleve.[24] Another significant anniversary occurred on February 9, 2009, the 200th anniversary of Abraham Lincoln's birth. The year-long national observance included a number of memorial activities involving institutions that the sixteenth president had a hand in founding. These, of course, included Gallaudet University, and in recognition of this association, Congress passed a concurrent resolution honoring Gallaudet. In view of all that had transpired just a few years earlier, the resolution represented a congressional vote of confidence in the university and the recovery it had made.

Davila Retires and a New Search Begins

As President Davila completed his term at the end of 2009, it became very important for Gallaudet to demonstrate to the federal government, MSCHE, and the rest of the world that it could successfully search for and install a new president. Given all that had happened as a result of the previous two searches, the stakes were very high for the board and the community to get it right. It was very clear that the process would be closely watched by observers both on and off the campus.

In late 2008, the board of trustees established the Presidential Search Advisory Committee (PSAC) to conduct a national search. Board member and alumnus James McFadden (BA 1962), chaired the committee comprised of board members, faculty, students, and staff. The PSAC carefully avoided issues that had been identified in the

3. CON. RES. 12
CONCURRENT RESOLUTION

Whereas in 2009, the United States honored the 200th anniversary of the birth of President Abraham Lincoln;

Whereas on July 4, 1861, President Lincoln stated in a message to Congress that a principal aim of the United States Government should be "to elevate the condition of men—to lift artificial weights from all shoulders—to clear the paths of laudable pursuit for all—to afford all, an unfettered start, and a fair chance, in the race of life";

Whereas on April 8, 1864, President Lincoln signed into law the legislation (Act of April 8, 1864, ch. 52, 13 Stat. 45) authorizing the conferring of collegiate degrees by the Columbia Institution for Instruction of the Deaf and Dumb and the Blind, which is now called Gallaudet University;

Whereas that law led for the first time in history to higher education for deaf students in an environment designed to meet their communication needs;

Whereas Gallaudet University was the first, and is still the only, institution in the world that focuses on educational programs for deaf and hard-of-hearing students from the pre-school through the doctoral level;

Whereas Gallaudet University has been a world leader in the fields of education and research for more than a century; and

Whereas since 1869, graduates of Gallaudet University have pursued distinguished careers of leadership in the United States and throughout the world: Now, therefore, be it

Resolved by the Senate (the House of Representatives concurring), That Congress—

(1) congratulates and honors Gallaudet University on the 145th anniversary of President Abraham Lincoln's signing of the legislation authorizing the establishment of collegiate programs at Gallaudet University; and

(2) congratulates Gallaudet University for 145 years of unique and exceptional service to the deaf people of the United States and the world deaf community.

PASSED THE SENATE MARCH 24, 2009.[25]

---

board's study of the 2006 search. It made sure that the job announcement clearly stated the requirements for the position and that the president's office did not become involved in the search.

The PSAC submitted a list of four finalists in late August, and on September 2, 2009, board chair Ben Soukup announced their names to the campus community: T. Alan Hurwitz, president of the National Technical Institute for the Deaf (NTID) and vice president/dean of Rochester Institute of Technology for NTID; Ronald J. Stern, superintendent/chief executive officer of the New Mexico School for the Deaf; Roslyn Rosen, director of the National Center on Deafness at California State University, Northridge; and Stephen F. Weiner, provost of Gallaudet University. All four finalists were well known at Gallaudet and, unlike in 2006, all four held terminal degrees.

On October 18, 2009, Soukup announced that the board had appointed T. Alan Hurwitz as Gallaudet's tenth president and that he would take office at the beginning of January 2010. Hurwitz, who was born deaf to deaf parents, had no previous affiliation with Gallaudet as either a student or an employee. He attended Central Institute for the Deaf in St. Louis, Missouri, and was mainstreamed in junior and senior high school in Iowa without support services, yet he is a fluent signer. After earning a bachelor's degree in electrical engineering at Washington University in St. Louis and a master's degree in engineering from St. Louis University, he began a career in engineering with the McDonnell Douglas Corporation. When

T. Alan Hurwitz took office on January 1, 2010, as the tenth president of Gallaudet University. He has been active in many professional and deafness-related organizations, and he is currently chair of the North Eastern Athletic Conference (NEAC) Presidents' Council, the first deaf person to hold this position in NEAC history. He is also the first deaf member of the Board of Directors for the DC Chamber of Commerce.

Alan Hurwitz and first lady Vicki Hurwitz. Photograph by Jessica Willoughby, September 28, 2010, in Ole Jim.

the fledgling NTID issued a call for instructors in 1970, Hurwitz applied and was hired. He subsequently earned a doctoral degree in education at the University of Rochester and rose through the administrative ranks at NTID. He is a past president of the National Association of the Deaf and a lifetime member of the Alexander Graham Bell Association. In many ways, he is a symbol of the possibilities of inclusiveness within the Deaf community.

Gallaudet organized a welcoming committee to familiarize the president-elect with members of the community and the issues that concerned them. The committee also gathered information Hurwitz had requested. The transition went smoothly, and Hurwitz took office as scheduled in January 2010 without incident.

GALLAUDET TRADITIONS: THE TOWER CLOCK AND BALD DAY

THE TOWER CLOCK

The Tower Clock is the prominent feature of Chapel Hall and an integral symbol of Gallaudet University's identity. According to the architect, Frederick C. Withers, the design "is liked by everyone who has seen it, and many say it is the best thing I have ever done." The construction of Chapel Hall began in 1867 and was completed by the end of 1870. U.S. President Ulysses S. Grant and Congressman James A. Garfield both attended the dedication ceremony in January 1871. However, the clock was not installed until 1874.

As a recognizable icon, the Tower Clock is woven into the fabric of the student body. It has played an essential role in several student traditions, and the university's yearbook is named in its honor. Graduating classes have incorporated the Tower Clock in their banners. Gallaudet alumni from the 1940s remember the annual New Year's Eve Dance held in the Old Jim, and how "just before twelve, the seniors slipped out to the Chapel Tower . . . [and] keeping up the college tradition, rang in the new year" with the number of clangs to match the incoming year. Many alumni have climbed up the winding staircase of the tower to write or carve their names on the walls, a tradition that has endured for decades.[28]

BALD DAY

Bald Day is a time-honored student tradition at Gallaudet University, though no one knows exactly when and why it started. It began as a preparatory student rite of passage that has long since been passed on to and sustained by the freshman classes. In the modern version of the tradition, freshman students, both male and female, dye and style their hair in various fashions during the fall semester. Then, in the last week of January or the first week of

◄ In 1911, a lightning strike broke the flagpole at the top of the Tower Clock, but the original iron crest work remained intact. Photograph 1917–1918.

A winding wooden staircase lines the interior of the Tower Clock. Generations of students have climbed the rickety structure to sign their names inside the tower. Photograph 1998.

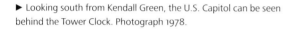

▶ Looking south from Kendall Green, the U.S. Capitol can be seen behind the Tower Clock. Photograph 1978.

February, they gather with upperclassmen and alumni to assist them in shaving their heads. Each year's class vies for bragging rights, comparing the number of students who have shaved their heads with the number from previous years. The class with the most shaved heads is said to have the most school spirit. Additionally, students feel the experience provides them with a unique opportunity to bond with other students, not only in their own class but with those of past generations. Participation in the custom is not mandatory and no one is pressured to shave their heads. In the past, students would gather off campus for this event, which often evolved into large parties. Beginning in 2010, in the interest of student safety, the administration allowed it to be hosted on campus, and it has done so ever since.[29]

In 1957, this group of male preparatory students gathered in College Hall to show off their newly shaven heads.

Preparatory student Don Lee Hanaumi (BA 1983) and junior Lucinda P. O'Grady (BA 1981) on Bald Day 1979.

Much to his credit, President Davila was able to retire knowing that stability had returned to Kendall Green. The university had regained the confidence of government officials, its accreditation had been reaffirmed, and the board and the university community had come together to conduct a thorough, open, and civil search for his successor.

The Administration of T. Alan Hurwitz

Alan Hurwitz took office in the midst of the worst economic recession in more than fifty years. The 2010 fiscal year federal budget included a three-year freeze on spending, and a Department of Education official warned that Gallaudet should not anticipate federal funding increases in coming years.[26] In an effort to secure the university's financial future, Hurwitz announced several new initiatives that pointed to an increased emphasis on partnerships and coalitions with local and national institutions and agencies. At the same time, Gallaudet began the difficult process of prioritizing, eliminating, and consolidating its programs and reducing staff for the purposes of long-term planning and strategic resource allocation. In January 2010 a fourteen-member Program Prioritization Task Force began reviewing undergraduate and graduate degree programs. After studying the final report, the board of trustees announced in February 2011 that it had approved a plan to close seventeen degree programs, effective in August 2013. At the same time, the university initiated plans to streamline its administrative operations. Soukup explained that "the university has an ambitious strategic plan in place requiring that we meet certain milestones by 2015. We feel these recommendations will help us meet those milestones and dramatically improve our offerings to ensure Gallaudet's continued growth and success."[27]

From Isolation to Innovation: Building an Open, Green, and Sustainable Campus

Every ten years, Gallaudet is required by the District of Columbia government to renew its campus facilities master plan. The university submitted its most recent plan in 2012 to cover the period until 2022. The master plan is a blueprint for the maintenance and development of Kendall Green beyond the university's sesquicentennial celebration and into its second 150 years. As it prepared the master plan, Gallaudet requested a study by the Urban Land Institute (ULI) to look at potential changes in the surrounding area. The university was especially interested in participating in and influencing the development occurring in its northeast Washington neighborhood, including the redeveloping H Street NE corridor and the "hot" new development area known as NoMa, for "North of Massachusetts Avenue." The plan focused not only on the campus itself but also undeveloped land it owned on Sixth Street across from the campus. A number of factors influenced the university's thinking—the increasingly rapid redevelopment of the surrounding area, the desire to integrate Kendall Green with the local neighborhood, and the need to reduce the traditional isolation of the campus.

The ULI conducted a series of interviews on campus and studied property development and land-use plans in the area around Kendall Green. In September 2011 it issued a report that included the following recommendations for how to open up the campus to the outside world:

- Build a new main entrance to the campus at the corner of Sixth Street and Florida Avenue;
- Keep the fences and walls around the campus but make more openings;
- Create more opportunities for students to interact with neighborhood residents and guests at the Kellogg Conference Center.

A second group of recommendations suggested taking greater advantage of the campus's historical heritage by refocusing activity around its core—Olmsted Green and the Mall—by removing the parking lot in front of College Hall and the driveway between the Green and College Hall; constructing new houses for honor students on the existing faculty row; demolishing the Merrill Learning Center and constructing a new library on the periphery of the

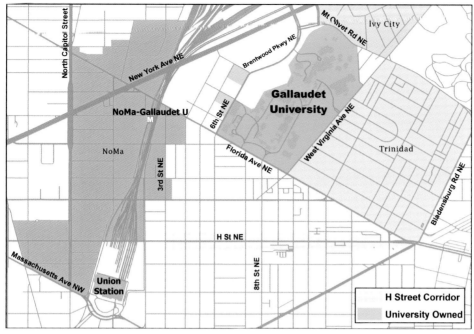

A street map of the area around Gallaudet showing the Trinidad, Ivy City, and NoMa neighborhoods, and the H Street corridor. Map by Charles H. Eckstein.

Mall. The ULI plan also recommended that the university form partnerships with developers to create space for student- and faculty-oriented businesses along Sixth Street and work with developers to build new residential and commercial space throughout the area around the campus, particularly along H Street Northeast and in the NoMa district.[30] All of these suggestions were incorporated into the university's new master plan, *From Isolation to Innovation*, and the District of Columbia government approved the new plan in January 2013.

Unlike most universities of its size and complexity, Gallaudet has never had to borrow money to fund new construction because the federal government's allocations paid for most it. However, faced with the freeze in its federal support, the university issued a $40 million bond to fund construction of a new building. Gallaudet used the bond issue to finance a new environmentally conscious dorm, the Living and Learning Residence Hall 6 (LLRH6). The residence hall, which was completed in 2012, has sustainable design features to support Leadership in Energy and Environmental Design (LEED) Silver Certification, including the use of a geothermal heating and cooling system located under Olmsted Green. The building also incorporates Deaf Space architectural design principles.

In general, green and sustainable designs have become more important to universities and other large organizations nationwide. The Sorenson Language and Communication Center, the first campus facility to receive LEED certification (in 2008), marked the beginning of Gallaudet's commitment to design and construct facilities in environmentally conscious ways. On February 29, 2012, President Hurwitz signed a pledge with Mayor Vincent Gray and eight other local university presidents to work together to make Washington, DC, the "Greenest College Town in America." The District of Columbia Mayor's College and University Sustainability Pledge (CUSP) is the first of its kind in the nation. As part of the CUSP agreement, Gallaudet pledged to achieve LEED Silver Certification or equivalent in all new construction projects and major renovations, reduce

Phase I
Phase II
Phase III

▲ Gallaudet's 2022 Campus Plan, showing the three planned phases of the plan.

▼ Gallaudet students, staff, and faculty have participated in the H Street Festival since 2011, as performers, vendors, and attendees. In 2012, the Gallaudet cheerleaders opened the festival by signing the "Star-Spangled Banner." Photograph courtesy Gallaudet Athletics.

energy usage in all campus buildings, increase energy usage from renewable sources, increase water conservation efforts, and publish a sustainability report, including measurements of progress on CUSP goals.

Looking into the future, Gallaudet will continue to expand its sustainability efforts through the work of a sustainability committee and Gallaudet students, staff, and faculty. Its 2022 goals include building a culture of sustainability on campus, developing a measurable and enforceable sustainability plan, ensuring that sustainability goals are achievable and agreed upon by a consensus, and developing a comprehensive approach to sustainability.[31]

Focus on Careers and Innovation

The mission statement that the board adopted in 2007 specifically called for Gallaudet to prepare its graduates for careers in an increasingly competitive and technologically complex world. Goal D, Objective 3 of Gallaudet's strategic plan states that the university will "strengthen students' preparation for employment and career success."[32] To achieve this goal, new undergraduate degree programs have been established in pre-med, pre-law, pre-business/ MBA, and pre-architecture to prepare students for graduate programs in these professional fields. The university has also instituted four new graduate degree programs—master's degrees in Public Administration and in Sign Language Education, and PhDs in Interpreting and in Educational Neuroscience. Gallaudet has long been a part of the Washington, DC, consortium of universities, which allows students to take courses elsewhere in the city, but renewed attention is being given to establishing external linkages. This has resulted in increased emphasis on student participation in internships at governmental agencies, other universities, and business organizations.

The Urban Land Institute's report recommended that Gallaudet establish an Innovation Lab that will serve as a multidisciplinary research and cultural center. The lab, which will be located

The James Lee Sorenson Language and Communication Center (SLCC), named for the founder of Sorenson Communications, houses the Departments of ASL and Deaf Studies; Linguistics; Hearing, Speech, and Language Sciences; Art, Communication, and Theatre, Communication Arts Research, the Hearing and Speech Center, and VL2. Together, these departments promote interdisciplinary and collaborative academic research. Photograph by Alain Jaramillo for Heery International, Inc., October 17, 2008.

Linguistics professor Julie A. Hochgesang (MA 2007, PhD 2013) lectures to students in her "Sign Language Linguistics" course in SLCC. The classrooms in the SLCC reflect the visu-centric design philosophy and provide maximum exposure to natural light. Photograph by Sara Moore (BA 2013), July 14, 2011.

On February 29, 2012, President Hurwitz joined DC Mayor Vincent Gray and eight other university presidents to sign the District of Columbia Mayor's College and University Sustainability Pledge.

▶ On August 2, 2012, Gallaudet became the first university in the Washington, DC, area to have a Capital Bikeshare station. President Hurwitz, who is an avid bicyclist, hailed the new station as one of many ways the university is implementing sustainability measures.

The 2022 Master Plan includes a pedestrian-friendly entrance to the campus that connects the historic part of campus to new, modern buildings. Courtesy of Dangermond Keane Architecture.

on the northeast corner of Florida Avenue NE and Sixth Street, will serve as a gateway between the Gallaudet campus and the Capital City Market area.[33]

President Hurwitz has also expressed an interest in having Gallaudet participate in innovative initiatives. To achieve this goal, the university joined nine other DC-area universities in June 2012 as part of the Chesapeake Crescent Innovation Alliance (CCIA). The other universities in the CCIA are the University System of Maryland, Johns Hopkins University, George Washington University, Georgetown University, Howard University, George Mason University, Virginia Tech, the University of Virginia, and James Madison University. The purpose of the CCIA is to use the wealth of research, knowledge, and technology in the Washington metropolitan area to promote the creation of jobs and investment in the region. The CCIA, which formed in 2008, helps its member universities communicate and share resources more efficiently and effectively while helping each university advance its mission.[34]

A New Gallaudet Brand

In July 2011, President Hurwitz announced the formation of a committee to design a new university logo. The Logo Redesign Committee included representatives from the university's many constituent groups, and they worked with artists Scott Carollo and Zhou Fang, both alumni, to create new designs. On September 15, 2011, the committee unveiled four new designs along with recommendations for new standards of use. After receiving input from the campus community, the committee chose two of the designs, both of which incorporated architectural features of university buildings. The Student Congress voted to reject all four of the designs because they thought the Victorian-era architectural features made the logo look old-fashioned. Instead, they urged the university to adopt a new logo that would reflect Gallaudet's bilingual heritage and would look to the future rather than the past. Hurwitz responded by asking

the redesign committee to work with a student subcommittee to find a satisfactory resolution. The artists created several new logos incorporating a graphic representation of the ASL sign for "Gallaudet," and the students, faculty, staff, and alumni participated in a survey to determine the final design. On December 7, 2011, the university announced the winning design.

The symbolic design of the logo represents the university's bilingual mission by portraying "Gallaudet University" in American Sign Language (ASL) as well as in English, the two languages contained in the mission. The ASL component is demonstrated by the two arches meeting at a point. . . . "This is an exciting time in Gallaudet's history. Our new logo promotes unity on our campus and beyond," said President Hurwitz. "Throughout the logo selection process we had an unprecedented level of participation by Gallaudet students, faculty, staff, and alumni as well as members of the deaf community throughout the country."[35]

Perhaps of greatest importance to the university was the way members of the Gallaudet community worked together cooperatively and in a civil manner to resolve what otherwise might have become a contentious issue.

MSCHE Reaccreditation

As the sesquicentennial anniversary of Gallaudet University approached, the university had to plan for a full reaccreditation process in 2013 (instead of 2011 because the last reaffirmation had occurred in 2008). During the 2011–2012 academic year the university community prepared a self-study report under the direction of Provost Weiner and Patricia Hulsebosch, Gallaudet's accreditation liaison. The final report presented to MSCHE in February 2013 sums up the many changes that occurred after the protests and probation shook the campus in 2006 and 2007. In particular, the report stressed the increased use of analytic data in decision making at the university that has occurred since that time, and it noted that

In 1986, Title 20 U.S. Code § 4301 declared the continuation of Gallaudet College as Gallaudet University. In recognition of this event, a new, unifying logo was designed in which the G is framed by three blocks, each one representing the schools of Kendall Green: KDES, MSSD, and the university. The logo was retired in December 2011.

Gallaudet's new logo represents the bilingual mission of the university. It was officially unveiled on December 7, 2011.

The sign meaning "Gallaudet" is incorporated in the new logo.

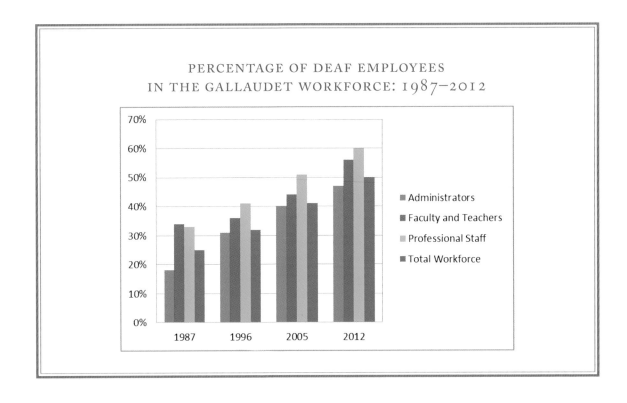

PERCENTAGE OF DEAF EMPLOYEES
IN THE GALLAUDET WORKFORCE: 1987–2012

- Administrators
- Faculty and Teachers
- Professional Staff
- Total Workforce

Another class enters the ranks of alumni after their graduation.

the percentage of Gallaudet University bachelor's degree graduates who are employed their first year after graduation has also increased or remained steady since implementing the new mission in 2007. In 2006 and 2007, employment rates were 73% and 70%, respectively. Rates improved to 80% in 2008 and rose again to 83% in 2009; they declined to 72% in 2010. In 2011 . . . 45% were pursuing additional education, and [only] 5% were neither employed nor pursuing additional education. Seventy-two percent (72%) of 2011 Alumni Survey respondents are working in fields that serve deaf and/or hard of hearing individuals.[36]

It is also significant that by 2012, the proportion of deaf people in the total Gallaudet workforce had increased to 50 percent: 47 percent of administrators, 49 percent of university faculty, 79 percent of Clerc Center teachers (56 percent of faculty and teachers combined), and 60 percent of the professional staff.[37] The percentage of all employees who were deaf had doubled in the quarter century since DPN in 1988 (see box on page 176).

The MSCHE visiting team came to Gallaudet in November 2012 and again in March 2013. In its report, it told the university community, "we commend you for your candid approach to self-evaluation and the openness with which you shared the challenges of continuous improvement as you work to analyze the strengths and effectiveness of your practices related to your strategic plan," and "for creating and sustaining a culture of assessment that is evident at all levels of the organization and governance structures." The report also mentioned that "Gallaudet community members should be commended for their self-reflective passion to fulfilling their mission and for the consistent articulation of that mission in interviews and documentation related to each of the 14 [MSCHE] standards."[38] The team concluded that the university was in compliance with all of MSCHE's standards, and on June 27, 2013, MSCHE reaffirmed Gallaudet's accreditation.[39]

With its ten-year facilities master plan in place and its strategic plan endorsed by its accreditors, Gallaudet is well positioned as it begins its second 150 years.

EPILOGUE

A Sense of Place

Since the earliest days of deaf education in the United States, deaf people have described their arrival at school as finding a home, even though they were among strangers.[1] For many of them, their school was the first place where they were not alone in a family of hearing people. Learning American Sign Language and living among other deaf people gave them a sense of place that led to the formation of the Deaf community. Now, almost two hundred years since the founding of the American School for the Deaf, societal and technological changes have resulted in the fragmentation of Deaf communities. Deaf people have moved out of their traditional occupations, such as printing, and into professions, including teaching, counseling, law, and computer programming. Changes in residential patterns have separated deaf people physically, and the technological revolution has allowed them to communicate with each other at a distance, rather than face-to-face.[2]

Communities and cultures are formed out of the innumerable encounters and the myriad negotiations and compromises that people engage in over time, measured in generations; and the construction of cultures has always relied upon physical proximity. We have already encountered anxiety about the future of Deaf communities and

their sign languages in this book, and this raises the question, "If our sense of 'place' is not derived from a physical space, how can our community be maintained?"[3] Carol Padden and Jennifer Rayman have given this considerable thought, and they assert that greater importance will accrue to Gallaudet University as a physical meeting place for deaf people in the face of all the new challenges that the future will certainly bring.

[There is] a photograph on the wall of the president's residence at Gallaudet University. It was taken most likely in the late 1880s or early 1890s, a panoramic wide shot of the main grounds of the campus, from the President's House to Faculty Row and includes the old Gymnasium and College Hall. A party of young men are standing, scattered around the lawn, nattily attired with walking canes and dark suits. As we look at their profiles and haughty arrangement across the lawn, we are struck by a sense of ownership that these men had of the land. The space of Gallaudet University is extraordinary indeed, 100 acres of land where deaf people have congregated since the founding of the university in 1864. Their confidence in place is palpable. But this stiffly proud collection of white men seems an anomaly, for now Gallaudet admits women and students of color. The old buildings in the photograph

◀ College Hall.

The 1889–1890 baseball team on the lawn in front of College Hall.

The concept drawing for the Innovation Lab and other new buildings that will form the campus in future years.
Courtesy of Dangermond Keane Architecture.

still exist, but interspersed among them are high-rise dormitories and modern brick structures. The pastoral campus of the waning years of the nineteenth century is gone as is segregation by race and gender. What we have to look forward to in the future is not that communities become fluid, but that as communities change and shift, they need to exist in the face of durable and stable places like Gallaudet. As communities become more fluid, the stability of places like this campus becomes even more significant.

As we face the challenges of maintaining cultural identity in the face of technological innovation, population diversity, and migration, we need to write a new description of the community that recognizes forces of regeneration and renewal and, at the same time, recognize the need for stability of place in different forms. As we continue to describe sign languages, especially those newly created and those existing for longer times, we will see that the human dimensions of language . . . depend deeply on cultural institutions such as the school and the deaf associations, whose crucial role is to make possible durability and complexity.[4]

If the passions that have been aroused in the Gallaudet community during recent years are an indication of the level of commitment deaf people have to the Institution, then it should have a long and successful future. Gallaudet University has always been and will continue to be both a physical reality and a cultural and educational ideal.

NOTES

PROLOGUE

1. McPherson, *A Fair Chance in the Race of Life*, 5.

2. Gallaudet, *History of the College for the Deaf*, 67.

3. Ibid., 36.

4. Thanks to Michael J. Olson for this observation.

CHAPTER ONE

1. See, for example, Van Cleve and Crouch, *A Place of Their Own*.

2. McCullough, *The Greater Journey*, 99.

3. Adapted from http://pr.gallaudet.edu/GallaudetHistory/page1.html.

4. Ibid. The story of the Institution's support by and close association with the Congress and government of the United States will be a recurring theme in this book. The continuous funding since 1858 is believed to make Gallaudet University the third oldest educational institution to receive federal support, following the United States Military Academy at West Point and the Naval Academy in Annapolis.

5. Gallaudet, *History of the College*, 32.

6. Ibid., 36.

7. Ibid., 227.

8. Ibid., 233. In the text, Goodwin is identified as "President," but the University of Pennsylvania did not create the position of president until 1930.

9. Ibid., 57.

10. Ibid., 59.

11. Ibid., 100.

12. Ibid., 107.

13. Boatner, *Voice of the Deaf*; Marilyn Daniels, *Benedictine Roots in the Development of Deaf Education: Listening with the Heart* (Westport, CT: Bergin and Garvey, 1997); First Church of Christ, *Historical Catalogue of the First Church in Hartford: 1633-1885* (Hartford, CT: Case, Lockwood and Brainard, 1885); Gallaudet, *History of the College*, 24, 38, 64; Francis R. Kowsky, "Gallaudet College: A High Victorian Campus," *Records of the Columbia Historical Society,* *Washington, D.C.* (1972): 439–467; Caroline Mills, Caroline Brewster, Helen Story, and Florence Snow, eds., *Catalog of Officers, Graduates and Nongraduates of Smith College* (Northampton, MA: Alumnae Association of Smith College, 1911); "Charitable Bequests," *New York Times*, January 8, 1888; "Mrs. Closson Dies; Daughter of D.C. College Founder," *New York Times*, December 28, 1942; "Dr. Gallaudet's Daughter Dies in New Haven: Special Dispatch to The Post," *Washington Post*, December 14, 1942; Winefield, *Never the Twain Shall Meet*; Oliver Norton Worden, *Some Records of Persons by the Name of Worden, Particularly of Over One Thousand of the Ancestors, Kin, and Descendants of John and Elizabeth Worden, of Washington County, Rhode Island* (Lewisburg, PA: Railway Press of J.R. Cornelius, 1868).

14. *Gallaudet Almanac*, 159.

15. "About the GUAA," accessed October 21, 2013, http://www.gallaudet.edu/development_and_alumni_relations/alumni_relations/alumni_association_(guaa)/about_the_guaa.html.

16. Jack R. Gannon, "Gallaudet College Alumni Association: Founding," in *Gallaudet Encyclopedia of Deaf People and Deafness*, vol. 1, ed. John V. Van Cleve (New York: McGraw Hill, 1987), 454.

17. Ibid., 455.

18. Stokoe, Bernard, and Padden, "An Elite Group in Deaf Society," 307.

19. "The Palisades, Washington, D.C.," retrieved from http://en.wikipedia.org/wiki/The_Palisades,_Washington,_D.C.; Gaston, "College Chronicle. Along the Road in Germany. Cane Rush. Et Cetera," *The Deaf-Mutes' Journal*, October 23, 1884; Olaf Hanson, "Gallaudet Athletics in the Early Eighties," *The Silent Worker* 36 no. 6 (1924): 274–276; Griffin O'Hara, "Class of 2012 Plants Their Class Tree," *The Buff and Blue*, November 18, 2010, retrieved from www.thebuffandblue.net/?p=4433; "Paper Chase (game)," retrieved from http://en.wikipedia.org/wiki/Paper_Chase_%28game%29; "A Grist of Graduates," *Washington Post*, June 22, 1881; "Beside the Class Tree," *Washington Post*, June 5, 1890; "Dance for Gallaudet Graduates," *Washington Post*, May 7, 1897; "Dancing with Deaf Mutes," *Washington Post*, June 18, 1884; "Easter Camp of Mutes," *Washington Post*, March 31. 1904;

"Mutes in Camp," *Washington Post*, March 28, 1907; "Presentation Hop at Gallaudet," *Washington Post*, May 10, 1903; "Split on Cane Rush," *Washington Post*, November 16, 1905.

20. Atwood, *Gallaudet College*, 35–36.

21. Gallaudet, *History of the College*, 188.

22. Ibid., 67.

23. Ibid., 76–96.

24. McCullough, *The Greater Journey*, 267–329.

25. Gallaudet, *History of the College*, 105.

26. Ibid., 180.

27. Gallaudet, *History of the College*, 19, 97, 105, 199; Boatner, *Voice of the Deaf*, 76, 163.

28. Ibid., 194–96.

29. Ibid., 193–94.

30. Ibid., 203.

31. Ibid., 211.

32. Garrick Mallery, *Sign Language among North American Indians Compared with That among Other Peoples and Deaf-Mutes.*

33. http://en.wikipedia.org/wiki/Second_International_Congress_on_Education_of_the_Deaf.

34. Gallaudet, *History of the College*, 140.

35. Baynton, "The Curious Death of Sign Language Studies."

36. Gallaudet, *History of the College*, 182–83.

37. Ibid.; Winefield, *Never the Twain Shall Meet*, 60. Deaf students were not admitted to the graduate school as regular degree-seeking students until 1960, although a few deaf students earned MS degrees, rather than MAs through programs of "home study" outside the Normal School program (Jones and Achtzehn, "A Century of Leadership," 7–8). See chapter 2 for more information about the Normal School.

38. Bahan and Bauman, "The Power of Place," 158–59.

39. Gallaudet, *History of the College*, 189.

40. Ibid., 184.

41. Olson, "The Thomas Hopkins Gallaudet and Alice Cogswell Statue," 33–34.

42. Ibid., 37.

43. Tom Harrington, "Lincoln Memorial Statue and Daniel Chester French," accessed November 8, 2013, http://libguides.gallaudet.edu/content.php?pid=352115.

44. Diary of Edward Miner Gallaudet, 24 February 1887.

45. Olson, "The Thomas Hopkins Gallaudet and Alice Cogswell Statue," 39–41.

46. Ibid., 43.

47. Ibid., 37.

48. Gallaudet, *History of the College*, 201–202.

49. Manuscript material, Vertical Files: African Americans—James Gilbert, Jr., Ennal Jerome Adams, Jr., Gallaudet University Archives; Elliot S. Waring, "Obituary of James Gilbert," *Buff and Blue* 12 no. 2 (1903): 57; alumni cards accessed at http://www.aladin0.wrlc.org/gsdl/collect/alumni/alumni.shtml.

50. W. J. Blount to E. M. Gallaudet, 8 December 1897, Gallaudet Archives, courtesy of Michael J. Olson.

51. Gallaudet, *History of the College*, 166–67.

52. Parker, "The Women of Kendall Green: Coeducation at Gallaudet," 99–101; *Herstory* (1892–2012), Phi Kappa Zeta Sorority, accessed November 5, 2013, http://phikappazeta.org/about/herstory/.

53. Gallaudet, *History of the College*, 205.

54. Boatner, *Voice of the Deaf.*

CHAPTER TWO

1. Atwood, *Gallaudet College*, 39.

2. http://en.wikipedia.org/wiki/Percival_Hall and http://www.gallaudet.edu/Library_Deaf_Collections_and_Archives/Collections/Manuscript_Collection/MSS_151.html.

3. Atwood, *Gallaudet College*, 43.

4. Gannon, *Deaf Heritage*, 73.

5. *Gallaudet Almanac*, 47.

6. *Eighty-ninth Annual Report of the Columbia Institution for the Deaf to the Federal Security Administrator, Year Ended June 30, 1946*, 9, 365.

7. Atwood, *Gallaudet College*, 60.

8. *Gallaudet Almanac*, 242.

9. Atwood, *Gallaudet College*, 47.

10. Ibid.

11. Ibid., 46.

12. *Annual Report of the Columbia Institution*, 1931, 3; Atwood, *Gallaudet College*, 47–48.

13. Parker, "The Women of Gallaudet," 101–102.

14. James Stewart, "The Beginning of the Buff and Blue," *Buff and Blue*, December 1932, vol. 41 no. 2: 52–54, http://www.thebuffandblue.net/?page_id=3153; "Gallaudet University-Buff and Blue Newspaper," https://archive.org/details/gu_buffandblue193405xx.

15. Sutcliffe, "George Detmold," 134.

16. http://www.gallaudet.edu/development_and_alumni_ relations/alumni_relations/alumni_association_(guaa)/ about_the_guaa/history/chronology_of_events.html.

17. Ibid.

18. *David Peikoff.* (2008, February 21). Retrieved August 19, 2013, from Find a Grave: www.findagrave.com/cgi-bin/fg .cgi?page=gr&GRid=24799785.

19. Supalla, "The Validity of the Gallaudet Lecture Films," 265.

20. Ibid., 269, 278.

21. Padden, "Translating Veditz," 248–49.

22. Ibid., 245.

23. *Gallaudet Almanac,* 139.

24. *Our Heritage,* 67.

25. *Gallaudet Almanac,* 139.

26. Atwood, *Gallaudet College,* 46.

27. Ibid., 49.

28. *Our Heritage,* 70.

29. Garretson, *My Yesterdays,* 61.

30. *Herstory* (1892–2012), Phi Kappa Zeta Sorority, http:// phikappazeta.org/about/herstory/, accessed November 5, 2013.

31. A. J. Roupp, "Alpha Sigma Pi" and "Delta Epsilon," in *Gallaudet University: Tower Clock* (Washington, DC: Gallaudet University, 1993), 176, 184.

32. "'Brother' of 'Rats' Dies," *Buff and Blue,* October 10, 1935; "Hurdy Gurdy," *Buff and Blue,* October 24, 1935; "Campers Peeved at All Rain, No Shine," *Buff and Blue,* April 30, 1940; Claudia M. Foy, "The Rat Funeral: Humorous Traditions Set by Colleges for the Deaf" (presentation at the World Humor and Irony Metaphor (WHIM) Conference, Arizona State University, Tempe, AZ, April 1, 1987); John Kelly, "Yes, the University of Maryland Has Traditions," *Washington Post,* August 29, 2012.

33. *Annual Reports of the Columbia Institution,* 1910–1945, Gallaudet University Archives.

34. Bureau of Labor Statistics, Consumer Price Index, All Urban Consumers, historical tables 1913–2012. ftp://ftp.bls .gov/pub/special.requests/cpi/cpiai.txt.

35. Atwood, *Gallaudet College,* 48.

36 John B. Wight, *A Tribute of Affection and Esteem to "Diamond,"* (Washington, DC: Kendall Green, 1888); "John Brewer Wight," http://www.findagrave.com; "Old Pamphlet Reveals Interesting Story of a Mascot, 'Diamond,'" *Buff and Blue* 45(3), November 5, 1936.

37. Ibid., 58; Garretson, *My Yesterdays,* 61.

38. Atwood, *Gallaudet College,* 59, 61; Gannon, *Deaf Heritage,* 231–36.

39. Atwood, *Gallaudet College,* 59.

40. Ibid., 59, 62.

41. Maher, *Seeing Language in Sign,* 29–30.

42. Atwood, *Gallaudet College,* 62.

43. George Detmold to Jane Maher, 19 January 1991.

44. Atwood, *Gallaudet College,* 64.

45. Ibid., 63.

46. Bahan and Bauman, "The Power of Place," 163–64.

47. Maher, *Seeing Language in Sign,* 44–45.

48. Lang, *Teaching from the Heart and Soul,* 101.

49. Atwood, *Gallaudet College,* 71.

50. Maher, *Seeing Language in Sign,* 49.

51. http://www.ntid.rit.edu/ntidweb/storycorps_audio/ transcript/ts.pdf.; Gannon, *Deaf Heritage,* 262–63.

52. Michael J. Olson to Ivey Wallace, 21 August 2013.

53. Harry Lang and Bonnie Meath-Lang, *Deaf Persons in the Arts and Sciences* (Westport, CT: Greenwood Press, 1995), 125–27.

54. Jowers-Barber, "The Struggle to Educate Black Deaf Schoolchildren," 24.

55. Edna P. Adler, "Boyce Robert Williams," in *Gallaudet Encyclopedia of Deaf People and Deafness,* vol. 3, ed. John V. Van Cleve (New York: McGraw Hill, 1987), 340–42; "Boyce Robert Williams," in Deaf Biographies, http://www .gallaudet.edu/library_deaf_collections_and_archives.html.

56. "Department of Business Names Computer Lab Suites in Honor of Dr. Alan B. Crammatte," January 28, 2012, https://www.gallaudet.edu/News?ABC_computer_lab .html; Armstrong, "Income and Occupations of Deaf Former College Students," 15.

57. "Lip-reading Skill Wins WAC Commission," *Washington Post,* March 27, 1945; Jean R. Hailey, "Elizabeth Benson, Ex-Dean at Gallaudet," *Washington Post,* December 15, 1972; "Elizabeth English Benson," in Deaf Biographies, http://www.gallaudet.edu/library_deaf_collections_and_ archives.html; Susie Tighe, "Do You Remember? Elizabeth Benson – Dean of Women," Gallaudet Class of 1972 e-Newsletter, September 14, 2010, http://gally72.blogspot. com/2010/09/do-you-remember-elizabeth-english.html, accessed on November 20, 2013.

58. "Terrence James O'Rourke, Activist for Deaf, Dies at 59," *Washington Post,* January 17, 1992; "T.J. O'Rourke (4/17/1932–1/10/1992)," www.deafpeople.com/history/ history_info/orourke.html, accessed November 22, 2013;

Stan Griffin, "A 'Deaf Man for All Seasons'," http://www .workersforjesus.com/dfi/965.htm.

59. "Dr. Robert R. Davila," http://www.gallaudet.edu/ history/presidents/davila_robert.html.

60. "The Class of 1947," *The Rochester Advocate*, Rochester School for the Deaf; "In a Manor of Speaking," *The Mill Neck Newsletter*, July 19, 2001.

61. Sutcliffe, "George Detmold," 137.

62. *Meeting the Challenges of Excellence and Cultural Diversity*, Gallaudet University Self-Study Report, submitted to the Middle States Association, January 1991, page ii, courtesy of the Gallaudet University Office of the Provost.

CHAPTER THREE

1. Gallaudet University Budget Office.

2. Gallaudet College Catalog 1955–56.

3. Atwood, *Gallaudet College*, 138.

4. See, for example, Armstrong, Karchmer, and Van Cleve, *The Study of Signed Languages*.

5. Stokoe, *Language in Hand*, 4.

6. Veditz, *Proceedings of the Ninth Convention of the NAD*.

7. Maher, *Seeing Language in Sign*, 71, 73–74.

8. Ibid., 73.

9. Sacks, *Seeing Voices*, 77.

10. David F. Armstrong, personal recollection.

11. http://maggieblanck.com/NewYork/GermanTheater NYC.html, http://www.jewishvirtuallibrary.org/jsource/ US-Israel/Yiddish.html, http://www.frizzilazzi.com/ italianexpierence.htm.

12. Schuchman, "The Silent Film Era," 233.

13. Baldwin, *Pictures in the Air*, 5–7.

14. Gannon, *Deaf Heritage*, 346.

15. Baldwin, *Pictures in the Air*, 10, 11, 16–17, 20–23.

16. Bragg, *Lessons in Laughter*, 105–107.

17. Baldwin, *Pictures in the Air*, 125–29; http://www .gallaudet.edu/library_deaf_collections_and_archives. html; http://digitalmusics.dartmouth.edu/~larry/cc2_2011/ readings/ntd%20at%20dartmouth/ML-81%20%2810 -4%29.pdf,, accessed 8/30/13.

18. Gannon, *Deaf Heritage*, 354.

19. Edward C. Merrill, Jr., to Jane Maher, 6 March 1991, in the author's possession.

20. http://www.gallaudet.edu/development_and_alumni_ relations/alumni_relations/alumni_association_(guaa)/ about_the_guaa/history/chronology_of_events.html.

21. *Our Heritage*, 100.

22. Gallaudet University Budget Office.

23. http://en.wikipedia.org/wiki/Demographics _of_Washington,_D.C.

24. http://pr.gallaudet.edu/otg/BackIssues.asp?ID=2830.

25. Gallaudet College, *New Challenges, New Responses*, 23–25.

26. Ibid., 30.

27. http://www.gallaudet.edu/gallaudet_research_institute .html.

28. Gallaudet College, *New Challenges, New Responses*, 30; http://gupress.gallaudet.edu/gupress30yrs.html.

29. Gannon, *Deaf Heritage*, 340–41.

30. The following sketch of important events is adapted from the Alumni Office on-line history: http://www .gallaudet.edu/development_and_alumni_relations/ alumni_relations/alumni_association_(guaa)/about_ the_guaa/history/chronology_of_events.html.

31. Gallaudet University Alumni Survey, 2006.

32. Armstrong, "Income and Occupations of Deaf Former College Students," 8–15.

33. http://www.gallaudet.edu/news/peace_corps_exhibit_ opens.html.

34. Kerstetter and Armstrong, "The Rubella Epidemic of 1963–65."

35. http://www.washingtonpost.com/ac2/wp-dyn/ A51912-2005Mar20?language=printer.

36. Edward C. Merrill, Jr., to Jane Maher, 6 March 1991, in the author's possession.

37. Gannon, *Deaf Heritage*, 439–42.

38. Garretson, *My Yesterdays in a Changing World of the Deaf*, Kindle locations 8211–19.

39. Christiansen and Barnartt, *Deaf President Now!*, xviii.

40. http://www.gallaudetathletics.com/news/2010-11/ hofrecap.

41. http://libguides.gallaudet.edu/content.php?pid =351760&sid=2877498.

42. http://www.presidency.ucsb.edu/ws/index.php?pid =37703#axzz2g1eQShQ8.

43. Several months after assuming his position at Bassett, Lee resigned, citing differences in corporate management style. He later became president of National University in La Jolla, California.

44. The author had this responsibility.

45. COED, *Toward Equality*, viii.

46. Ibid., 45, 74, 77–81.

47. Gannon, *Deaf Heritage*, 439–42.

48. Stokoe, Bernard, Padden, "An Elite Group in Deaf Society," 315.

49. Alan B. Crammatte to David F. Armstrong, ca. 1983.

50. Christiansen and Barnartt, *Deaf President Now!*, 2.

51. Ibid., 4–16.

52. Garretson, *My Yesterdays in a Changing World of the Deaf*, Kindle locations 9091–98.

53. See chapter 4 for a detailed description of the Ducks and their activities in support of a deaf president.

54. Gannon, *Deaf Heritage*, 20.

CHAPTER FOUR

Note: This chapter is based primarily on the papers and personal recollections of the author and two book-length treatments of the Deaf President Now protest: *The Week the World Heard Gallaudet* by Jack R. Gannon, published in 1989 by Gallaudet University Press, and *Deaf President Now!: The 1988 Revolution at Gallaudet University* by John B. Christiansen and Sharon M. Barnartt published in 1995, also by Gallaudet University Press. Both books are highly readable, well researched, and strongly recommended for readers who want to experience DPN on an almost minute-by-minute basis. Oliver Sacks, the neurologist and nonfiction writer, spent some time at Gallaudet during the DPN protest and recorded his observations in the book *Seeing Voices: A Journey into the World of the Deaf*, published in 1989 by the University of California Press.

1. Christiansen and Barnartt, *Deaf President Now!*, 45, 48–49; Gannon, *The Week the World Heard Gallaudet*, 37.

2. Christiansen and Barnartt, *Deaf President Now!*, 52.

3. See Christiansen and Barnartt, *Deaf President Now!*, 54–56, for a detailed account of this meeting.

4. Ibid., 56–62.

5. See Gannon, *The Week the World Heard Gallaudet*, and Christiansen and Barnartt, *Deaf President Now!*

6. Christiansen and Barnartt, *Deaf President Now!*, 192.

7. David F. Armstrong, personal recollection.

8. Garretson, *My Yesterdays in a Changing World of the Deaf*, Kindle locations 9111–18.

9. David F. Armstrong, personal recollection.

10. Christiansen and Barnartt, *Deaf President Now!*, 11–12.

Recent research has revealed that there were seven Ducks. Both Gannon's and Christiansen and Barnartt's accounts of DPN omitted Dwight Benedict, who worked in the Office of Student Life during DPN (Ben Jarashow, "Deaf History Lecture: Ducks," March 7, 2013). Gallaudet history professor Brian Greenwald interviewed several of the Ducks in 2012, and they were not unanimous on the origin of the group's name (personal communication to the author). However, it does no harm to the historical record to repeat the version given to Christiansen and Barnartt shortly after the event itself.

11. Gannon, *The Week the World Heard Gallaudet*, 25.

12. Mitchell and Karchmer, "Chasing the Mythical Ten Percent."

13. Christiansen and Barnartt, *Deaf President Now!*, 180.

14. Ibid., 71, 73.

15. Commission on Education of the Deaf, *Toward Equality*, 80.

16. Christiansen and Barnartt, *Deaf President Now!*, 120.

17. Bonior, foreword to *The Week the World Heard Gallaudet*, by Gannon, 10.

18. Christiansen and Barnartt, *Deaf President Now!*, 97–101, 107.

19. Ibid., 134, 136.

20. Ibid., 136.

21. Gannon, *The Week the World Heard Gallaudet*, 96.

22. Christiansen and Barnartt, *Deaf President Now!*, 153–54.

23. Sacks, *Seeing Voices*, 156.

24. Gannon, *The Week the World Heard Gallaudet*, 141–43.

25. Ibid., 144.

26. Ibid., 166–70.

27. Commission on Education of the Deaf, *Toward Equality*, 78–80.

28. See Christiansen and Barnartt, *Deaf President Now!*, 213–15.

29. Weiner, "Deaf President Now," 1.

30. Dr. Martin Luther King, Jr., "I Have a Dream" (speech, Washington, DC, August 28, 1963).

CHAPTER FIVE

1. "Panel Calls Education of Deaf Unsatisfactory," *New York Times*, March 22, 1988.

2. Molly Sinclair, "Panel Criticizes U.S. on Education of the Deaf; In Debate on the Hill, 'Mainstreaming' of

Hearing-Impaired Students Is Reexamined," *Washington Post*, March 22, 1988.

3. See chapter 3 for a full account of the COED recommendations.

4. John E. Smith, "Request Satisfies Gallaudet President," *Washington Times*, February 22, 1990.

5. Valerie Strauss, "Fearing Funding Cuts, New Howard U. President Starts Lobbying Hill Leaders," *Washington Post*, June 21, 1995.

6. William Jefferson Clinton, "Gallaudet, A National Treasure" (Gallaudet University 125th Commencement Address, Washington, DC, May 13, 1994).

7. Personal recollection of the author.

8. Gallaudet Budget Office, *Gallaudet University Congressional Budget Justifications*, 1990–1997.

9. Gallaudet University, *Integrated Postsecondary Education Data System (IPEDS) Report to the U.S. Department of Education*, 1997.

10. Delaporte, *Les sourds*.

11. Goodstein, *The Deaf Way II Reader*, xiii.

12. Joyner, "Douglas Craig," 72.

13. Office of the Provost, *Vision Implementation Plan Steering Committee Recommendations*, December 22, 1994.

14. Roz Prickett, *On the Green*, April 8, 2002.

15. Wayne Coffey, *Winning Sounds Like This: A Season with the Women's Basketball Team at Gallaudet, the World's Only Deaf University* (New York: Crown, 2002).

16. "They Can't Hear But They Can Win: The Triumph of a Deaf Basketball Team," *New York Daily News*, March 31, 2002. http://www.nydailynews.com/archives/news/hear-win-triumph-deaf-basketball-team-article-1.476798?pgno=2#ixzz2nfil4p5G.

17. "Ronda Jo Miller, Teacher and Coach," http://www.zoominfo.com/p/Ronda-Miller/612061.

18. "Team USA Looks to Reclaim Gold at the XXII Deaflympiad," July 24, 2013, http://usadeafbasketball.org/womennews.php.

19. Gallaudet University Financial Statement FY 2005, courtesy of William Hughes.

20. Bahan and Bauman, "Power of Place," 167.

21. David Van Biema, "Murder in a Silent Place," *Time*, June 17, 2001, http://www.time.com/time/magazine/article/0,9171,130940,00.html.

22. Amy Argetsinger, "Gallaudet to Admit Hearing Freshmen; Number Limited to 2% of Class," *Washington Post*, October 14, 2000.

23. Education of the Deaf Act of 1986, Pub. L. No. 99-371, https://www.govtrack.us/congress/bills/99/s1874/tcxt.

24. Gallaudet University Office of Enrollment Services, *2005 Enrollment Report*, January 2006.

25. *Student Organization Manual 2012–2013*, http://www.gallaudet.edu/Documents/StudentOrganizationManual2012-2013.pdf.

26. "GUAA History," http://www.gallaudet.edu/development_and_alumni_relations/alumni_relations/alumni_association_%28guaa%29/about_the_guaa/history.html.

27. Gallaudet Research Institute, *Gallaudet University Alumni Survey*, Winter 2006.

28. *Student Organization Manual 2012–2013*, http://www.gallaudet.edu/Documents/StudentOrganizationManual2012-2013.pdf; http://ccosd.org/2010/12/20/1914-banner-donated-to-gallaudet-university.

29. David F. Armstrong, "Interview with I. King Jordan," *Sign Language Studies* 7, no. 3 (2007): 262–68.

30. "Program Assessment," http://www.whitehouse.gov/sites/default/files/omb/assets/omb/expectmore/summary/10003306.2006.html.

31. Gallaudet eventually succeeded in convincing OMB to reverse its decision, raising the rating to "adequate" in early 2007.

32. Christiansen, *Reflections*, 190–91, 204, 205.

33. Susan Kinzie, "Student Rebellion Boils Over at Gallaudet," *Washington Post*, October 12, 2006, http://www.washingtonpost.com/wp-dyn/content/article/2006/10/12/AR2006101200217.html.

34. Editorial, "Standoff at Gallaudet: The Wrong Way to Shape the University's Future," *Washington Post*, October 10, 2006, http://www.washingtonpost.com/wp-dyn/content/article/2006/10/09/AR2006100901141.html.

35. Krentz, Review of *Open Your Eyes*, 127.

CHAPTER SIX

1. Personal recollection of the author.

2. *Report to the Faculty, Staff, Students, and Administration of Gallaudet University by a Team Representing the Middle States Commission of Higher Education*, Dr. Stephen Sweeny, President, College of New Rochelle, Team Chair, Dr. David Rubino, Special Assistant to the President, Seton Hill University, Ms. Lisa Marsh Ryerson, President, Wells College, January 10, 2007.

3. Ibid.

4. Gallaudet Board of Trustees, *Task Force to Review the 2006 Presidential Search Report*, November 15, 2007.

5. Bauman, "Postscript: Gallaudet Protests of 2006," 93.

6. Christiansen, "The 2006 Protest at Gallaudet University," 86.

7. Bauman, "Postscript: Gallaudet Protests of 2006," 95–96.

8. Christiansen, "The 2006 Protest at Gallaudet University," 85.

9. Ibid., 85–86.

10. Gallaudet University, *Meeting the Challenges of Academic Excellence and Cultural Diversity*, January 1991, ii.

11. Personal recollection of the author.

12. Tim Krepp, *Capitol Hill Haunts* (Charleston, SC: The History Press, 2012), 102.

13. *Gallaudet University Monitoring Report to MSCHE*, April 2008.

14. http://www.gallaudet.edu/about_gallaudet/mission_and_goals.html.

15. Ibid.

16. MSCHE, *Report to the Faculty, Staff, Students, and Administration of Gallaudet University by a Team Representing the Middle States Commission of Higher Education*, October 9–10, 2007.

17. http://www.gallaudetathletics.com/sports/wvball/coaches/boren_lynnray; http://www.gallaudetathletics.com/sports/wvball/index.

18. http://en.wikipedia.org/wiki/Curtis_Pride.

19. "Gallaudet University Coach Curtis Pride Selected to President Obama's Delegation for the 2012 Olympic Games Closing Ceremony," *On the Green*, August 11, 2012.

20. http://www.gallaudetathletics.com/sports/fball/index.

21. Gallaudet Office of Institutional Research, *Fall Enrollment Reports*, 2009 and 2011.

22. Office of the Provost, *Gallaudet University Annual Report of Achievements Fiscal Year 2010–2011*.

23. See Office of the Provost, *Gallaudet University Annual Reports of Achievements*.

24. Greenwald and Van Cleve, *A Fair Chance in the Race of Life*, 2008.

25. http://www.gpo.gov/fdsys/pkg/BILLS-111sconres12es/pdf/BILLS-111sconres12es.pdf.

26. Office of the Provost, *Gallaudet University Annual Report of Achievements Fiscal Year 2010*, 113; http://www.gallaudet.edu/Documents/Academic/2010 percent20 Gallaudet percent20Annual percent20Report.pdf.

27. http://www.gallaudet.edu/news/mr_gallaudet_university_announces_elimination_of_17_academic_programs.html.

28. Francis R. Kowsky, "Gallaudet College: A High Victorian Campus," In *Records of the Columbia Historical Society, Washington, D.C.*, Vol. 71/72, (1971/1972): 45–51, retrieved from http://www.jstor.org/stable/40067785; "Storm Wreaks Havoc," *Washington Post*, June 1, 1911; "Gay Party Rings in the New Year," *The Buff and Blue*, October 23, 1945; http://www.gallaudet.edu/museum/museum_news_archives/antique_stereocard.html.

29. Jessica Feldman, "The Freshmen Go Bald!" *The Buff and Blue*, February 9, 2010; Bethany Weiner, "Bald Day 2012," *The Buff and Blue*, February 1, 2012; Heather Breitbach, "Bald Day," *gBlog-how we see it . . .*, April 17, 2011, retrieved from http://gallaudetblog.wordpress.com/tag/bald-day.

30. Urban Land Institute, *Repositioning the Institution, Renewing the Community*, September 12–17, 2011.

31. The preceding paragraphs were adapted from the Gallaudet website, http://www.gallaudet.edu/news/campus_sustainability.html.

32. http://www.gallaudet.edu/office_of_the_president/strategic_plan/goals_and_strategies.html.

33. http://www.gallaudet.edu/campus_design/projects/innovation_lab.html.

34. "Gallaudet Joins Alliance to Drive Innovation, Economic Growth in D.C. Region," *On the Green*, July 3, 2012.

35. http://www.gallaudet.edu/news/announcing_new_logo.html.

36. Gallaudet University, *Selected Topics Self-Study: Gallaudet Strategic Plan (GSP)*, Submitted to the Middle States Commission on Higher Education, February 8, 2013, 21–22.

37. Office of the Provost, *Gallaudet University Annual Report of Achievements*, 2012.

38. MSCHE, *Report to the Faculty, Administration, Trustees, and Students of Gallaudet University by an Evaluation Team Representing the Middle States Commission on Higher Education Prepared after Study of the Institution's Self-Study Report and Visits to the Campus on November 26, 2012, and March 24–27, 2013*.

39. https://www.msche.org/documents/sas/237/Statement percent20of percent20Accreditation percent20Status.htm.

EPILOGUE

1. Harry G. Lang, *Edmund Booth: Deaf Pioneer* (Washington, DC: Gallaudet University Press, 2004), 5–6.

2. Adapted from Padden and Rayman, "Concluding Thoughts."

3. Padden and Rayman, "Concluding Thoughts," 257.

4. Ibid., 259.

SELECTED, ANNOTATED BIBLIOGRAPHY

Author's note: The following is a partial list of the works and sources I consulted in preparing this book. It contains those books and articles I found most useful in writing this history.

Armstrong, David F. "Deep Roots: The Historical Context for Gallaudet's Birth and Growth." *Gallaudet Today* (Spring 1987): 10–17.
   A brief article on the history of Gallaudet within the context of the growth of American higher education during the late nineteenth and early twentieth centuries.

———. "Income and Occupations of Deaf Former College Students." *Journal of Rehabilitation of the Deaf* 17, no. 1 (1983): 8–15.
   A report on a comprehensive follow-up survey of Gallaudet alumni, graduates, and former students who left before completing a degree.

Armstrong, David F., Michael A. Karchmer, and John Vickrey Van Cleve, eds. *The Study of Signed Languages: Essays in Honor of William C. Stokoe.* Washington, DC: Gallaudet University Press, 2002.
   This volume contains essays by many leading scholars and researchers on the linguistics and neurolinguistics of signed languages and on the Deaf community.

Atwood, Albert. W. *Gallaudet College: Its First One Hundred Years.* Washington, DC: Gallaudet College, 1964.
   This is a detailed account of the first century of operations of the college, based upon the records of the Gallaudet Board of Trustees and annual reports to the federal government, compiled by a longtime chairman of the board.

Bahan, Benjamin, and Hansel Bauman. "The Power of Place: The Evolution of Kendall Green." In Greenwald and Van Cleve, *A Fair Chance in the Race of Life,* 154–69.
   Deaf Studies professor Ben Bahan and campus architect Hansel Bauman describe the architectural development of the Gallaudet campus from Frederick Law Olmsted through Deaf Space.

Baldwin, Stephen C. *Pictures in the Air: The Story of the National Theatre of the Deaf.* Washington, DC: Gallaudet University Press, 1994.

Bauman, H-Dirksen L. "Postscript: Gallaudet Protests of 2006 and the Myths of In/exclusion." *Sign Language Studies* 10, no.1 (2009): 90–104.
   Deaf Studies professor Dirksen Bauman discusses possible causes of the 2006 protests at Gallaudet.

Baynton, Douglas C. "The Curious Death of Sign Language Studies in the Nineteenth Century." In Armstrong, Karchmer, and Van Cleve, *The Study of Signed Languages,* 13–34.
   Baynton's chapter recounts how the rise of oralism led to the demise of serious linguistic study of signed languages in the United States and Europe at the end of the nineteenth century.

Baynton, Douglas C., Jack R. Gannon, and Jean Lindquist Bergey. *Through Deaf Eyes: A Photographic History of an American Community.* Washington, DC: Gallaudet University Press, 2007.
   This book is the companion volume to the PBS television documentary, *History through Deaf Eyes.* It is a beautifully illustrated, very readable history of the signing Deaf community in America.

Boatner, Maxine Tull. *Voice of the Deaf: A Biography of Edward Miner Gallaudet.* Washington, DC: Public Affairs Press, 1959.
   The life and work of the founder of Gallaudet College.

Bonior, David. Foreword to *The Week the World Heard Gallaudet,* by Jack Gannon, 10–11. Washington, DC: Gallaudet University Press, 1989.

Bragg, Bernard. *Lessons in Laughter: The Autobiography of a Deaf Actor.* Washington DC: Gallaudet University Press, 1989.

Christiansen, John B. "The 2006 Protest at Gallaudet University: Reflections and Explanations." *Sign Language Studies* 10, no.1 (2009): 69–89.

Christiansen, a sociology professor at Gallaudet and member of the original 2006 presidential search committee, reflects on possible causes of the protest that led to the retraction of the appointment of Jane Fernandes.

Christiansen, John B., and Sharon N. Barnartt. *Deaf President Now!: The 1988 Revolution at Gallaudet University.* Washington, DC: Gallaudet University Press, 1995.

A detailed and well-researched account of DPN and the events leading up to it during the first few months of 1988.

Commission on Education of the Deaf. *Toward Equality: Education of the Deaf.* Washington, DC: Commission on Education of the Deaf, 1988.

The Commission's report contains data about and a number of recommendations concerning Gallaudet University and its Pre-College Programs.

Crammatte, Alan B. *Deaf Persons in Professional Employment.* Springfield, IL: Charles C. Thomas, 1968.

Crammatte, a Gallaudet alumnus and faculty member, conducted a survey during the 1960s of one hundred deaf people engaged in professional occupations, about half of whom had attended Gallaudet for at least part of their higher education.

Delaporte, Yves. *Les sourds, c'est comme ça.* Paris: Éditions de la maison des sciences de l'homme, 2003.

A history and ethnography of the signing Deaf community in France. The book's title and the sign that represents it can be translated into English as "The Deaf Way."

Erting Carol J., Robert C. Johnson, Dorothy L. Smith, and Bruce D. Snider, eds. *The Deaf Way: Perspectives from the International Conference on Deaf Culture.* Washington, DC: Gallaudet University Press, 1994.

The Deaf Way documents the vast scholarly and artistic endeavors that took place in July 1989 when more than 6,000 deaf people from around the world met at Gallaudet University to celebrate Deaf culture.

Gallaudet Almanac. Compiled by Wallace Edington, David Peikoff, and Hans-Dieter Baumert, edited by Jack Gannon. Washington, DC: Gallaudet College Alumni Association, 1974.

An invaluable compendium of facts and figures concerning the first 110 years of the college, including class lists, names and years of service of faculty, athletic teams and their records, etc.

Gallaudet College. *New Challenges, New Responses: A Report on the Mission of Gallaudet College.* Washington, DC: Gallaudet College, 1977.

Gallaudet, Edward Miner. *History of the College for the Deaf, 1857–1907.* Edited by Lance J. Fischer and David L. de Lorenzo. Washington, DC: Gallaudet College Press, 1983 (1907).

This is EMG's own account of the first fifty years of the Columbia Institution, told in an extremely engaging, even intimate, style. It was not published during his lifetime, but it is a must-read for anyone interested in the history of the Institution, the operation of the federal government during the post–Civil War era, and much more.

Gannon. Jack R. *Deaf Heritage: A Narrative History of Deaf America.* Silver Spring, MD: National Association of the Deaf, 1981.

Gannon's groundbreaking work on the history of the Deaf community.

———. *The Week the World Heard Gallaudet.* Washington, DC: Gallaudet University Press, 1989.

A day-by-day account of DPN, illustrated by a particularly fine collection of black-and-white and color photographs of the week's events.

Garretson, Mervin D. *My Yesterdays in a Changing World of the Deaf.* Xlibris Corporation, 2010. Kindle edition.

A memoir by a Gallaudet alumnus, educator, Gallaudet administrator, and longtime leader of the Deaf community.

Goodstein, Harvey, ed. *The Deaf Way II Reader: Perspectives from the Second International Conference on Deaf Culture.* Washington, DC: Gallaudet University Press, 2006.

This volume contains papers documenting the second Deaf Way conference.

Greenwald, Brian H., and John Vickrey Van Cleve, eds. *A Fair Chance in the Race of Life: The Role of Gallaudet in Deaf History.* Washington, DC: Gallaudet University Press, 2008.

Historians Greenwald and Van Cleve selected papers presented at a conference celebrating the 150th anniversary of the founding of the Columbia Institution. Several of the essays are cited separately in this bibliography.

Jones, Thomas W., and James C. Achtzehn, Jr. "A Century of Leadership: Gallaudet's Teacher Education Program Celebrates 100 Years of Advancement." *Gallaudet Today* (Spring 1992): 4–13.

Jowers-Barber, Sandra. "The Struggle to Educate Black Deaf Schoolchildren in Washington, DC." In Greenwald and Van Cleve, *A Fair Chance in the Race of Life*, 113–31.

    This article examines racial segregation in the Kendall School and the ultimately successful attempts to end it.

Joyner, Marieta. "Douglas Craig, 186?–1936." In Greenwald and Van Cleve, *A Fair Chance in the Race of Life*, 65–84.

    The life story of a longtime African American employee of the college during the years of segregation in the educational program.

Kerstetter, Philip P., and David F. Armstrong. "The Rubella Epidemic of 1963–65: Impacts on Postsecondary Education of a Large Group of Deaf Adolescents." *Directions* 2 (1981): 55–66.

    This article describes the demographics of the population born deaf as a result of the rubella epidemic of the mid-1960s and projects enrollments at Gallaudet University during the mid- to late 1980s.

Krentz, Christopher. Review of *Open Your Eyes: Deaf Studies Talking*, by H-Dirksen L. Bauman, ed. *Sign Language Studies* 10, no. 1 (2009): 110–32.

    This review and essay discusses *Open Your Eyes* in light of Krentz's personal observations of the 2006 protest.

Lang, Harry G. *Teaching from the Heart and Soul: The Robert F. Panara Story.* Washington, DC: Gallaudet University Press, 2007.

    This biography of Robert Panara, a Gallaudet alumnus and faculty member at both Gallaudet and NTID, provides much information about the institutional changes that led to Gallaudet's accreditation in 1957.

Lang, Harry G., Oscar P. Cohen, and Joseph E. Fischgrund. *Moments of Truth: Robert R. Davila: The Story of a Deaf Leader.* Rochester, NY: RIT Press, 2007.

    The often dramatic life story of Gallaudet's ninth president.

Maher, Jane. *Seeing Language in Sign: The Work of William C. Stokoe.* Washington, DC: Gallaudet University Press, 1996.

    An account of the life and work of the founder of the modern linguistic study of signed languages.

Mallery, Garrick. *Sign Language Among North American Indians Compared With That Among Other Peoples And Deaf-Mutes.* First Annual Report of the Bureau of Ethnology to the Secretary of the Smithsonian Institution, 1879–1880. Washington, DC: Smithsonian Institution, 1880.

    The definitive study of Plains Indian Sign Language, carried out while these languages were still used extensively. The report includes Mallery's account of his visit to Gallaudet with a group of American Indians fluent in this sign language.

McCullough, David. *The Greater Journey: Americans in Paris.* New York: Simon and Schuster, 2011.

    A book about well-known Americans who visited Paris during the nineteenth century. One of these visitors was Elihu Washburne, EMG's nemesis while he was in Congress, who won praise for his actions as American minister to Paris during the Franco-Prussian War and the Paris Commune.

McPherson, James M. "A Fair Chance in the Race of Life: Thoughts on the 150th Anniversary of the Founding of the Columbia Institution." In Greenwald and Van Cleve, *A Fair Chance in the Race of Life*, 1–11.

    The Pulitzer Prize–winning historian considers the founding of the College for the Deaf within the historical perspective of the ongoing Civil War and the expansion of higher education in America.

Mitchell, Ross E., and Michael A. Karchmer. "Chasing the Mythical Ten Percent: Parental Hearing Status of Deaf and Hard of Hearing Students in the United States." *Sign Language Studies* 4, no. 3 (2004): 138–63.

    It is commonly believed that about 10 percent of deaf people have deaf parents. In this report, Mitchell and Karchmer reexamine the data and conclude that the percentage is actually lower than this, probably about 8 percent, including those whose parents are hard of hearing. This low percentage has a profound impact on the way most deaf people acquire a sign language.

National Association of the Deaf. *Proceedings of the Ninth Convention of the National Association of the Deaf and the Third World's Congress of the Deaf, 1910.* Philadelphia: Philocophus Press, 1912.

Olson, Michael J. "The Thomas Hopkins Gallaudet and Alice Cogswell Statue: Controversies and Celebrations." In Greenwald and Van Cleve, *A Fair Chance in the Race of Life*, 33–49.

    Gallaudet archivist Olson documents an early instance of deaf resistance to a move by a hearing administrator (EMG) that seemed contrary to the interests of deaf people.

Our Heritage: Gallaudet College Centennial 1864–1964. Compiled by the Centennial Souvenir Book Committee: Reuben Altziger, Richard Wright, Vilas Johnson, Clyde Morton, Marwood Burr, Al Sonnenstrahl, Willard Madsen, Marcellus Kleberg, Elizabeth Miller, August Herdtfelder, Robert Panara, and Francis Higgins. Washington, DC: Graphic Arts Press, 1964.

This makes a good companion piece to Atwood's centennial history, as this volume presents the story from the point of view of students and alumni.

Padden, Carol. "Translating Veditz." *Sign Language Studies* 4, no. 3 (2004): 244–60.

Padden attempts to get at the meaning of George Veditz's classic sign language film on preserving the sign language.

Padden, Carol A., and Jennifer Rayman. "Concluding Thoughts: The Future of American Sign Language." In Armstrong, Karchmer, and Van Cleve, *The Study of Signed Languages*, 247–62.

As Deaf associations diminish in importance, places like Gallaudet become more important to the formation and continuity of Deaf culture.

Parker, Lindsey M. "The Women of Kendall Green: Coeducation at Gallaudet, 1860–1910." In Greenwald and Van Cleve, *A Fair Chance in the Race of Life*, 85–112.

This article documents the contributions of female students at Gallaudet before they were excluded and after they were readmitted during the nineteenth century.

Sacks, Oliver. *Seeing Voices: A Journey into the World of the Deaf*. Berkeley: University of California Press, 1989.

Among other things, this book includes a chapter on William Stokoe's work on ASL and a chapter recounting Sacks's experiences at Gallaudet during the DPN protest.

Schuchman, John S. "The Silent Film Era: Silent Films, NAD Films, and the Deaf Community's Response." *Sign Language Studies* 4, no. 3 (2004): 231–38.

Historian and former chief academic officer John Schuchman discusses the importance of deaf actors in silent films and that of sign language films before the appearance of captioned "talkies."

Stokoe, William C. *Language in Hand: Why Sign Came before Speech*. Washington, DC: Gallaudet University Press, 2001.

Stokoe's posthumous memoir of his linguistic work at Gallaudet contains many observations about the importance of signed languages in the education of deaf children and on the role they may have played in human evolution.

Stokoe, William C., H. Russell Bernard, and Carol Padden. "An Elite Group in Deaf Society." In *Sign and Culture: A Reader for Students of American Sign Language*, edited by William C. Stokoe, 295–316. Silver Spring, MD: Linstok Press, 1980.

In this article, Stokoe, Padden, and anthropologist Russell Bernard discuss the demographic characteristics and intragroup dynamics of a Gallaudet-educated leadership group.

Supalla, Ted. "The Validity of the Gallaudet Lecture Films." *Sign Language Studies* 4, no. 1 (2004): 261–92.

Linguist Ted Supalla assesses the extent to which the Gallaudet/NAD films can be considered representative of ASL in the early twentieth century.

Sutcliffe, Ronald E. "George Detmold, The Reformer." In Greenwald and Van Cleve, *A Fair Chance in the Race of Life*, 132–39.

Sutcliffe gives Dean Detmold considerable credit for improving the academic standards of Gallaudet College and gaining accreditation.

Van Cleve, John Vickrey, and Barry A. Crouch. *A Place of Their Own: Creating the Deaf Community in America*. Washington, DC: Gallaudet University Press, 1989.

Gallaudet history professors Van Cleve and Crouch give a comprehensive account of the formation of the American Deaf community, including histories of the founding of the residential schools and Gallaudet College.

Winefield, Richard. *Never the Twain Shall Meet: Bell, Gallaudet and the Communications Debate*. Washington, DC: Gallaudet University Press, 1987.

This book describes the often contentious relationship between two of the major figures in American deaf education during the latter part of the nineteenth century.

INDEX